Pillsbury

Christmas

Pillsbury Christmas

published by

Taste of Home Books
Reiman Media Group, Inc.
5400 S. 60th St., Greendale WI 53129

Taste of Home® is a registered trademark of Reiman Media Group, Inc.

Bake-Off® is a registered trademark of General Mills.

All recipes were previously published in a slightly different form.

Front Cover Photograph:
Triple-Chocolate Torte, p. 298.

Title Page Photograph:
Festive Ham and Cheese Wreath, p. 51.

Back Cover Photographs:
Cinnamon French Toast Bake, p. 191;
Chocolate Buttersweets, p. 246;
Three-Cheese Beef Pasta Shells, p. 111;
Key Lime Cream Torte, p. 308;
Turkey with Cornmeal-Thyme Dumplings, p. 122.

credits

GENERAL MILLS, INC.

EDITORIAL DIRECTOR: Jeff Nowak
PUBLISHING MANAGER: Christine Gray
COOKBOOK EDITOR: Grace Wells
DIGITAL ASSETS MANAGER: Carrie Jacobson
PRODUCTION MANAGER: Michelle Tufts
RECIPE DEVELOPMENT AND TESTING: Pillsbury Test Kitchens
PHOTOGRAPHY: General Mills Photo Studio

REIMAN MEDIA GROUP, INC.

EDITOR IN CHIEF: Catherine Cassidy
VICE PRESIDENT, EXECUTIVE EDITOR/BOOKS: Heidi Reuter Lloyd
CREATIVE DIRECTOR: Ardyth Cope
SENIOR EDITOR/BOOKS: Mark Hagen
EDITOR: Michelle Bretl
ART DIRECTOR: Gretchen Trautman
CONTENT PRODUCTION SUPERVISOR: Julie Wagner
LAYOUT DESIGNERS: Kathy Crawford, Nancy Novak
PROOFREADER: Linne Bruskewitz
EDITORIAL INTERN: Danielle Calkins
COVER PHOTOGRAPHY: Reiman Publications Photo Studio
  PHOTOGRAPHER: Jim Wieland
  FOOD STYLIST: Jennifer Janz
  SET STYLIST: Melissa Haberman

CREATIVE DIRECTOR/CREATIVE MARKETING: Jim Palmen
VICE PRESIDENT, BOOK MARKETING: Dan Fink
CHIEF MARKETING OFFICER: Lisa Karpinski

READER'S DIGEST ASSOCIATION, INC.

PRESIDENT AND CHIEF EXECUTIVE OFFICER: Mary G. Berner
PRESIDENT, FOOD & ENTERTAINING: Suzanne M. Grimes
PRESIDENT, CONSUMER MARKETING: Dawn Zier
SVP, CHIEF MARKETING OFFICER: Amy J. Radin

For additional holiday recipes and other delicious dishes, visit
Pillsbury.com.

International Standard Book Number (10): 1-61765-177-X
International Standard Book Number (13): 978-1-61765-177-9
International Standard Serial Number: 1930-1685
Printed in U.S.A.
1 3 5 7 9 10 8 6 4 2

contents

Savor the Foods of the Season!

It's so easy to make your Christmas celebrations extra special when you have more than 300 scrumptious holiday recipes and helpful cooking tips from Pillsbury.

p. 34

p. 84

p. 34

p. 279

p. 117

p. 119

In a twinkling, Christmastime arrives each year spreading joy, warmth and cheer in every heart and home. And this magical season just wouldn't be the same without bountiful tables, platters and trays filled with favorite holiday flavors and yummy Yuletide delights.

From the most elegant December feasts to merry cookie exchanges and school classroom parties, every festive event on your family's calendar will be the best yet when you rely on the rave-winning recipes in Pillsbury Christmas.

The third edition in our popular series of Christmas cookbooks, this brand-new treasury gives you all of the tempting delicacies your family and friends have come to cherish. Whether you prefer traditional holiday tastes or exciting new twists, you'll find mouthwatering sensations from cover to cover.

Over 300 recipes include eye-catching main dishes and complementary sides, dazzling appetizers and beverages to get parties started, and cute Christmas cookies and desserts guests will long remember. Every recipe was tested and approved in the Pillsbury Kitchens, so you can be confident your creations will be perfect when you set them on the table.

It's a cinch to locate exactly the types of dishes you're looking for thanks to 10 big chapters. Turn to "Memorable Main Courses" (p. 104) to choose the star attraction for your menu, then page through "Special Soups, Salads & Sides" (p. 76) and "Yuletide Breads & Baked Goods" (p. 52) to select just the right accompaniments.

Christmas morning will be unforgettable when you serve the wonderful breakfast and brunch items in "Seasonal Sunrise Specialties" (p. 188). And everyone on your list will be thrilled to receive the irresistible snacks, goodies and more from "Gifts of Good Taste" (p. 214).

Celebrate your family's heritage—or give your recipe lineup a bit of international flair—with Rich Tiramisu, Quesadilla Pie, Apple-Cranberry Strudel and other selections from "Christmas Around the World" (p. 162). You'll also want to see "Merry Nibblers & Sippers" (p. 6) and "Jolly Holiday Gatherings" (p. 126) when you need crowd-pleasers for get-togethers.

Of course, sweet treats are a must during the holiday season…and you'll find indulgences to satisfy everyone in "Festive Cookies & Confections" (p. 230) and "Heavenly Desserts" (p. 272). Make eyes light up with delectable cakes, pies, cheesecakes and tarts, plus dozens of clever cookies and candies for your holiday trays and tins.

Most of the recipes in this cookbook feature handy hints to help ensure success. The *cook's notes* offer speedy shortcuts, ingredient substitutions and more. Many *kitchen tips* provide sensible advice on everything from streamlining cleanup to selecting the best produce, and *special touches* suggest ways of dressing up your creations. We've also included winners of our famous Bake-Off® Contest—the very best of the best!

With all of that and much, much more, this indispensable holiday collection gives you everything you need to make the season as bright, memorable and delicious as can be. So let the tongue-tingling tastes and festive fun of Pillsbury Christmas bring glad tidings to you and yours this year…and for many years to come. *Merry Christmas!*

p. 292

Merry Nibblers & Sippers

Spread good cheer at every holiday event with the delightful bites in this chapter. From casual munchies to elegant appetizers, they'll get a seasonal party started.

p. 34

p. 10

p. 34

p. 18

p. 9

thai turkey lettuce wraps p. 29

smoked salmon cheese cups

smoked salmon cheese cups

READY IN: 20 Minutes ✳ SERVINGS: 15

- 1 package (2.1 oz.) frozen mini phyllo (filo) shells (15 shells)
- 3 oz. chèvre (goat) cheese, crumbled
- 1 package (3 oz.) cream cheese, softened
- 2 oz. smoked salmon, flaked (from 4.5-oz. pkg.)
- 2 tablespoons shredded fresh Parmesan cheese
- 1 tablespoon chopped fresh basil leaves
- 1 tablespoon whipping cream
- 1/4 teaspoon salt
- 1/8 teaspoon freshly ground black pepper
- 2 tablespoons chopped pecans, toasted

1 Thaw phyllo shells as directed on package. In medium bowl, mix all remaining ingredients except pecans until well mixed. Spoon into 1-quart resealable food-storage plastic bag. Seal bag; cut 1/2 inch off one corner of bag.

2 To serve, pipe or spoon cheese-salmon mixture into each phyllo cup. Sprinkle each with toasted pecans.

NUTRITION INFORMATION PER SERVING: Calories 80 • Total Fat 6g • Saturated Fat 3g • Cholesterol 15mg • Sodium 135mg • Total Carbohydrate 2g • Dietary Fiber 0g • Sugars 0g • Protein 3g. DIETARY EXCHANGES: 1/2 Lean Meat • 1 Fat.

kitchen tip

As a general rule, when a recipe calls for 1 tablespoon of a fresh herb, you may substitute 1 teaspoon of the dried herb or 1/4 teaspoon of the powdered or ground form.

spinach and jalapeño roll-ups

PREP TIME: 25 Minutes ✳ READY IN: 1 Hour 25 Minutes ✳ SERVINGS: 32

- 1 package (9 oz.) Green Giant® frozen spinach
- 1 package (8 oz.) cream cheese, softened
- 2 jalapeño chiles, minced
- 4 flour tortillas (8-inch)
- Roasted red bell pepper (from 7.25-oz. jar), cut into 4 (8-inch) strips

1 Cook spinach as directed on package. Place in colander or strainer; rinse with cold water to cool. Squeeze spinach to remove as much moisture as possible.

2 In food processor bowl with metal blade, combine cream cheese and chiles; process until smooth. Add spinach; process until just blended.

3 Place 1 tortilla on work surface. Spread 1/4 of spinach mixture over tortilla, leaving 1/2-inch border on one side. Place strips of roasted pepper, piecing together if necessary, across middle of tortilla.

4 Roll tortilla toward border, making sure beginning is tightly rolled, but easing pressure as rolling continues to avoid forcing out filling. Wrap in plastic wrap; repeat with remaining tortillas, spinach mixture and roasted peppers. Refrigerate at least 1 hour before serving.

5 To serve, remove plastic wrap from tortilla rolls. Cut each roll diagonally into 8 slices, trimming ends.

NUTRITION INFORMATION PER SERVING: Calories 45 • Total Fat 3g • Saturated Fat 2g • Cholesterol 10mg • Sodium 60mg • Total Carbohydrate 3g • Dietary Fiber 0g • Sugars 0g • Protein 1g. DIETARY EXCHANGES: 1/2 Vegetable • 1/2 Fat.

cook's notes

Allow the cooked spinach to cool before squeezing it dry. Keeping the spinach in the colander, use clean hands to squeeze the water out of the spinach.

stuffed date roll-ups

PREP TIME: 20 Minutes ✳ READY IN: 35 Minutes ✳ SERVINGS: 16

16 whole large dates	**GLAZE**
3 oz. soft chèvre (goat) cheese (1/3 cup)	1/2 cup powdered sugar
1 tablespoon chopped toasted almonds	1/2 teaspoon grated orange peel
1 can (8 oz.) Pillsbury® refrigerated crescent dinner rolls	1 tablespoon orange juice
	Fresh currants, if desired

1 Cut each date lengthwise along one side; remove pit. Place cheese and almonds in quart-size resealable freezer plastic bag or decorating bag fitted with tip with large end; seal bag. Squeeze bag to mix almonds into cheese. Cut small hole in 1 corner of plastic bag. Squeeze bag to pipe about 1 teaspoon cheese mixture into each split date.

2 Heat oven to 375°F. Unroll dough and separate into 4 rectangles; firmly press perforations to seal. Cut each into 4 short strips (about 3x1 inch); wrap each stuffed date with 1 dough strip. Place 2 inches apart, seam side down, on ungreased large cookie sheet.

3 Bake 10 to 15 minutes or until golden brown. Meanwhile, in small bowl, mix glaze ingredients. Immediately drizzle glaze over hot roll-ups. Remove from cookie sheet. Cool 10 minutes. Serve warm or at room temperature. Garnish with currants.

NUTRITION INFORMATION PER SERVING: Calories 110 • Total Fat 4.5g • Saturated Fat 2g • Cholesterol 0mg • Sodium 130mg • Total Carbohydrate 16g • Dietary Fiber 0g • Sugars 10g • Protein 2g. DIETARY EXCHANGES: 1 Other Carbohydrate • 1 Fat • 1 Carb Choice.

garlic beef cubes

READY IN: 25 Minutes ✳ SERVINGS: 24

1 lb. beef tenderloin, cut into 48 (about 1 inch) cubes	1/3 cup mayonnaise or salad dressing
1/2 teaspoon salt	3 tablespoons sour cream
1/8 teaspoon pepper	1/4 cup finely chopped drained sun-dried tomatoes in oil
2 tablespoons olive or vegetable oil	1 tablespoon prepared horseradish
2 garlic cloves, pressed	1 tablespoon chopped fresh parsley

1 Sprinkle beef cubes with salt and pepper. In 10-inch skillet, heat oil and pressed garlic over medium-high heat, stirring frequently, until garlic is toasted (be careful not to burn garlic). Remove as much garlic as possible from skillet; discard.

2 Add beef cubes to skillet. Cook 4 to 5 minutes, stirring occasionally, until brown on all sides and desired doneness; drain.

3 Meanwhile, in small bowl, mix mayonnaise, sour cream, tomatoes and horseradish. Spoon beef cubes into serving bowl or onto platter; sprinkle with parsley. Serve with toothpicks for dipping into sauce.

NUTRITION INFORMATION PER SERVING: Calories 70 • Total Fat 5g • Saturated Fat 1g • Cholesterol 10mg • Sodium 80mg • Total Carbohydrate 0g • Dietary Fiber 0g • Sugars 0g • Protein 5g. DIETARY EXCHANGES: 1/2 Medium-Fat Meat • 1/2 Fat.

stuffed date roll-ups

grilled cheese quesadillas

grilled cheese quesadillas

READY IN: 40 Minutes ✳ SERVINGS: 32

- 1 package (11.5 oz.) (8 tortillas) Old El Paso® Flour Tortillas for Burritos
- 3/4 cup spicy black bean dip (from 16-oz. jar)
- 2 cups shredded Mexican cheese blend or Monterey Jack cheese (8 oz.)

- 1/4 cup chopped fresh cilantro
- 3 to 4 pickled jalapeño chiles, sliced
- 1 jar (16 oz.) Old El Paso® Thick 'n Chunky salsa
- 1 container (12 oz.) guacamole

1 For each quesadilla, spread tortilla with 3 tablespoons bean dip. Top with 1/2 cup cheese, 1 tablespoon cilantro and another tortilla.

2 Heat large skillet over medium-high heat until hot. Place 1 quesadilla in skillet; cook 2 to 4 minutes or until bottom of tortilla is golden brown. Turn quesadilla; cook 1 to 2 minutes or until thoroughly heated and cheese is melted. Remove from skillet; place on cutting board.

3 Repeat with remaining quesadillas. Cut each into 8 wedges. Garnish each with 1 jalapeño chile slice. Serve with salsa and guacamole.

NUTRITION INFORMATION PER SERVING: Calories 95 • Total Fat 5g • Saturated Fat 2g • Cholesterol 10mg • Sodium 240mg • Total Carbohydrate 9g • Dietary Fiber 1g • Sugars 1g • Protein 3g. DIETARY EXCHANGES: 1/2 Starch • 1 Fat • 1/2 Carb Choice.

cook's notes

When you're having soup, try these quesadillas as a side in place of the usual sandwich.

grands!® meatball pops

READY IN: 30 Minutes ✳ SERVINGS: 10

- 1 can (10.2 oz.) Pillsbury® Grands!® refrigerated southern-style or buttermilk biscuits (5 biscuits)
- 1/3 cup shredded Monterey Jack or Cheddar cheese (1-1/3 oz.)
- 10 refrigerated or frozen cooked beef meatballs, thawed

- 1/4 cup margarine or butter, melted
- 2/3 cup finely crushed seasoned croutons
- 10 large appetizer picks or lollipop sticks, if desired

1 Heat oven to 375°F. Line cookie sheet with parchment paper or spray with nonstick cooking spray. Separate dough into 5 biscuits. With serrated knife, cut each biscuit in half horizontally to make 10 rounds. Press out each biscuit half to form 3-inch round.

2 Sprinkle each biscuit round with cheese to within 1/2 inch of edge. Top each with meatball. Bring up sides of dough over meatball; pinch edges to seal. Brush rounded tops and sides of dough with margarine; coat with croutons. Place seam side down on paper-lined cookie sheet.

3 Bake at 375°F for 10 to 15 minutes or until golden brown. To serve, place appetizer pick in each warm biscuit-wrapped meatball to form meatball pop.

NUTRITION INFORMATION PER SERVING: Calories 275 • Total Fat 16g • Saturated Fat 5g • Cholesterol 35mg • Sodium 690mg • Total Carbohydrate 22g • Dietary Fiber 1g • Sugars 5g • Protein 9g. DIETARY EXCHANGES: 1-1/2 Starch • 1/2 High-Fat Meat • 2 Fat OR 1-1/2 Carbohydrate • 1/2 High-Fat Meat • 2 Fat • 1-1/2 Carb Choices.

special touch

A fun way to serve these pops is with warm tomato pasta sauce for dipping and grated Parmesan cheese for sprinkling on top.

ANN WALLER
Conroe, Texas
Bake Off® Contest 42, 2006

spinach-cheese balls with pasta sauce

READY IN: 1 Hour ✳ SERVINGS: 20

1 box (9 oz.) frozen spinach	1/2 cup sour cream
1 egg, beaten	2 tablespoons extra-virgin olive oil
1 cup shredded Parmesan cheese (4 oz.)	1 container (15 oz.) ricotta cheese
1 cup shredded mozzarella cheese (4 oz.)	2 cups all-purpose flour
1 teaspoon salt	Vegetable oil for deep frying
1 teaspoon onion powder	3/4 cup Italian-style dry bread crumbs
1 teaspoon garlic powder	1 jar (25.5 oz.) organic garden vegetable pasta sauce, heated
1 teaspoon dried oregano leaves	

1 Remove frozen spinach from pouch; place in colander. Rinse with warm water until thawed; drain well. Squeeze spinach dry with paper towel.

2 Meanwhile, in large bowl, mix egg, both cheeses, salt, onion powder, garlic powder, oregano, sour cream, oil and ricotta cheese until well blended. Add spinach to cheese mixture; mix well. Stir in flour, 1 cup at a time, until well blended.

3 Fill 10-inch skillet half full with oil; heat over medium heat until candy/deep-fry thermometer reads 350°F. (Or use deep fryer; add oil to fill line and heat to 350°F.)

4 Meanwhile, place bread crumbs in small bowl. Shape spinach-cheese mixture into 1-1/2-inch balls (about 40), using about 1-1/2 tablespoons for each; roll in bread crumbs and place on cookie sheet.

5 Fry 6 balls at a time 4 to 6 minutes, turning as necessary, until golden brown. With slotted spoon, remove balls from skillet; place on paper towels to drain. Cool 2 minutes before serving; serve with warm pasta sauce for dipping.

NUTRITION INFORMATION PER SERVING: Calories 220 • Total Fat 12g • Saturated Fat 4.5g • Cholesterol 30mg • Sodium 450mg • Total Carbohydrate 18g • Dietary Fiber 1g • Sugars 2g • Protein 9g. DIETARY EXCHANGES: 1 Starch • 1 Medium-Fat Meat • 1-1/2 Fat • 1 Carb Choice.

italian cheesy chex® mix

PREP TIME: 15 Minutes ✳ READY IN: 1 Hour 30 Minutes ✳ SERVINGS: 20

3 cups Wheat Chex® cereal	1/2 cup olive oil
3 cups Rice Chex® cereal	3 tablespoons balsamic vinegar
1 cup pretzel nuggets	2 teaspoons garlic salt
2 cups small cheese-flavor crackers	3 teaspoons Italian seasoning
1 cup salted roasted soy nuts	1/3 cup grated Parmesan cheese

1 Heat oven to 300°F. In large bowl, mix cereals, pretzel nuggets, cheese-flavor crackers and roasted soy nuts.

2 In small bowl, mix oil, vinegar, garlic salt and Italian seasoning. Pour over cereal mixture, stirring to coat. Spread in ungreased 15x10x1-inch pan.

3 Bake about 30 minutes, stirring twice, until toasted. Sprinkle with cheese; toss to coat. Cool completely, about 45 minutes. (Cereal will crisp as it cools.) Store in airtight container.

NUTRITION INFORMATION PER SERVING: Calories 170 • Total Fat 9g • Saturated Fat 2g • Cholesterol 0mg • Sodium 340mg • Total Carbohydrate 18g • Dietary Fiber 2g • Sugars 2g • Protein 5g. DIETARY EXCHANGES: 1 Starch • 2 Fat • 1 Carb Choice.

cook's notes

Make an extra batch of this irresistible mix and give bags of it to the snack lovers on your Christmas list.

spinach-cheese balls
with pasta sauce

tomato-artichoke crostini

PREP TIME: 25 Minutes ✳ READY IN: 45 Minutes ✳ SERVINGS: 20

40 slices (1/2 inch thick) baguette French bread
  Cooking spray
1 jar (6 oz.) marinated artichoke hearts, drained
2 cups chopped, seeded plum (Roma) tomatoes (6 to 7 medium)

2 tablespoons chopped fresh basil leaves
1/2 teaspoon salt
1/8 teaspoon coarse ground black pepper

1 Heat oven to 325°F. Line cookie sheet with foil. Place bread slices on cookie sheet; lightly spray bread with cooking spray.

2 Bake 6 to 9 minutes or until crisp. Remove from cookie sheet to cooling rack. Cool completely, about 20 minutes.

3 Meanwhile, coarsely chop artichokes. In medium bowl, mix artichokes and remaining ingredients. Serve artichoke mixture with toasted bread slices.

NUTRITION INFORMATION PER SERVING: Calories 45 • Total Fat 1g • Saturated Fat 0g • Cholesterol 0mg • Sodium 150mg • Total Carbohydrate 8g • Dietary Fiber 0g • Sugars 0g • Protein 1g. DIETARY EXCHANGES: 1/2 Starch • 1/2 Carb Choice.

warm roasted pepper and artichoke spread

PREP TIME: 15 Minutes ❄ READY IN: 40 Minutes ❄ SERVINGS: 52

1 cup grated Parmesan cheese
1/2 cup fat-free mayonnaise or salad dressing
1 package (8 oz.) cream cheese, softened
1 small garlic clove

1 can (14 oz.) artichoke hearts, drained, finely chopped
1/3 cup finely chopped roasted red bell peppers (from 7.25-oz. jar)

1 Heat oven to 350°F. In food processor bowl with metal blade, combine Parmesan cheese, mayonnaise, cream cheese and garlic; process until smooth.

2 Place mixture in large bowl. Add artichoke hearts and roasted peppers; mix well. Spread in ungreased 9-inch quiche dish or glass pie pan.

3 Bake at 350°F for 20 to 25 minutes or until thoroughly heated. Serve warm with crackers, cut-up fresh vegetables or cocktail bread slices.

NUTRITION INFORMATION PER SERVING: Calories 25 • Total Fat 2g • Saturated Fat 1g • Cholesterol 5mg • Sodium 85mg • Total Carbohydrate 1g • Dietary Fiber 0g • Sugars 0g • Protein 1g. DIETARY EXCHANGES: 1/2 Vegetable • 1/2 Fat.

cook's notes

Have leftovers of this snack from a party? Spread some on the bread of your sandwich for lunch the next day.

apple cheese ball

PREP TIME: 15 Minutes ❄ READY IN: 1 Hour 15 Minutes ❄ SERVINGS: 28

1 package (8 oz.) cream cheese, softened
1 cup shredded Cheddar cheese (4 oz.)
1/4 teaspoon cinnamon
3/4 cup finely chopped dried apples

1/3 cup finely chopped nuts
1 bay leaf
1 cinnamon stick, halved

1 In large bowl, combine cream cheese, Cheddar cheese and cinnamon; beat until well blended. Stir in apples.

2 Shape mixture into ball; roll in nuts. Insert bay leaf and cinnamon stick on top of ball to resemble stem and leaf of apple. Refrigerate at least 1 hour or until firm. Serve with crackers. Store in refrigerator up to 2 weeks.

NUTRITION INFORMATION PER SERVING: Calories 60 • Total Fat 5g • Saturated Fat 3g • Cholesterol 15mg • Sodium 50mg • Total Carbohydrate 2g • Dietary Fiber 0g • Sugars 1g • Protein 2g. DIETARY EXCHANGE: 1 Fat.

cook's notes

For coating this yummy cheese ball, try nuts such as pecans or walnuts.

french onion meatballs

PREP TIME: 5 Minutes ❄ READY IN: 3 Hours 35 Minutes ❄ SERVINGS: 18

2 bags (18 oz. each) frozen cooked original-flavor meatballs
1 jar (12 oz.) beef gravy

1 package (1 oz.) dry onion soup mix
1 tablespoon dry sherry, if desired

1 In 4- to 5-quart slow cooker, place meatballs. In medium bowl, mix gravy, soup mix and sherry; gently stir into meatballs.

2 Cover; cook on Low heat setting 3-1/2 to 4-1/2 hours. Serve meatballs with fondue forks or long toothpicks.

NUTRITION INFORMATION PER SERVING: Calories 160 • Total Fat 8g • Saturated 3g • Cholesterol 60mg • Sodium 570mg • Total Carbohydrate 8g • Dietary Fiber 0g • Sugars 2g • Protein 12g. DIETARY EXCHANGES: 1/2 Starch • 1-1/2 Medium-Fat Meat • 1/2 Carb Choice.

MICHAEL W. WEAVER
San Francisco, California
Bake-Off® Contest 42, 2006

deviled crab and cheese rolls

PREP TIME: 10 Minutes ✳ READY IN: 50 Minutes ✳ SERVINGS: 6

1/2 cup whipped cream cheese (from 8-oz. container)

1 tablespoon fresh lemon juice

1 to 2 teaspoons red pepper sauce

1/4 cup finely shredded mild Cheddar cheese (1 oz.)

2 tablespoons finely chopped green onions (2 medium)

1 teaspoon paprika

1/2 cup garlic-herb dry bread crumbs

3 cans (6 oz. each) white crabmeat, well drained

1 can (11 oz.) refrigerated original breadsticks

1 egg, slightly beaten

1 Heat oven to 350°F. Spray cookie sheet with cooking spray or line with a silicone baking mat. In medium bowl, mix cream cheese, lemon juice and red pepper sauce until smooth. Stir in Cheddar cheese, onions and paprika. Reserve 2 tablespoons bread crumbs for topping; stir remaining bread crumbs into cream cheese mixture. Gently stir in crabmeat. Shape crabmeat mixture into 6 balls, using about 1/3 cup mixture for each; flatten slightly.

2 Unroll dough; separate into 6 (2-breadstick) portions. Seal seam halfway up length of each portion; place 1 ball on sealed side of each. Holding dough and ball in one hand, stretch dough strips over balls, crisscrossing and tucking ends under opposite side; place on cookie sheet.

3 Lightly brush tops and sides of dough with beaten egg; sprinkle with reserved 2 tablespoons bread crumbs. Bake 20 to 30 minutes or until golden brown. Cool 10 minutes. Serve warm.

NUTRITION INFORMATION PER SERVING: Calories 330 • Total Fat 11g • Saturated Fat 5g • Cholesterol 120mg • Sodium 890mg • Total Carbohydrate 33g • Dietary Fiber 0g • Sugars 4g • Protein 24g. DIETARY EXCHANGES: 2 Starch • 2-1/2 Lean Meat • 1/2 Fat • 2 Carb Choices.

baked brie and brandied mushrooms

PREP TIME: 10 Minutes ✳ READY IN: 25 Minutes ✳ SERVINGS: 16

1 tablespoon butter or margarine

2 tablespoons slivered almonds

1 cup chopped fresh mushrooms

2 garlic cloves, finely chopped

1 teaspoon chopped fresh or 1/4 teaspoon dried tarragon leaves

1/8 teaspoon pepper

1 tablespoon brandy

1 round (8 oz.) Brie cheese

2 sprigs fresh tarragon, if desired

1 Heat oven to 375°F. In medium skillet, melt butter over medium heat. Add almonds; cook and stir 2 to 3 minutes or until almonds are browned. Stir in mushrooms, garlic, tarragon, pepper and brandy. Cook and stir 1 to 2 minutes or until mushrooms are tender. Remove from heat.

2 In ungreased decorative shallow baking dish or 8- or 9-inch glass pie plate, place cheese; spoon mushrooms over top.

3 Bake 10 to 12 minutes or until cheese is soft. Garnish with tarragon sprigs. Serve as a dip, or spread on melba toast rounds or crackers.

NUTRITION INFORMATION PER SERVING: Calories 60 • Total Fat 5g • Saturated Fat 3g • Cholesterol 15mg • Sodium 95mg • Total Carbohydrate 0g • Dietary Fiber 0g • Sugars 0g • Protein 3g. DIETARY EXCHANGE: 1/2 High-Fat Meat.

kitchen tip

When an appetizer buffet is the main food event of your party, include heartier selections and a wider array of spreads and dips. For six to eight people, plan on four to six different appetizers.

deviled crab and cheese rolls

elegant cheese grape cluster

elegant cheese grape cluster

PREP TIME: 1 Hour 5 Minutes ✳ READY IN: 2 Hours 5 Minutes ✳ SERVINGS: 48 Appetizers

1-1/2 cups slivered almonds (8 oz.)
    1 package (8 oz.) cream cheese, softened
  1/2 cup Gorgonzola cheese or other blue cheese, crumbled (2 oz.)
    3 tablespoons chopped fresh chives or parsley
   48 small red seedless grapes (about 9 oz.)

1 Heat oven to 350°F. Place slivered almonds in single layer in shallow baking pan with sides. Bake at 350°F for 8 to 12 minutes or until golden brown, stirring once. Remove from pan; cool about 5 minutes. Finely chop almonds.

2 In medium bowl, combine cream cheese, Gorgonzola cheese and chives; mix well. Wrap about 1 teaspoon cheese mixture around each grape to cover; roll in chopped almonds. Place in single layer in 13x9-inch pan. Cover; refrigerate at least 1 hour or up to 8 hours before serving.

3 To serve, if desired, arrange on serving platter in shape of grape cluster; garnish with parsley or grape leaves.

NUTRITION INFORMATION PER SERVING: Calories 50 • Total Fat 4g • Saturated Fat 1g • Cholesterol 5mg • Sodium 30mg • Total Carbohydrate 2g • Dietary Fiber 0g • Sugars 1g • Protein 2g. DIETARY EXCHANGE: 1 Fat.

penguin meatballs

PREP TIME: 40 Minutes ✳ READY IN: 55 Minutes ✳ SERVINGS: 16 (1 penguin each)

   16 strips bell pepper or onion, 1/2 inch by 3 inches
    1 large carrot (1 to 1-1/2 inches in diameter)
    1 bag (16 oz.) frozen cooked plain or Italian-style meatballs (32 count), thawed
   16 mini bamboo skewers (6 inches)

1 Heat oven to 350°F. Bell pepper or onion strips make the breast of each penguin. Blanch peppers or onions by placing in boiling water 20 seconds; plunge into ice water. Drain; set aside.

2 Cut 16 diagonal slices (1/4 inch thick) from carrot. To make beaks, cut a small triangle from edge of each carrot slice; set aside. Place the carrot slices for the feet in small microwavable bowl. Cover; microwave on High 30 seconds. Uncover; set aside. For head of each penguin, make small hole in each of 16 meatballs to hold beak; push skewer through meatball, starting at top of head. To place beak, insert carrot triangle into small hole of each meatball, inserting tip of skewer into carrot to secure in place.

3 Count out 16 additional meatballs to use for body of each penguin. Push skewer with first meatball (head) through 1 end of pepper or onion, then 1 meatball (body) and then through opposite end of pepper or onion. Continue pushing point of skewer into carrot slice with cutout facing forward as the feet. Place penguins in ungreased shallow pan. Bake 10 to 12 minutes or until hot.

NUTRITION INFORMATION PER SERVING: Calories 90 • Total Fat 7g • Saturated Fat 2.5g • Cholesterol 15mg • Sodium 170mg • Total Carbohydrate 3g • Dietary Fiber 0g • Sugars 0g • Protein 4g. DIETARY EXCHANGES: 1/2 Medium-Fat Meat • 1 Fat.

cook's notes

If you're a fan of cilantro, chop

1 tablespoon and add it to

the filling of these empanadas.

beef and chile empanadas

PREP TIME: 30 Minutes ❋ READY IN: 50 Minutes ❋ SERVINGS: 16

1 box (15 oz.) Pillsbury® refrigerated pie crusts, softened as directed on box

1/2 lb. lean (at least 80%) ground beef

1 can (4 oz.) Old El Paso® chopped green chiles

1 cup shredded Cheddar cheese (4 oz.)

1 cup Old El Paso® Thick 'n Chunky salsa

1 Heat oven to 425°F. Line large cookie sheet with cooking parchment paper, or spray with cooking spray. Unroll crusts. Cut each into 4 wedges.

2 In 10-inch nonstick skillet, cook beef over medium-high heat 5 to 7 minutes, stirring frequently, until thoroughly cooked; drain. Stir in chiles. Spoon about 2 tablespoons mixture over half of each crust wedge to within 1/4 inch of edges. Top each with 1 tablespoon cheese. Brush edges of crust with water. Fold untopped dough over filling, forming triangle; press edges to seal. Place on cookie sheet.

3 Bake 12 to 17 minutes or until golden brown. Remove from cookie sheet to cooling rack. Cool 10 minutes. Spoon salsa into small bowl. Place bowl in center of serving platter. Cut each warm empanada in half, forming 2 triangles. Arrange around bowl.

NUTRITION INFORMATION PER SERVING: Calories 180 • Total Fat 11g • Saturated Fat 4.5g • Cholesterol 20mg • Sodium 390mg • Total Carbohydrate 15g • Dietary Fiber 0g • Sugars 0g • Protein 4g. DIETARY EXCHANGES: 1/2 Starch • 1/2 Other Carbohydrate • 1/2 High-Fat Meat • 1-1/2 Fat • 1 Carb Choice.

spicy praline pecans

PREP TIME: 20 Minutes ❋ READY IN: 50 Minutes ❋ SERVINGS: 32

2 tablespoons butter

2 tablespoons dark brown sugar

2 tablespoons maple-flavored syrup or real maple syrup

1/4 teaspoon ground red pepper (cayenne), if desired

2 cups pecan halves (8 oz.)

1 Heat oven to 350°F. Line cookie sheet with parchment paper. Melt butter in large skillet over medium heat. Add brown sugar, syrup and ground red pepper; mix well. Cook until bubbly, stirring constantly.

2 Add pecans; cook 2 to 3 minutes or until coated, stirring constantly. Spread mixture onto parchment-lined cookie sheet.

3 Bake at 350°F for 5 to 10 minutes or until golden brown. Cool 30 minutes or until completely cooled. Store in tightly covered container for up to 2 weeks.

NUTRITION INFORMATION PER SERVING: Calories 135 • Total Fat 12g • Saturated Fat 2g • Cholesterol 5mg • Sodium 15mg • Total Carbohydrate 6g • Dietary Fiber 1g • Sugars 3g • Protein 1g. DIETARY EXCHANGES: 1/2 Other Carbohydrate • 2-1/2 Fat • 1/2 Carb Choice.

kitchen tip

Pecans are more than 70%

fat and are difficult to keep

fresh because they can become

rancid.

beef and chile empanadas

caramel apple baked brie

PREP TIME: 20 Minutes ✳ READY IN: 1 Hour 40 Minutes ✳ SERVINGS: 12

1 tablespoon butter

1/2 cup chopped peeled firm apple (Braeburn, Gala or Granny Smith)

1/4 cup sweetened dried cranberries

1/4 cup packed brown sugar

2 tablespoons chopped shelled pistachios or pecans

2 tablespoons brandy or apple juice

1 round (8 oz.) Brie cheese

Baguette French bread slices, assorted crackers or fresh apple slices

1 Heat oven to 350°F. In 8-inch skillet, melt butter over low heat. Add apple, cranberries, brown sugar, pistachios and brandy; cook 3 minutes or just until apples are tender, stirring frequently.

2 Cut Brie round in half horizontally; place bottom half in ungreased 9-inch pie pan. Spoon half of fruit mixture over cheese; place top half of cheese over fruit. Top with remaining fruit mixture. Secure with 3 toothpicks.

3 Bake 15 to 20 minutes or until cheese is soft. With broad spatula, slide Brie from pie pan onto serving platter. Spoon any syrup and fruit from pan over top of Brie. Serve warm with baguette bread slices.

NUTRITION INFORMATION PER SERVING: Calories 180 • Total Fat 8g • Saturated Fat 4g • Cholesterol 20mg • Sodium 300mg • Total Carbohydrate 22g • Dietary Fiber 1g • Sugars 7g • Protein 7g. DIETARY EXCHANGES: 1 Starch • 1/2 High-Fat Meat • 1/2 Fat • 1-1/2 Carb Choices.

cranberry-glazed appetizer meatballs

PREP TIME: 40 Minutes ✳ READY IN: 1 Hour 10 Minutes ✳ SERVINGS: 30

MEATBALLS

1-1/2 lbs. ground beef

1/2 cup finely chopped onion

1/2 cup unseasoned dry bread crumbs

1/2 teaspoon salt

1/8 teaspoon pepper

2 eggs, slightly beaten

SAUCE

1 bottle (12 oz.) chili sauce (1-1/2 cups)

1 can (8 oz.) jellied cranberry sauce (about 1 cup)

1 Heat oven to 375°F. In large bowl, combine all meatball ingredients; blend well. Shape into 1-inch balls; place in ungreased 15x10x1-inch baking pan.

2 Bake at 375°F for 25 to 30 minutes or until meatballs are browned and no longer pink in center. Meanwhile, in large saucepan, combine sauce ingredients; blend well. Bring to a boil over medium heat. Reduce heat to low; simmer 5 minutes, stirring occasionally.

3 Add meatballs to sauce; stir to coat. Cook over medium heat for 5 minutes or until thoroughly heated, stirring occasionally.

NUTRITION INFORMATION PER SERVING: Calories 80 • Total Fat 4g • Saturated Fat 1g • Cholesterol 30mg • Sodium 220mg • Total Carbohydrate 7g • Dietary Fiber 0g • Sugars 5g • Protein 5g. DIETARY EXCHANGES: 1/2 Fruit • 1/2 Lean Meat • 1/2 Fat OR 1/2 Carbohydrate • 1/2 Lean Meat • 1/2 Fat.

ham and asparagus squares

PREP TIME: 20 Minutes ✳ READY IN: 40 Minutes ✳ SERVINGS: 24

1/2 lb. fresh thin asparagus spears

1 can (8 oz.) Pillsbury® refrigerated crescent dinner rolls

1-1/2 cups finely shredded Swiss cheese (6 oz.)

1-1/2 oz. thinly sliced prosciutto or deli ham, cut into 1-inch strips

2 teaspoons olive oil

1/4 teaspoon crushed red pepper flakes

1 Heat oven to 375°F. In 10-inch skillet, heat 1/2 inch water to boiling. Add asparagus; reduce heat to medium-low. Cover; simmer 2 to 3 minutes or until crisp-tender. Drain. Plunge asparagus into bowl of ice water to cool; drain on paper towels.

2 Unroll dough on ungreased cookie sheet; press into 11x8-inch rectangle, firmly pressing perforations to seal. With fork, prick crust generously. Bake 6 to 9 minutes or until light golden brown.

3 Remove partially baked crust from oven. Sprinkle with 1/2 cup of the cheese; top with prosciutto strips. Sprinkle with remaining 1 cup cheese. Arrange cooked asparagus spears in rows over cheese, alternating tips. Brush with oil; sprinkle with pepper flakes.

4 Return to oven; bake 5 to 7 minutes longer or until edges of crust are deep golden brown and cheese is melted. Cool 5 minutes. With serrated knife, cut into squares. Serve warm.

HIGH ALTITUDE (3500-6500 FT): Bake untopped crust at 375°F 8 to 11 minutes. Continue as directed above.

NUTRITION INFORMATION PER SERVING: Calories 70 • Total Fat 4g • Saturated Fat 2g • Cholesterol 5mg • Sodium 150mg • Total Carbohydrate 5g • Dietary Fiber 0g • Sugars 1g • Protein 3g. DIETARY EXCHANGE: 1/2 High-Fat Meat.

cook's notes

To make dry bread crumbs, simply break slices of dried bread into pieces and process them in a blender or food processor until you have fine crumbs.

kitchen tip

Prosciutto is very thinly sliced. When you open the package, separate the paper-thin slices carefully. Running a table knife between layers helps separate them.

chicken peanut kabobs

READY IN: 30 Minutes ✳ SERVINGS: 20 Kabobs

20 bamboo or wooden skewers (6 inches)	1/4 cup soy sauce
10 slices bacon	1/4 cup apple juice or water
4 boneless skinless chicken breasts	1/4 to 1/2 teaspoon crushed red pepper flakes
1/4 cup peanut butter	

1 Soak skewers in water 15 minutes. Meanwhile, cut each bacon slice into 4 pieces; cook in 10-inch nonstick skillet over medium heat about 5 minutes or until partially cooked but not crisp. Remove bacon from skillet; drain on paper towels.

2 Cut each chicken breast lengthwise into 5 strips, each about 1/2 inch thick. Cut each strip into 3 pieces. Alternately thread 3 chicken pieces and 2 cooked bacon pieces onto each skewer; place on broiler pan.

3 In small bowl, mix all remaining ingredients until well blended. Pour half of sauce mixture into small serving bowl; set aside until serving time.

4 Brush about half of remaining sauce evenly over kabobs. Broil kabobs 4 to 6 inches from heat 3 to 4 minutes. Brush remaining sauce over kabobs; turn kabobs. Broil 3 to 4 minutes longer or until chicken is no longer pink in center. Serve with reserved sauce.

NUTRITION INFORMATION PER SERVING: Calories 60 • Total Fat 3g • Saturated Fat 1g • Cholesterol 15mg • Sodium 160mg • Total Carbohydrate 1g • Dietary Fiber 0g • Sugars 0g • Protein 7g. DIETARY EXCHANGES: 1 Very Lean Meat • 1/2 Fat.

barbecue chicken crescent pinwheels

PREP TIME: 15 Minutes ✳ READY IN: 35 Minutes ✳ SERVINGS: 6

1 can (15.5 oz.) Pillsbury® Grands!® refrigerated crescent dinner rolls	6 thin slices mozzarella cheese (3/4 oz.)
1/2 lb. thinly sliced roasted chicken breast	1 egg white, beaten
1 to 2 tablespoons barbecue sauce	1 tablespoon sesame seed
	Barbecue sauce

1 Heat oven to 375°F. Spray large cookie sheet with nonstick cooking spray. Separate dough into 3 rectangles. Firmly press perforations to seal. Cut rectangles in half crosswise to make 6 pieces, each about 5-1/2x4 inches. Place dough pieces on sprayed cookie sheet. Press each to form 5-1/2-inch square.

2 Arrange chicken evenly on dough squares, folding under edges of chicken as necessary to fit dough. Spread chicken with 1 to 2 tablespoons barbecue sauce. Top each with mozzarella cheese slice to fit.

3 With kitchen scissors, cut into each sandwich from each corner to within 1 inch of center. Fold alternating points to center of each, overlapping and pressing center to seal. Brush each with egg white. Sprinkle dough with sesame seed.

4 Bake at 375°F for 13 to 18 minutes or until golden brown. Serve sandwiches with additional barbecue sauce.

NUTRITION INFORMATION PER SERVING: Calories 400 • Total Fat 20g • Saturated Fat 6g • Cholesterol 30mg • Sodium 1230mg • Total Carbohydrate 34g • Dietary Fiber 1g • Sugars 6g • Protein 20g. DIETARY EXCHANGES: 2-1/2 Starch • 2 Very Lean Meat • 3 Fat OR 2-1/2 Carbohydrate • 2 Very Lean Meat • 3 Fat • 2 Carb Choices.

chicken peanut kabobs

thai turkey lettuce wraps

thai turkey lettuce wraps

READY IN: 30 Minutes ✳ SERVINGS: 12

1-1/4 lbs. ground turkey	2 teaspoons garlic and red chile paste
1/4 cup chopped green onions (4 medium)	1 teaspoon sugar
3 tablespoons chopped fresh cilantro	1/2 teaspoon crushed red pepper flakes
1 tablespoon chopped fresh mint	1 cup shredded carrots
2 tablespoons fresh lime juice	1/3 cup chopped salted peanuts
2 tablespoons fish sauce	12 medium Bibb lettuce leaves, rinsed, patted dry with paper towel
3 tablespoons creamy peanut butter	

1 In 10-inch nonstick skillet, cook turkey over medium-high heat, stirring frequently, until thoroughly cooked; drain and return to skillet. Stir in green onions, cilantro, mint, lime juice, fish sauce, peanut butter, chile paste, sugar and red pepper flakes. Cook 3 to 4 minutes longer or until hot.

2 To serve, spoon 2 heaping tablespoons turkey mixture, 2 tablespoons carrots and 1 teaspoon peanuts onto each lettuce leaf; wrap around filling. Serve warm.

NUTRITION INFORMATION PER SERVING: Calories 140 • Total Fat 9g • Saturated Fat 2g • Cholesterol 30mg • Sodium 320mg; • Total Carbohydrate 3g • Dietary Fiber 1g • Sugars 2g • Protein 12g. DIETARY EXCHANGE: 2 Medium-Fat Meat.

cook's notes

We recommend Bibb lettuce for this recipe because of its sturdiness.

stuffed party mushrooms

PREP TIME: 20 Minutes ✳ READY IN: 45 Minutes ✳ SERVINGS: 10

1 lb. medium-sized fresh whole mushrooms	1/2 teaspoon dried oregano leaves
1/4 cup grated Parmesan cheese	1/4 teaspoon salt
1/4 cup unseasoned dry bread crumbs	1/8 teaspoon pepper
1/4 cup finely chopped onion	1 garlic clove, minced

1 Heat oven to 350°F. Brush or wipe mushrooms with damp cloth. Remove stems from mushrooms; set caps aside. Finely chop mushroom stems.

2 In medium bowl, combine chopped stems and all remaining ingredients; mix well. Press mixture firmly into mushroom caps, mounding on top. Place in ungreased 13x9-inch pan. Bake at 350°F for 18 to 23 minutes or until thoroughly heated. Serve warm.

NUTRITION INFORMATION PER SERVING: Calories 30 • Total Fat 1g • Saturated Fat 0g • Cholesterol 0mg • Sodium 95mg • Total Carbohydrate 3g • Dietary Fiber 1g • Sugars 1g • Protein 2g. DIETARY EXCHANGE: 1 Vegetable.

cook's notes

After placing the mushrooms in the baking pan, you can cover and refrigerate them for up to 4 hours before baking as directed.

red bell pepper and olive pizza sticks

PREP TIME: 15 Minutes ✳ READY IN: 30 Minutes ✳ SERVINGS: 28 servings

1 can (13.8 oz.) Pillsbury® refrigerated classic pizza crust	3 tablespoons thinly slivered pitted ripe olives
1 tablespoon extra-virgin olive oil	1 tablespoon chopped fresh rosemary
1/3 cup red bell pepper strips (1x1/8 inch)	1/4 teaspoon kosher (coarse) salt
	1 cup tomato pasta sauce, heated

1 Heat oven to 400°F. Grease cookie sheet with shortening or spray with cooking spray. Unroll dough; place on cookie sheet. Starting from center, press out dough to form 14x9-inch rectangle. With fingertips, make indentations over surface of dough.

2 Drizzle oil over dough. Top with remaining ingredients except pasta sauce; press lightly into dough.

3 Bake 13 to 18 minutes or until golden brown. Cut pizza in half lengthwise; cut each half crosswise into 14 sticks. Serve warm sticks with warm pasta sauce for dipping.

NUTRITION INFORMATION PER SERVING: Calories 50 • Total Fat 1.5g • Saturated Fat 0g • Cholesterol 0mg • Sodium 170mg • Total Carbohydrate 8g • Dietary Fiber 0g. DIETARY EXCHANGES: 1/2 Starch • 1/2 Carb Choice.

cranberry-raspberry wine coolers

PREP TIME: 20 Minutes ✳ READY IN: 3 Hours 50 Minutes ✳ SERVINGS: 12

1 package (10 oz.) frozen raspberries in syrup, thawed	3 cups white zinfandel wine, chilled
2 cups raspberry-cranberry juice drink blend, chilled	1-1/2 cups lemon-lime flavored carbonated beverage, chilled
	12 fresh orange or star fruit slices

1 In medium bowl, combine raspberries and 1/2 cup of the raspberry-cranberry drink; mix well. Spoon into 12 sections of ice cube tray. Freeze 3-1/2 hours or until firm.

2 To serve, place 1 ice cube in each of 12 wine glasses. In large pitcher, combine remaining raspberry-cranberry drink, wine and carbonated beverage; stir gently. Pour into glasses. Garnish with orange slices.

NUTRITION INFORMATION PER SERVING: Calories 110 • Total Fat 0g • Saturated Fat 0g • Cholesterol 0mg • Sodium 5mg • Total Carbohydrate 18g • Dietary Fiber 1g • Sugars 16g • Protein 0g. DIETARY EXCHANGES: 1 Fruit • 1 Fat OR 1 Carbohydrate • 1 Fat.

olive cheese nuggets

PREP TIME: 30 Minutes ✳ READY IN: 45 Minutes ✳ SERVINGS: 24 Snacks

1 cup shredded sharp Cheddar cheese (4 oz.)	1/8 teaspoon salt
1/4 cup butter or margarine, softened	1/2 teaspoon paprika
3/4 cup all-purpose flour	24 small stuffed green olives

1 Heat oven to 400°F. In medium bowl, mix Cheddar cheese and butter. In small bowl, mix flour, salt and paprika. Add to cheese mixture in medium bowl; mix with hands to form dough (mixture will be stiff). Shape dough around olives, using about a teaspoonful of dough for each olive. Place on ungreased cookie sheet. Bake 12 to 15 minutes or until firm. Serve hot or cold.

HIGH ALTITUDE (3500-6500 FT): Add 1 to 2 tablespoons water to make a dough.

NUTRITION INFORMATION PER SERVING: Calories 60 • Total Fat 4g • Saturated Fat 2.5g • Cholesterol 10mg • Sodium 120mg • Total Carbohydrate 3g • Dietary Fiber 0g. DIETARY EXCHANGE: 1/2 High-Fat Meat.

red bell pepper and olive pizza sticks

mozzarella and pesto crescent tarts

mozzarella and pesto crescent tarts

PREP TIME: 20 Minutes ✳ READY IN: 35 Minutes ✳ SERVINGS: 16

1 can (8 oz.) Pillsbury® refrigerated crescent dinner rolls	1 to 2 teaspoons chopped fresh rosemary or 1/2 teaspoon dried rosemary leaves
2 tablespoons purchased pesto	2 oz. diced fresh mozzarella cheese or shredded mozzarella cheese (1/2 cup)
2 medium tomatoes, seeded, sliced	1 oz. shredded fresh Parmesan cheese (1/4 cup)
1 small red onion, thinly sliced	

1 Heat oven to 425°F. Unroll dough into 2 long rectangles. Place 3 inches apart on ungreased cookie sheet. Firmly press perforations to seal. Press to form two 10x3-inch strips, forming rim around edge of dough.

2 Spread each strip with 1 tablespoon pesto. Top each with tomatoes, onion and rosemary. Sprinkle each with mozzarella and Parmesan cheese.

3 Bake at 425°F for 10 to 14 minutes or until edges are golden brown and cheese is melted. Cut each into crosswise slices. Serve warm or cool.

NUTRITION INFORMATION PER SERVING: Calories 90 • Total Fat 5g • Saturated Fat 2g • Cholesterol 0mg • Sodium 170mg • Total Carbohydrate 7g • Dietary Fiber 0g • Sugars 2g • Protein 3g. DIETARY EXCHANGES: 1/2 Starch • 1 Fat • 1/2 Carb Choice.

TRACIE OJAKANGAS
Springfield, Missouri
Bake-Off® Contest 39, 2000

cook's notes

Four medium plum (Roma) tomatoes may be substituted for the regular tomatoes.

beef fondue and dipping sauces

READY IN: 20 Minutes ✳ SERVINGS: 8

AÏOLI DIP
- 1/2 cup mayonnaise
- 1 large garlic clove, minced
- 3 tablespoons olive oil
- 1/4 teaspoon salt

CURRY DIP
- 3/4 cup mayonnaise
- 1 teaspoon lemon juice
- 2 teaspoons curry powder
- 1/8 teaspoon ground ginger

HORSERADISH SAUCE
- 1/3 cup mayonnaise
- 1/3 cup sour cream
- 1 tablespoon prepared horseradish
- 1 tablespoon Dijon mustard

STEAK SAUCE
- 1/2 cup ketchup
- 2 tablespoons Worcestershire sauce
- 1/2 teaspoon garlic salt

FONDUE
- 1 quart peanut oil (4 cups)
- 1 beef tenderloin (3 lbs.), cut into 1-1/2-inch cubes
- 8 oz. fresh whole mushrooms

cook's notes

Feel free to use a less-expensive cut of beef, such as boneless beef top sirloin steak, in place of the tenderloin.

1 To prepare aïoli dip, in small bowl, combine mayonnaise and garlic; blend well. With wire whisk, beat in olive oil and salt until well blended.

2 To prepare curry dip, in small bowl, combine all ingredients; blend well. To prepare horseradish sauce, in small bowl, combine all ingredients; blend well.

3 To prepare steak sauce, in small bowl, combine all ingredients; blend well. Cover each dip or sauce tightly. Refrigerate until serving time.

4 At serving time, heat peanut oil in fondue pot over medium heat until oil reaches 350°F. Place on warmer to maintain heat. Place beef cubes and mushrooms on serving platters.

5 Pass beef and mushrooms to guests. Place 1 or 2 pieces beef and/or mushrooms on fondue fork. Place in hot oil; cook until beef is of desired doneness and mushrooms are tender. Serve with dips and sauces.

NUTRITION INFORMATION PER SERVING: Calories 315 • Total Fat 18g • Saturated Fat 6g • Cholesterol 95mg • Sodium 90mg • Total Carbohydrate 1g • Dietary Fiber 0g • Sugars 0g • Protein 37g. DIETARY EXCHANGES: 5 Lean Meat • 1 Fat.

cook's notes

If you have time, make your own guacamole. Simply mash a ripe avocado and throw in a dash of salt, lime juice and chopped garlic.

pita tree appetizer

READY IN: 25 Minutes ✳ SERVINGS: 32

4 flavored or plain pita folds or pita (pocket) breads (about 6 inches in diameter)	1/2 cup guacamole
16 thin pretzel sticks, halved	2 tablespoons finely chopped parsley
1/2 cup fat-free sour cream	1/4 teaspoon garlic-pepper blend
	1/4 cup very finely chopped red bell pepper

1 Cut each pita fold into 8 wedges. Insert pretzel stick half into center of bottom of each wedge to form "tree trunk."

2 In small bowl, mix sour cream, guacamole, parsley and garlic-pepper blend. Spread about 1 teaspoon sour cream mixture on each pita wedge.

3 Blot bell pepper with paper towel to remove excess moisture. Sprinkle about 1/4 teaspoon bell pepper on each wedge or arrange to form a garland. If desired, cover and refrigerate up to 8 hours before serving.

NUTRITION INFORMATION PER SERVING: Calories 30 • Total Fat 0.5g • Saturated Fat 0g • Cholesterol 0mg • Sodium 60mg • Total Carbohydrate 5g • Dietary Fiber 0g • Sugars 0g • Protein 0g. DIETARY EXCHANGES: 1/2 Starch • 1/2 Carb Choice.

grilled cheese appetizer sandwiches

PREP TIME: 20 Minutes ✳ READY IN: 25 Minutes ✳ SERVINGS: 12

2 tablespoons butter or margarine

24 slices cocktail rye or sourdough bread

12 slices cracker-cut sharp Cheddar cheese (from 6-oz. pkg.)

3 slices (about 1 oz. each) American cheese, cut into quarters

1 Set oven control to broil. Place butter in small microwavable bowl; cover with microwavable paper towel. Microwave on High 30 to 50 seconds or until melted. Brush butter on 1 side of each bread slice.

2 On ungreased cookie sheet, place 12 bread slices, buttered sides down. Top each with 1 slice Cheddar cheese and 1 quarter-slice American cheese. Add remaining bread slices, buttered sides up.

3 Broil with tops 4 to 6 inches from heat 2 minutes. Turn sandwiches over. Broil about 1 minute longer or until golden brown and cheese is melted.

NUTRITION INFORMATION PER SERVING: Calories 120 • Total Fat 8g • Saturated Fat 5g • Cholesterol 20mg • Sodium 270mg • Total Carbohydrate 7g • Dietary Fiber 0g • Sugars 0g • Protein 5g. DIETARY EXCHANGES: 1/2 Starch • 1/2 High-Fat Meat • 1/2 Fat • 1/2 Carb Choice.

cook's notes

These mini sandwiches may be assembled up to 8 hours before broiling. Place them on a cookie sheet, cover them with plastic wrap and refrigerate. Broil as directed.

pita tree appetizer

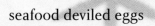

seafood deviled eggs

seafood deviled eggs

PREP TIME: 1 Hour ✳ READY IN: 2 Hours ✳ SERVINGS: 24

12 eggs	1/2 teaspoon ground mustard
1/2 cup mayonnaise or salad dressing	1/2 cup cooked salad shrimp, chopped (4 oz.)
1 teaspoon seafood seasoning (from 6-oz. container)	1 can (6 oz.) lump crabmeat, drained
1/2 teaspoon paprika	3 slices bacon, crisply cooked, crumbled
	2 tablespoons chopped fresh parsley

1 Place eggs in 4-quart Dutch oven. Add cold water until it reaches 1 inch above eggs. Heat to boiling; remove from heat. Cover and let stand 18 minutes. Immediately cool eggs about 10 minutes in cold water to prevent further cooking.

2 Tap egg to crack shell; roll egg between hands to loosen shell, then peel. Cut eggs lengthwise in half. Slip out yolks into medium bowl; reserve egg white halves. Mash yolks with fork. Stir in mayonnaise, seasoning, paprika and ground mustard until well blended. Stir in shrimp and crab.

3 Spoon heaping teaspoonfuls of yolk mixture into egg white halves. Refrigerate at least 30 minutes before serving. Just before serving, sprinkle with bacon and parsley.

HIGH ALTITUDE (3500-6500 FT): Heat water to boiling; boil 5 minutes. Remove from heat; cover and let stand 15 minutes.

NUTRITION INFORMATION PER SERVING: Calories 90 • Total Fat 7g • Saturated Fat 1.5g • Cholesterol 125mg • Sodium 140mg • Total Carbohydrate 0g • Dietary Fiber 0g • Sugars 0g • Protein 6g. DIETARY EXCHANGE: 1 High-Fat Meat.

kitchen tip

You can prepare these stuffed eggs up to 24 hours ahead of time. Cover and refrigerate them until serving time. Wait to add the bacon and parsley until just before serving.

curry-mustard glazed meatballs

PREP TIME: 10 Minutes ✳ READY IN: 4 Hours 10 Minutes ✳ SERVINGS: 40

1 jar (12 oz.) pineapple preserves	1/2 cup firmly packed dark brown sugar
1 jar (8 oz.) Dijon mustard	1 teaspoon curry powder
1 can (8 oz.) pineapple tidbits in unsweetened juice, undrained	2-1/2 lbs. frozen cooked Italian meatballs (about 80 meatballs)

1 In small saucepan, combine all ingredients except meatballs. Bring to a boil. Place meatballs in 2-1/2- to 3-quart slow cooker. Stir in preserves mixture. Cover; cook on High setting for 4 hours, stirring twice. Stir well before serving.

HIGH ALTITUDE (3500-6500 FT): Defrost meatballs and continue as directed.

NUTRITION INFORMATION PER SERVING: Calories 120 • Total Fat 5g • Saturated Fat 2g • Cholesterol 30mg • Sodium 310mg • Total Carbohydrate 13g • Dietary Fiber 0g • Sugars 8g • Protein 6g. DIETARY EXCHANGES: 1 Starch • 1 Medium-Fat Meat • 1 Carb Choice.

cook's notes

Use a slow cooker to serve meatballs during a party. Hot meatballs can be held for two hours in a slower cooker set on the Low heat setting with the lid removed. Provide small forks, pretzel sticks or cocktail toothpicks for easy eating.

cook's notes

One can (4 oz.) Old El Paso® whole green chiles, drained and cut into 16 pieces, may be substituted for the whole jalapeño chiles.

crescent jalapeño poppers

PREP TIME: 25 Minutes ✷ READY IN: 40 Minutes ✷ SERVINGS: 16

4 jalapeño chiles (about 3 inches long)

1/3 cup Boursin cheese with garlic and herbs (from 5.2-oz. container)

8 slices packaged precooked bacon (from 2.2-oz. pkg.), halved

1 can (8 oz.) Pillsbury® refrigerated crescent dinner rolls

1/2 cup pineapple or fruit salsa, if desired

1 Heat oven to 375°F. Carefully remove stems from chiles; cut each in half lengthwise and again horizontally to make 4 pieces. Remove and discard seeds. Spoon about 1 teaspoon cheese into each chile quarter. Wrap half slice of bacon around each.

2 On cutting board, unroll dough; separate dough into 8 triangles. From center of longest side to opposite point, cut each triangle in half, making 16 triangles. Place chile, cheese side down, on dough triangle. Fold 1 point of triangle over filling; fold 2 remaining points over first point. Place on ungreased cookie sheet.

3 Bake 12 to 15 minutes or until golden brown. Immediately remove from cookie sheet. Serve with pineapple salsa.

HIGH ALTITUDE (3500-6500 FT): Bake 9 to 12 minutes.

NUTRITION INFORMATION PER SERVING: Calories 90 • Total Fat 6g • Saturated Fat 2.5g • Cholesterol 10mg • Sodium 220mg • Total Carbohydrate 6g • Dietary Fiber 0g • Sugars 1g • Protein 3g. DIETARY EXCHANGES: 1/2 Starch • 1 Fat • 1/2 Carb Choice.

cook's notes

Cambozola is a German cheese similar to Gorgonzola and Camembert. Like Camembert, Cambozola is soft-ripened and has an edible white rind. Its delightful creamy interior is veined with blue. Cambozola is particularly nice for this recipe because it's easy to slice.

pecan and blue cheese crescent bites

READY IN: 35 Minutes ✷ SERVINGS: 24

1 can (8 oz.) Pillsbury® refrigerated crescent dinner rolls

1/4 cup plum jam

1/2 cup diced dried fruit and raisin mixture, chopped

4 oz. Cambozola cheese, cut into 24 small slices

24 pecan halves

1 Heat oven to 375°F. Line cookie sheet with parchment paper or spray lightly with nonstick cooking spray. Unroll dough into 1 long rectangle. Gently press perforations to seal. Stir jam to soften; spread over dough. Sprinkle with dried fruits.

2 Starting with one long side, roll up dough jelly-roll fashion. With serrated knife, cut roll into 24 slices; place, cut side down, on paper-lined cookie sheet.

3 Bake at 375°F for 13 to 15 minutes or until golden brown. Immediately remove from cookie sheet; place on wire rack. Cool about 2 minutes or until slightly cooled.

4 Top each with slice of Cambozola cheese and pecan half. Serve appetizers warm or at room temperature.

NUTRITION INFORMATION PER SERVING: Calories 75 • Total Fat 4g • Saturated Fat 1g • Cholesterol 5mg • Sodium 180mg • Total Carbohydrate 9g • Dietary Fiber 1g • Sugars 4g • Protein 2g. DIETARY EXCHANGES: 1/2 Starch • 1 Fat OR 1/2 Carbohydrate • 1 Fat.

crescent jalapeño poppers

broccoli-bacon crescent spiral

broccoli-bacon crescent spiral

PREP TIME: 20 Minutes ✳ READY IN: 40 Minutes ✳ SERVINGS: 32

1/4 cup garlic and herb cream cheese spread (from 8-oz. container)

1 tablespoon grated Parmesan cheese

1 can (8 oz.) Pillsbury® refrigerated crescent dinner rolls

4 slices bacon, crisply cooked, crumbled

1 cup frozen broccoli florets, thawed, finely chopped and patted dry with paper towel

1/4 cup coarsely chopped drained roasted red bell peppers (from a jar)

1 egg, beaten

1 teaspoon sesame seed

Sprigs fresh rosemary, if desired

1 Heat oven to 375°F. In small bowl, mix cream cheese spread and cheese. Unroll dough and separate into 2 long rectangles. Place and pinch 2 short ends of rectangles together; pat or press into 22x4-1/2-inch rectangle, pressing perforations to seal.

2 Spread cream cheese mixture lengthwise down center 1-1/2 inches of rectangle. Top with crumbled bacon, broccoli and roasted peppers.

3 With kitchen scissors or sharp knife, make 30 cuts about 3/4 inch apart on long sides of rectangle to about 1/4 inch of filling. Alternately cross strips over filling. Press ends together to seal. Coil braid into spiral shape (see photo). Gently slide ungreased cookie sheet under spiral and move to center of cookie sheet. Carefully brush dough with beaten egg; sprinkle with sesame seed.

4 Bake 11 to 13 minutes or until deep golden brown. Cool 5 minutes. With broad spatula, carefully loosen from cookie sheet; slide onto serving platter. Cut into thin slices. Garnish platter with rosemary. Serve warm.

HIGH ALTITUDE (3500-6500 FT): Bake 13 to 15 minutes.

NUTRITION INFORMATION PER SERVING: Calories 45 • Total Fat 3g • Saturated Fat 1g • Cholesterol 10mg • Sodium 90mg • Total Carbohydrate 3g • Dietary Fiber 0g • Sugars 0g • Protein 1g. DIETARY EXCHANGES: 1/2 Other Carbohydrate • 1/2 Fat.

cook's notes

You can prepare this snack up to 2 hours before baking. Just cover it in plastic wrap and refrigerate.

maple-apple party riblets

PREP TIME: 25 Minutes ✳ READY IN: 1 Hour 25 Minutes ✳ SERVINGS: 8

2 lbs. pork back ribs, cut across bones to form riblets

1/2 cup real maple syrup

1/4 cup apple jelly

1 tablespoon soy sauce

1/4 cup chopped fresh chives

1/2 teaspoon dry mustard

1 Heat oven to 450°F. Line 15x10x1-inch baking pan with foil. Cut ribs into individual riblets. Place, meaty side down, in foil-lined pan; cover with foil. Bake at 450°F for 30 minutes.

2 Meanwhile, in small saucepan, combine syrup, jelly, soy sauce, chives and dry mustard; mix well. Cook over low heat for 8 to 10 minutes or until hot and well blended, stirring occasionally. Remove from heat.

3 Reduce oven temperature to 350°F. Remove ribs from oven. Uncover; drain liquid from ribs. Turn ribs meaty side up; brush with syrup mixture.

4 Bake, uncovered, at 350°F for 30 minutes. Brush with syrup mixture; bake an additional 10 to 15 minutes or until ribs are tender and glazed.

NUTRITION INFORMATION PER SERVING: Calories 280 • Total Fat 16g • Saturated Fat 6g • Cholesterol 65mg • Sodium 190mg • Total Carbohydrate 20g • Dietary Fiber 0g • Sugars 17g • Protein 14g. DIETARY EXCHANGES: 1-1/2 Fruit • 2 High-Fat Meat OR 1-1/2 Carbohydrate • 2 High-Fat Meat.

Kitchen tip

Serve hot appetizers promptly after cooking or reheating, or keep them at an appropriate temperature with electric trays, chafing dishes, slow cookers or fondue pots.

apple-cherry brie appetizer

PREP TIME: 20 Minutes ✳ READY IN: 1 Hour 45 Minutes ✳ SERVINGS: 16

1 round (8 oz.) Brie cheese	1/4 teaspoon ground cinnamon
1 medium apple, peeled, chopped	1 tablespoon orange-flavored liqueur or orange juice
1/4 cup dried cherries	
1/4 cup sugar	1/4 cup chopped walnuts, toasted
1/2 cup water	1 can (8 oz.) Pillsbury® refrigerated crescent dinner rolls
1 tablespoon cornstarch	

1 With sharp knife, carefully remove rind from cheese. Wrap cheese in plastic wrap; freeze 30 minutes.

2 Meanwhile, in 1-quart saucepan heat apple, cherries, sugar and 1/4 cup of the water to boiling. Reduce heat to low; simmer 2 to 3 minutes, stirring occasionally, until fruit is tender.

3 In small bowl, mix cornstarch, cinnamon, remaining 1/4 cup water and the liqueur until well blended. Add to apple mixture, stirring constantly. Simmer 2 to 3 minutes or until sauce thickens. Remove from heat; stir in walnuts.

4 Heat oven to 375°F. Line 15x10x1-inch pan with foil. On foil in pan, unroll dough into 1 large rectangle; firmly press perforations to seal. Press into 11x9-inch rectangle. Cut 11x3-inch strip from 1 side of rectangle; set aside.

5 Cut cheese round horizontally to make 2 rounds. Place cheese rounds next to each other in center of dough rectangle. Roll sides of dough up next to cheese, forming a rim around cheese. Top cheese evenly with apple mixture. Cut remaining strip of dough into 6 (1/2-inch wide) strips. Place 3 strips lengthwise across cheese. Cut remaining strips in half; place across other strips to make lattice; press edges to seal, tucking under if necessary. Fold foil edges up about 1 inch from dough; pinch corners of foil together.

6 Bake uncovered 30 minutes. Cover with foil; bake about 5 minutes longer or until golden brown and cheese is softened. Let stand 10 minutes. To serve, cut in half lengthwise, then into crosswise strips. Serve warm.

NUTRITION INFORMATION PER SERVING: Calories 140 • Total Fat 8g • Saturated Fat 3.5g • Cholesterol 15mg • Sodium 200mg • Total Carbohydrate 12g • Dietary Fiber 0g • Sugars 6g • Protein 4g. DIETARY EXCHANGES: 1/2 Starch • 1/2 Other Carbohydrate • 1/2 High-Fat Meat • 1/2 Fat • 1 Carb Choice.

new england mulled cider

PREP TIME: 10 Minutes ✳ READY IN: 40 Minutes ✳ SERVINGS: 8

2 quarts (8 cups) apple cider	1/2 teaspoon nutmeg
1/4 cup firmly packed brown sugar	2 cinnamon sticks
1/2 teaspoon cardamom	Peel from 1 orange

1 In large saucepan, combine all ingredients; mix well. Bring to a boil. Reduce heat; simmer 30 minutes. Remove cinnamon sticks and orange peel. Keep warm in hot pot or coffee pot.

NUTRITION INFORMATION PER SERVING: Calories 140 • Total Fat 0g • Saturated Fat 0g • Cholesterol 0mg • Sodium 10mg • Total Carbohydrate 36g • Dietary Fiber 0g • Sugars 31g • Protein 0g. DIETARY EXCHANGES: 2-1/2 Fruit OR 2-1/2 Carbohydrate.

apple-cherry brie appetizer

smoked salmon wraps

READY IN: 30 Minutes ✳ SERVINGS: 20

4 oz. thinly sliced smoked salmon (lox)	20 small sprigs fresh dill
1/4 cup whipped cream cheese (from 8-oz. container)	20 fresh sugar snap peas

1 Carefully separate slices of salmon; place individually on work surface. Spread slices with thin layer of cream cheese.

2 Cut each slice of salmon into about 3x1-inch strips (because salmon slices are irregular shape, some strips may need to be cut in one direction and some in another direction). Top each strip with dill. Place 1 sugar snap pea crosswise on each strip; roll up.

NUTRITION INFORMATION PER SERVING: Calories 15 • Total Fat 1g • Saturated Fat 0g • Cholesterol 5mg • Sodium 50mg • Total Carbohydrate 0g • Dietary Fiber 0g • Sugars 0g • Protein 1g. DIETARY EXCHANGES: Free.

salami veggie roll-ups

PREP TIME: 20 Minutes ❊ READY IN: 1 Hour 20 Minutes ❊ SERVINGS: 32

cook's notes

These appetizer roll-ups can be made a day ahead and sliced just before serving.

1/2 cup light garden vegetable cream cheese spread (from 8-oz. container)

4 flour or tomato tortillas (10 inch)

3 oz. very thinly sliced salami (about 24 slices)

3/4 cup creamy coleslaw (from deli), drained

1/4 medium red bell pepper, cut into very thin strips

4 large leaves leaf lettuce

1 Spread light garden vegetable cream cheese spread evenly over tortillas, covering tortillas completely.

2 Arrange salami over cheese spread, covering bottom half of each tortilla. Top salami with coleslaw, bell pepper and lettuce.

3 Roll up each tightly; wrap individually in plastic wrap. Refrigerate until completely chilled, at least 1 hour. To serve, trim off ends of each roll; cut each into 8 slices.

NUTRITION INFORMATION PER SERVING: Calories 50 • Total Fat 2g • Saturated Fat 1g • Cholesterol 5mg • Sodium 110mg • Total Carbohydrate 6g • Dietary Fiber 0g • Sugars 1g • Protein 2g. DIETARY EXCHANGES: 1/2 Starch • 1/2 Fat • 1/2 Carb Choice.

zesty margarita shrimp cocktail

zesty margarita shrimp cocktail

READY IN: 10 Minutes ✳ SERVINGS: 32

- 1/2 cup mayonnaise
- 2 tablespoons refrigerated honey mustard salad dressing
- 1 teaspoon grated lime peel
- 1 tablespoon fresh lime juice
- 1 tablespoon tequila, if desired
- 32 deveined shelled cooked extra-large shrimp with tails on (about 2 lbs.)

1 In medium bowl, mix all ingredients except cooked extra-large shrimp. Serve mixture as dip for shrimp.

NUTRITION INFORMATION PER SERVING: Calories 35 • Total Fat 3g • Saturated 0g • Cholesterol 20mg • Sodium 45mg • Total Carbohydrate 0g • Dietary Fiber 0g • Sugars 0g • Protein 2g.

cook's notes

Tequila adds depth of flavor but isn't absolutely necessary for the success of this recipe.

rich and creamy eggnog

PREP TIME: 10 Minutes ✳ READY IN: 1 Hour 10 Minutes ✳ SERVINGS: 10

- 4 cups milk
- 1 package (3.4 oz.) instant vanilla pudding and pie filling mix
- 1 carton (8 oz.) refrigerated or frozen fat-free egg product, thawed (1 cup)
- 1 teaspoon vanilla
- 1 teaspoon rum extract or 1/4 cup light rum
- 1/4 teaspoon salt
- 1/4 teaspoon nutmeg
  - Whipped cream, if desired
  - Nutmeg, if desired

1 In large bowl, combine 2 cups of the milk and vanilla pudding mix; beat 1 minute or until smooth.

2 Add remaining 2 cups milk, egg product, vanilla, rum extract, salt and 1/4 teaspoon nutmeg; beat well. Cover; refrigerate at least 1 hour before serving. Serve topped with whipped cream and a sprinkle of nutmeg.

NUTRITION INFORMATION PER SERVING: Calories 130 • Total Fat 5g • Saturated Fat 3g • Cholesterol 20mg • Sodium 280mg • Total Carbohydrate 16g • Dietary Fiber 0g • Sugars 14g • Protein 6g. DIETARY EXCHANGES: 1/2 Starch • 1/2 Low-Fat Milk • 1/2 Fat OR 1 Carbohydrate • 1/2 Fat.

cook's notes

To make sweetened whipped cream, add 2 tablespoons confectioners' sugar to each cup of cream before whipping.

tomato and basil bruschetta

READY IN: 15 Minutes ✳ SERVINGS: 2

- 4 slices (1/2 inch thick) coarse-textured bread (about 4x3 inches)
- 1 garlic clove, peeled, cut in half
- 8 teaspoons extra-virgin olive oil
- 1/4 teaspoon salt
- 1/8 teaspoon coarsely ground black pepper
- 1 small tomato, cut into 8 thin slices
- 1 tablespoon chopped fresh basil

1 Grill, broil or toast bread slices on both sides until light golden brown. While hot, rub cut side of garlic over 1 side of each bread slice.

2 Drizzle 1 teaspoon oil over garlic-rubbed side of each bread slice; sprinkle with salt and pepper. Top each with tomato slices; sprinkle with basil. Drizzle remaining oil over tomato slices. Serve immediately.

NUTRITION INFORMATION PER SERVING: Calories 310 • Total Fat 20g • Saturated Fat 3g • Cholesterol 0mg • Sodium 580mg • Total Carbohydrate 28g • Dietary Fiber 2g • Sugars 3g • Protein 5g. DIETARY EXCHANGES: 2 Starch • 3-1/2 Fat OR 2 Carbohydrate • 3-1/2 Fat.

kitchen tip

Extra-virgin olive oil loses much of its distinctive flavor when heated, but its flavor shines in cold dishes, in salad dressings and when drizzled on salads or breads.

holiday appetizer tree

PREP TIME: 15 Minutes ✻ READY IN: 45 Minutes ✻ SERVINGS: 16

1 can (8 oz.) Pillsbury® refrigerated crescent dinner rolls	1/4 medium yellow bell pepper
1 container (8 oz.) chives-and-onion cream cheese spread	1/2 cup chopped fresh broccoli
1 tablespoon milk	2 tablespoons sliced ready-to-eat baby-cut carrots
3/4 medium red bell pepper	1 tablespoon chopped cucumber
	2 tablespoons sliced almonds

1 Heat oven to 375°F. Remove dough from can in 1 long roll; do not unroll or separate. Cut roll into 16 slices.

2 Place slices, cut side down, on ungreased cookie sheet. To form tree, start by placing 1 slice for top; arrange 2 slices just below, with sides touching. Continue arranging a row of 3 slices, then a row of 4 slices, ending with a row of 5 slices. Use remaining slice for tree trunk.

3 Bake 11 to 13 minutes or until golden brown. Cool 1 minute; carefully loosen from cookie sheet with spatula and slide onto wire rack. Cool completely, about 15 minutes.

4 Place tree on serving platter or tray. In small bowl, mix cream cheese spread and milk until smooth. Spread mixture over baked tree.

5 Cut strips from red bell pepper for garland of tree; chop any remaining red pepper. With small star-shaped canapé cutter, cut star from yellow bell pepper; chop remaining yellow pepper. Decorate tree with bell peppers, broccoli, carrots, cucumber and almonds. Serve immediately or cover loosely and refrigerate up to 24 hours before serving.

NUTRITION INFORMATION PER SERVING: Calories 100 • Total Fat 7g • Saturated Fat 3.5g • Cholesterol 15mg • Sodium 210mg • Total Carbohydrate 7g • Dietary Fiber 0g • Sugars 2g • Protein 2g. DIETARY EXCHANGES: 1/2 Starch • 1-1/2 Fat • 1/2 Carb Choice.

mini chicken caesar cups

PREP TIME: 20 Minutes ✻ READY IN: 35 Minutes ✻ SERVINGS: 20

1 cup finely chopped cooked chicken	1/4 cup finely sliced romaine lettuce
3 tablespoons Caesar salad dressing	1 oz. shaved Parmesan cheese
1 can (12 oz.) Pillsbury® Golden Layers® refrigerated flaky or buttermilk flaky biscuits	

1 Heat oven to 400°F. In small bowl, mix chicken and salad dressing. Separate dough into 10 biscuits; divide each into 2 rounds. Press dough rounds in bottom and up sides of 20 ungreased mini muffin cups, extending dough 1/4 inch above edge of cups. Fill each cup with about 2 teaspoons chicken mixture.

2 Bake 8 to 11 minutes or until crust is deep golden brown. Remove from cups. Top each with lettuce and Parmesan cheese. Serve warm.

HIGH ALTITUDE (3500-6500 FT): Bake at 400°F 10 to 13 minutes.

NUTRITION INFORMATION PER SERVING: Calories 80 • Total Fat 4g • Saturated Fat 1g • Cholesterol 10mg • Sodium 250mg • Total Carbohydrate 8g • Dietary Fiber 0g • Sugars 2g • Protein 4g. DIETARY EXCHANGES: 1/2 Starch • 1/2 Lean Meat • 1/2 Fat • 1/2 Carb Choice.

holiday appetizer tree

festive ham and cheese wreath

festive ham and cheese wreath

PREP TIME: 45 Minutes ✳ READY IN: 1 Hour 10 Minutes ✳ SERVINGS: 40

2 cups finely shredded Swiss cheese (8 oz.)

1-1/2 cups (about 8 oz.) chopped cooked ham

1/4 cup sliced green onions

2 tablespoons honey mustard

2 cans (12 oz. each) Pillsbury® Grands!® Jr. Golden Layers® refrigerated buttermilk or flaky biscuits

1 egg, beaten

1 tablespoon sesame seed or poppy seed

2 tablespoons diced red and green bell pepper, if desired

1 green onion fan, if desired

1 Heat oven to 375°F. Spray large cookie sheet with nonstick cooking spray. In large bowl, combine cheese, ham, onions and mustard; mix well.

2 Separate 1 can of dough into 10 biscuits; leave second can in refrigerator. Separate each biscuit into 2 layers. Press each biscuit layer to form 3-1/2-inch round.

3 Place 1 rounded tablespoon cheese mixture on each dough round. Wrap dough around cheese mixture, pinching edges to seal. Repeat with remaining can of dough and cheese mixture.

4 Arrange 8 balls, seam side down and sides almost touching, to form ring on sprayed cookie sheet, leaving 3-inch hole in center. Arrange 14 balls, sides almost touching, around outside of first ring. Arrange remaining 18 balls around outside of second ring. Brush wreath with beaten egg. Sprinkle with sesame seed.

5 Bake at 375°F for 18 to 25 minutes or until golden brown. Carefully slide wreath from cookie sheet onto 14-inch serving platter. Sprinkle with bell pepper. Place onion fan in center of wreath. Serve warm.

NUTRITION INFORMATION PER SERVING: Calories 95 • Total Fat 5g • Saturated Fat 2g • Cholesterol 15mg • Sodium 310mg • Total Carbohydrate 9g • Dietary Fiber 0g • Sugars 3g • Protein 4g. DIETARY EXCHANGES: 1/2 Starch • 1 Fat • 1/2 Carb Choice.

cook's notes

To make a green-onion brush, place the tip of a knife at the onion's middle and slit through the green ends. Place the onion in ice water, which will cause the "leaves" to curl; keep the green-onion brush in water until you're ready to use it.

chicken-chutney-cucumber cups

READY IN: 20 Minutes ✳ SERVINGS: 36

1-1/2 cups finely chopped cooked chicken

1/4 cup finely chopped unpeeled red apple

1/4 cup chopped peanuts

1/2 cup mango chutney, chopped

3 medium English (seedless) cucumbers

1 In medium bowl, mix all ingredients except cucumbers. Cut tapered ends from cucumbers. Draw tines of fork lengthwise through cucumber peel to score; cut into 3/4-inch-thick slices.

2 With small melon baller, scoop and discard center portion of each slice; do not go through bottom. Fill each with 1 tablespoon chicken mixture.

NUTRITION INFORMATION PER SERVING: Calories 25 • Total Fat 1g • Saturated Fat 0g • Cholesterol 5mg • Sodium 10mg • Total Carbohydrate 2g • Dietary Fiber 0g • Sugars 2g • Protein 2g. DIETARY EXCHANGE: 1/2 Lean Meat.

Yuletide Breads & Baked Goods

From golden loaves to gooey breakfast rolls, special breads are a must at Christmastime. Your family will love the bakery-worthy, homemade goodies featured here.

p. 54

p. 63

p. 70

p. 56

p. 59

sticky chewy chocolate
pecan rolls p. 66

cherry-cinnamon crisps

PREP TIME: 20 Minutes ✳ READY IN: 40 Minutes ✳ SERVINGS: 6

1 can (8 oz.) Pillsbury® refrigerated crescent dinner rolls

1/3 cup chopped dried cherries

1/4 cup butter or margarine, melted

1/4 cup sugar

1 teaspoon ground cinnamon

1 Heat oven to 375°F. Grease 2 cookie sheets with shortening or spray with cooking spray. Separate dough into 2 rectangles, about 7x6 inches each; press perforations to seal. Sprinkle cherries evenly over dough, pressing into dough. Brush rectangles with half of the butter.

2 In small bowl, mix sugar and cinnamon. Sprinkle half of cinnamon-sugar mixture evenly over dough.

3 Starting with one short side of each rectangle, roll up; pinch edge to seal. With serrated knife, cut each roll into 3 slices. Place each slice, cut side down, between 2 sheets of plastic wrap or waxed paper; roll or press each into 5-inch round. Remove plastic wrap; place 2 inches apart on cookie sheets.

4 Brush rounds with remaining butter; sprinkle with remaining cinnamon-sugar mixture. Cover rounds with plastic wrap or waxed paper; press or roll sugar mixture into dough.

5 Bake 14 to 16 minutes or until golden brown. Immediately remove from cookie sheets. Serve warm or cool.

NUTRITION INFORMATION PER SERVING: Calories 255 • Total Fat 13g • Saturated Fat 6g • Cholesterol 20mg • Sodium 510mg • Total Carbohydrate 32g • Dietary Fiber 1g • Sugars 19g • Protein 3g. DIETARY EXCHANGES: 1 Starch • 1 Other Carbohydrate • 2-1/2 Fat • 2 Carb Choices.

cracked wheat raisin bread

PREP TIME: 40 Minutes ✴ READY IN: 3 Hours 55 Minutes ✴ SERVINGS: 2 Loaves (20 slices each)

1-1/2 cups uncooked cracked wheat	2 cups boiling water
1 cup raisins	2 packages active dry yeast
1/2 cup firmly packed brown sugar	2/3 cup warm water
2 teaspoons salt	5 to 6 cups all-purpose flour
3 tablespoons margarine or butter	1 egg, beaten

1 In large bowl, combine cracked wheat, raisins, brown sugar, salt, margarine and 2 cups boiling water; mix well. Let cool to 105°F to 115°F.

2 In small bowl, dissolve yeast in warm water (105°F to 115°F). Add dissolved yeast and 2 cups flour to cracked wheat mixture; blend at low speed until moistened. Beat 2 minutes at medium speed. By hand, stir in an additional 2-1/2 to 3 cups flour until dough pulls cleanly away from sides of bowl.

3 On floured surface, knead in remaining 1/2 to 1 cup flour until dough is smooth and elastic, about 10 minutes. Place dough in greased bowl; cover loosely with greased plastic wrap and cloth towel. Let rise in warm place (80°F to 85°F) until light and doubled in size, 45 to 60 minutes.

4 Grease large cookie sheet. Punch down dough several times to remove all air bubbles. Divide dough in half; shape each into a ball. Place on greased cookie sheet. Cover; let rise in warm place until light and doubled in size, 45 to 60 minutes.

5 Heat oven to 350°F. Uncover dough. With sharp knife, slash a 1/2-inch-deep lattice design on top of each loaf. Brush with beaten egg. Bake at 350°F for 35 to 45 minutes or until loaves sound hollow when lightly tapped. Immediately remove from cookie sheet; cool on wire racks for 1 hour or until completely cooled.

NUTRITION INFORMATION PER SERVING: Calories 120 • Total Fat 1g • Saturated Fat 0g • Cholesterol 5mg • Sodium 120mg • Total Carbohydrate 24g • Dietary Fiber 2g • Sugars 5g • Protein 3g. DIETARY EXCHANGES: 1 Starch • 1/2 Fruit OR 1-1/2 Carbohydrate.

kitchen tip

When yeast bread dough is doubled in size, an indentation will remain in the dough when poked lightly with two fingers. If the indentation rapidly fills up, let the dough rise a little bit longer.

brown bread

PREP TIME: 20 Minutes ✴ READY IN: 2 Hours 20 Minutes ✴ SERVINGS: 2 Loaves (16 slices each)

2 cups raisins	1/2 cup molasses
Boiling water	2 cups buttermilk
1/2 cup firmly packed brown sugar	1 egg
1/4 cup margarine or butter, softened	3 cups all-purpose flour
1 cup cornmeal	2 teaspoons baking soda

1 Heat oven to 350°F. Grease and flour bottoms only of two 1-quart casseroles or two 8x4-inch loaf pans. In small bowl, cover raisins with boiling water; let stand 5 minutes. Drain.

2 In large bowl, combine brown sugar and margarine; beat until light and fluffy. Add cornmeal, molasses, buttermilk and egg; blend well. Stir in flour and baking soda until well mixed. Fold in raisins. Pour batter into greased and floured casseroles.

3 Bake at 350°F for 40 to 50 minutes or until toothpick inserted in center comes out clean. Cool 10 minutes; remove from casseroles. Cool 1 hour or until completely cooled. Wrap tightly and store in refrigerator.

NUTRITION INFORMATION PER SERVING: Calories 140 • Total Fat 2g • Saturated Fat 0g • Cholesterol 5mg • Sodium 120mg • Total Carbohydrate 27g • Dietary Fiber 1g • Sugars 13g • Protein 3g. DIETARY EXCHANGES: 1 Starch • 1 Fruit OR 2 Carbohydrate.

kitchen tip

Press brown sugar firmly into a standard dry measuring cup. Level it off at the top using a spatula or the flat side of a table knife.

FRANCES SHEPPARD
Corsicana, Texas
Bake-Off® Contest 35, 1992

cook's notes

Yeast breads fall into two main categories: batter breads and kneaded breads. Batter breads are quicker to prepare because they do not require kneading.

mexican cilantro batter bread

PREP TIME: 25 Minutes ✳ READY IN: 2 Hours 30 Minutes ✳ SERVINGS: 16

4-1/2	cups all-purpose flour	1	cup milk
2	tablespoons sugar	2	tablespoons butter or margarine
1	teaspoon salt	1/2	cup chopped fresh cilantro
1	teaspoon garlic powder	3	teaspoons freeze-dried chopped chives
1	package regular active dry yeast	1	can (4.5 oz.) chopped green chiles, drained
1	cup water	1	tablespoon poppy seed

1 In large bowl, mix 2 cups flour, the sugar, salt, garlic powder and yeast. In 1-quart saucepan, heat water, milk and butter until very warm (120°F to 130°F). Add warm liquid to flour mixture; beat with electric mixer on medium speed 2 minutes. By hand, stir in remaining 2-1/2 cups flour, the cilantro, chives and green chiles to make stiff batter. Cover; let rise in warm place (80°F to 85°F) 45 to 60 minutes or until light and doubled in size.

2 Generously grease 12-cup fluted tube cake pan or 10-inch angel food (tube) cake pan. Sprinkle bottom and sides of pan with poppy seed. Stir down dough to remove all air bubbles. Carefully spoon into pan. Cover loosely with greased plastic wrap and cloth towel. Let rise in warm place 30 to 45 minutes or until light and doubled in size.

3 Heat oven to 375°F. Uncover dough. Bake 35 to 40 minutes or until deep golden brown. Cool 5 minutes; remove from pan. Serve warm or cool.

NUTRITION INFORMATION PER SERVING: Calories 160 • Total Fat 2.5g • Saturated Fat 1g • Cholesterol 5mg • Sodium 280mg • Total Carbohydrate 30g • Dietary Fiber 1g. DIETARY EXCHANGES: 1-1/2 Starch • 1/2 Other Carbohydrate • 1/2 Fat • 2 Carb Choices.

cook's notes

Greased standard muffin pans can be substituted for the popover cups. Pour the batter into alternating greased cups in the muffin pan to prevent the sides of the popovers from touching.

perfect popovers

PREP TIME: 10 Minutes ✳ READY IN: 1 Hour ✳ SERVINGS: 10

3	eggs, room temperature
1-1/4	cups milk, room temperature
1-1/4	cups all-purpose flour
1/4	teaspoon salt

1 Heat oven to 450°F. Generously grease 10 popover cups or 6-oz. custard cups. In small bowl, beat eggs with eggbeater or wire whisk until lemon-colored and foamy. Add milk; blend well.

2 Add flour and salt; beat with eggbeater just until batter is smooth and foamy on top. Pour batter into greased cups, filling about full.

3 Bake at 450°F for 15 minutes. (Do not open oven.) Reduce oven temperature to 350°F; bake an additional 25 to 35 minutes or until high, hollow and deep golden brown. Remove from oven; insert sharp knife into each popover to allow steam to escape. Remove from cups. Serve warm.

HIGH ALTITUDE (ABOVE 3500 FT): Increase flour to 1-1/4 cups plus 2 tablespoons. Bake at 450°F for 15 minutes. Reduce oven temperature to 350°F; bake an additional 20 to 30 minutes.

NUTRITION INFORMATION PER SERVING: Calories 90 • Total Fat 2g • Saturated Fat 1g • Cholesterol 65mg • Sodium 90mg • Total Carbohydrate 14g • Dietary Fiber 0g • Sugars 2g • Protein 5g. DIETARY EXCHANGES: 1 Starch • 1/2 Fat OR 1 Carbohydrate • 1/2 Fat.

mexican cilantro batter bread

cranberry-walnut scones

MICHELLE DECOY
Pittsburg, California
Bake-Off® Contest 37, 1996

cranberry-walnut scones

PREP TIME: 20 Minutes ✳ READY IN: 50 Minutes ✳ SERVINGS: 12 Scones

2 cups all-purpose flour	1/2 cup unsalted butter, butter or margarine
2 tablespoons sugar	1 package (3.53 oz.) sweetened dried cranberries (1/2 cup)
2 teaspoons baking powder	1/2 cup chopped walnuts
1 teaspoon freshly grated nutmeg or ground nutmeg	3/4 cup buttermilk
1/2 teaspoon baking soda	1 egg, separated
1/2 teaspoon salt	2 teaspoons sugar

1 Heat oven to 375°F. Lightly grease cookie sheet or line with parchment paper. In large bowl, mix flour, 2 tablespoons sugar, the baking powder, nutmeg, baking soda and salt. With pastry blender or fork, cut in butter until mixture looks like coarse crumbs. Stir in cranberries and walnuts.

2 In small bowl, mix buttermilk and egg yolk. Add to flour mixture; stir just until dry ingredients are moistened.

3 Place dough on lightly floured surface; gently knead 12 times. Divide dough in half; place on cookie sheet. Pat each half into 6-inch round. Cut each into 6 wedges; do not separate.

4 In small bowl, beat egg white slightly. Brush over tops of scones. Sprinkle with 2 teaspoons sugar. Bake 15 to 20 minutes or until golden brown. Remove from cookie sheet. Cool 10 minutes. Cut into wedges. Serve warm.

NUTRITION INFORMATION PER SERVING: Calories 220 • Total Fat 12g • Saturated Fat 5g • Cholesterol 40mg • Sodium 250mg • Total Carbohydrate 25g • Dietary Fiber 1g. DIETARY EXCHANGES: 1 Starch • 1/2 Other Carbohydrate • 2-1/2 Fat • 1-1/2 Carb Choices.

cook's notes

Need to substitute for the buttermilk? Use 2 teaspoons vinegar or lemon juice plus milk to make 3/4 cup.

herb focaccia

PREP TIME: 25 Minutes ✳ READY IN: 1 Hour 35 Minutes ✳ SERVINGS: 16

3-1/2 cups all-purpose flour	2 tablespoons oil
1 teaspoon sugar	1 egg
1 teaspoon salt	3 to 4 tablespoons olive oil
1 package fast-acting yeast	1 teaspoon dried rosemary or basil leaves, crushed
1 cup water	

1 Grease cookie sheet. In large bowl, combine 1 cup flour, sugar, salt and yeast; mix well. In small saucepan, heat water and oil until very warm (120°F to 130°F). Add warm liquid and egg to flour mixture; blend at low speed until moistened. Beat 2 minutes at medium speed. By hand, stir in an additional 1-3/4 cups flour until dough pulls cleanly away from sides of bowl.

2 On floured surface, knead in 3/4 cup flour until dough is smooth and elastic, about 5 minutes. Cover with large bowl; let rest 5 minutes.

3 Place dough on greased cookie sheet. Roll or press to 12-inch round. Cover loosely with greased plastic wrap and cloth towel. Let rise in warm place (80°F to 85°F) until light and doubled in size, about 30 minutes.

4 Heat oven to 400°F. Uncover dough. With fingers or handle of wooden spoon, poke holes in dough at 1-inch intervals. Drizzle 3 to 4 tablespoons olive oil over top of dough. Sprinkle evenly with rosemary.

5 Bake at 400°F for 17 to 27 minutes or until golden brown. Immediately remove from cookie sheet; cool on wire rack for 10 minutes. Serve warm or cool.

NUTRITION INFORMATION PER SERVING: Calories 150 • Total Fat 6g • Saturated Fat 1g • Cholesterol 15mg • Sodium 140mg • Total Carbohydrate 21g • Dietary Fiber 1g • Sugars 1g • Protein 3g. DIETARY EXCHANGES: 1 Starch • 1/2 Fruit • 1 Fat OR 1-1/2 Carbohydrate • 1 Fat.

cook's notes

For two smaller loaves, grease two cookie sheets. Divide the dough in half and roll or press each half into an 8-inch round. Continue as directed in the recipe, then bake for 10 to 20 minutes.

dilly casserole bread

PREP TIME: 20 Minutes ✶ READY IN: 3 Hours ✶ SERVINGS: 18

2 to 2-2/3 cups all-purpose flour	1/4 cup water
2 tablespoons sugar	1 tablespoon margarine or butter
2 to 3 teaspoons instant minced onion	1 cup small-curd creamed cottage cheese
2 teaspoons dill seed	1 egg
1 teaspoon salt	2 teaspoons margarine or butter, melted
1/4 teaspoon baking soda	1/4 teaspoon coarse salt, if desired
1 package active dry yeast	

1   In large bowl, combine 1 cup flour, sugar, onion, dill seed, 1 teaspoon salt, baking soda and yeast; mix well.

2   In small saucepan, heat water, 1 tablespoon margarine and cottage cheese until very warm (120°F to 130°F). Add warm liquid and egg to flour mixture; blend at low speed until moistened. Beat 3 minutes at medium speed.

3   By hand, stir in remaining 1 to 1-2/3 cups flour to form a stiff batter. Cover loosely with greased plastic wrap and cloth towel. Let rise in warm place (80°F to 85°F) until light and doubled in size, 45 to 60 minutes.

4   Generously grease 1-1/2 or 2-quart casserole. Stir down batter to remove all air bubbles. Turn batter into greased casserole. Cover; let rise in warm place until light and doubled in size, 30 to 45 minutes.

5   Heat oven to 350°F. Uncover dough. Bake 30 to 40 minutes or until loaf is deep golden brown and sounds hollow when lightly tapped. If necessary, cover with foil to prevent overbrowning. Remove from casserole; place on wire rack. Brush loaf with melted margarine; sprinkle with coarse salt. Cool 15 minutes. Serve warm or cool.

HIGH ALTITUDE (ABOVE 3500 FT): Bake at 375°F for 35 to 40 minutes.

NUTRITION INFORMATION PER SERVING: Calories 100 • Total Fat 2g • Saturated Fat 1g • Cholesterol 15mg • Sodium 230mg • Total Carbohydrate 16g • Dietary Fiber 1g • Sugars 2g • Protein 4g. DIETARY EXCHANGES: 1 Starch • 1/2 Fat OR 1 Carbohydrate • 1/2 Fat.

olive-feta pinwheels

PREP TIME: 20 Minutes ✶ READY IN: 40 Minutes ✶ SERVINGS: 16

1 can (8 oz.) refrigerated crescent dinner rolls	1/4 cup chopped pitted kalamata olives
2 tablespoons cream cheese spread (from 8-oz. container)	2 tablespoons chopped fresh oregano leaves or parsley
1/4 cup crumbled feta cheese (1 oz.)	

1   Heat oven to 350°F. Spray cookie sheet with cooking spray. Unroll dough and separate into 2 long rectangles; press each into 12x4-inch rectangle, firmly pressing perforations to seal.

2   Spread cream cheese over each rectangle. Sprinkle evenly with feta cheese, kalamata olives and oregano.

3   Starting with one short side, roll up each rectangle. With serrated knife, cut each roll into 8 slices; place cut side down on cookie sheet.

4   Bake 15 to 20 minutes or until edges are golden brown. Immediately remove from cookie sheet. Serve warm.

HIGH ALTITUDE (3500-6500 FT): Bake 13 to 18 minutes.

NUTRITION INFORMATION PER SERVING: Calories 70 • Total Fat 4g • Saturated Fat 1.5g • Cholesterol 0mg • Sodium 160mg • Total Carbohydrate 6g • Dietary Fiber 0g • Sugars 1g • Protein 1g. DIETARY EXCHANGES: 1/2 Starch • 1/2 Fat • 1/2 Carb Choice.

crunchy banana-colada bread

PREP TIME: 15 Minutes ✳ READY IN: 3 Hours 40 Minutes ✳ SERVINGS: 16

3/4 cup sugar	1-1/2 cups all-purpose flour
1/2 cup unsalted or regular butter, softened	1 teaspoon baking soda
2 eggs	1 teaspoon salt
1 cup mashed very ripe bananas (2 medium)	4 Nature Valley® Banana Nut Crunchy Granola Bars (2 pouches from 8.9-oz. box), coarsely crushed
1 container (6 oz.) Yoplait® Original 99% Fat Free Piña Colada Yogurt	1/4 cup flaked coconut

1 Heat oven to 350°F. (If using dark pan, decrease oven temperature to 325°F.) Generously grease 9x5-inch loaf pan with shortening or spray with cooking spray. In large bowl, beat sugar and butter with electric mixer on medium speed until well blended. Beat in eggs, bananas and yogurt.

2 Add flour, baking soda and salt; beat until combined. Stir in 1/2 cup of the crushed granola bars until well combined. Pour batter into greased pan.

3 In small bowl, mix remaining 1/4 cup crushed granola bars and the coconut. Sprinkle evenly over batter in pan; press in lightly.

4 Bake at 350°F for 60 to 70 minutes or until toothpick inserted in center comes out clean, covering with foil during last 15 to 20 minutes of baking to prevent excessive browning. Cool in pan on wire rack 15 minutes. Remove loaf from pan; place on rack. Cool completely, about 2 hours. Wrap tightly and store in refrigerator.

HIGH ALTITUDE (3500-6500 FT): Bake at 350°F for 65 to 70 minutes.

NUTRITION INFORMATION PER SERVING: Calories 190 • Total Fat 8g • Saturated Fat 4.5g • Cholesterol 40mg • Sodium 260mg • Total Carbohydrate 28g • Dietary Fiber 1g. DIETARY EXCHANGES: 1/2 Starch • 1-1/2 Other Carbohydrate • 1-1/2 Fat • 2 Carb Choices.

Pillsbury
Bake-Off

SUSAN ADAMS
Naperville, Illinois
Bake-Off® Contest 41, 2004
Prize Winner

kitchen tip

To easily crush granola bars,

leave them unwrapped and

crush them with a rolling pin.

crunchy banana muffins

crunchy banana muffins

PREP TIME: 15 Minutes ✴ READY IN: 1 Hour ✴ SERVINGS: 8 Muffins

LORRAINE MAGGIO
Manlius, New York
Bake-Off® Contest 40, 2002

1 box (14 oz.) Pillsbury® banana quick bread & muffin mix	1/2 cup low-fat granola cereal
1 cup milk	1/2 cup coconut
1/2 cup butter or unsalted butter, melted, cooled	1/4 cup quick-cooking oats
2 teaspoons vanilla	2 tablespoons wheat germ, if desired
2 eggs	1 small banana, diced (about 1/2 cup)
1/2 cup finely chopped walnuts	2 tablespoons coarse sugar

1 Heat oven to 375°F. Place paper baking cup in each of 8 jumbo muffin cups, or spray with cooking spray. In large bowl, mix quick bread mix, milk, melted butter, vanilla and eggs 50 to 75 strokes with spoon until mix is moistened.

2 Add remaining ingredients except coarse sugar; mix well. Divide batter evenly among muffin cups. Sprinkle batter in each cup with coarse sugar.

3 Bake 22 to 32 minutes or until toothpick inserted in center comes out clean. Cool 2 minutes; remove from muffin cups. Cool 10 minutes. Serve warm or cool.

HIGH ALTITUDE (3500–6500 FT): Add 2 tablespoons all-purpose flour to dry bread mix.

NUTRITION INFORMATION PER SERVING: Calories 460 • Total Fat 22g • Saturated Fat 10g • Cholesterol 85mg • Sodium 420mg • Total Carbohydrate 57g • Dietary Fiber 1g. DIETARY EXCHANGES: 2 Starch • 2 Other Carbohydrate • 4 Fat • 4 Carb Choices.

kitchen tip

Muffins do best with a light touch. Mix the batter gently, stirring only enough to moisten the dry ingredients, in order to keep the muffins tender and avoid a "peaked" shape.

spinach dip crescent wreath

PREP TIME: 30 Minutes ✴ READY IN: 1 Hour 10 Minutes ✴ SERVINGS: 20

2 cans (8 oz. each) refrigerated crescent dinner rolls	2 tablespoons chopped green onions (2 medium)
1-1/2 cups spinach dip	1 tablespoon chopped fresh parsley
1/4 cup chopped red bell pepper	Green bell pepper, cut into holly leaf shapes
	Small cherry tomatoes

1 Heat oven to 375°F. Invert 10-ounce custard cup on center of ungreased large cookie sheet. Remove dough from 1 can, keeping dough in 1 piece; do not unroll. (Keep remaining can of dough in refrigerator.) With hands, roll dough in one direction to form 12-inch log. Cut log into 20 slices. Arrange 16 slices, slightly overlapping, around custard cup on cookie sheet.

2 Repeat with second can of dough, cutting log into 20 slices. Arrange slices from second can and remaining 4 slices from first can (total of 24 slices), slightly overlapping each other, next to but not overlapping first ring. Remove custard cup from center of wreath shape.

3 Bake 14 to 18 minutes or until light golden brown. Gently loosen wreath from cookie sheet; carefully slide onto cooling rack. Cool completely, about 30 minutes.

4 Place cooled wreath on serving tray or platter. Spread spinach dip over wreath. Sprinkle with red bell pepper, onions and parsley. Decorate with bell pepper "holly leaves" and cherry tomato "berries." Serve immediately, or cover and refrigerate up to 2 hours before serving.

NUTRITION INFORMATION PER SERVING: Calories 120 • Total Fat 8g • Saturated Fat 2.5g • Cholesterol 0mg • Sodium 280mg • Total Carbohydrate 11g • Dietary Fiber 0g • Sugars 3g • Protein 2g. DIETARY EXCHANGES: 1/2 Starch • 1/2 Other Carbohydrate • 1-1/2 Fat • 1 Carb Choice.

cook's notes

A 4-1/2-inch round ovenproof bowl (inverted), empty can or ball of crumpled foil can be used in place of a 10-ounce custard cup.

braided pumpkin wreaths

PREP TIME: 50 Minutes ✳ READY IN: 3 Hours 45 Minutes ✳ SERVINGS: 2 Wreaths (24 slices each)

BREAD
5-3/4 to 6-1/2 cups all-purpose flour
1/3 cup sugar
1-1/2 teaspoons salt
2 packages regular active dry yeast
1 cup canned pumpkin (not pie filling mix)
1/4 cup butter or margarine
1-1/2 cups apple cider or apple juice

TOPPING
1 egg
1 tablespoon water
2 teaspoons sesame seed, if desired
2 teaspoons poppy seed, if desired

1 In large bowl, stir 2 cups of the flour, sugar, salt and yeast. In 2-quart saucepan, heat pumpkin, butter and cider over medium heat, until 120°F to 130°F. Add to flour mixture; beat on medium speed 3 minutes, scraping bowl occasionally.

2 Stir in enough of the remaining flour to make a soft dough. On floured surface, knead until smooth and elastic, 3 to 5 minutes. Place dough in greased bowl, turning to grease top. Cover with plastic wrap and cloth towel; let rise in warm place until doubled in size, about 1 hour.

3 Grease large cookie sheet. Punch down dough. Divide in half; divide each half into 3 pieces. On lightly floured surface, roll each piece into 24-inch-long rope. On cookie sheet, place 3 ropes close together. Braid loosely; pinch ends together, forming a circle. Repeat with remaining dough. Cover; let rise in warm place until almost doubled in size, 20 to 30 minutes.

4 Heat oven to 375°F. In small bowl, beat egg and water until well blended; brush over braids; sprinkle with sesame and poppy seed.

5 Bake 18 to 24 minutes or until golden brown. Remove from cookie sheet to wire racks. Cool about 1 hour.

HIGH ALTITUDE (3500-6500 FT): Use 1 package regular active dry yeast. Bake at 375°F 22 to 26 minutes.

NUTRITION INFORMATION PER SERVING: Calories 75 • Total Fat 1g • Saturated Fat 1g • Cholesterol 5mg • Sodium 80mg • Total Carbohydrate 14g • Dietary Fiber 0g • Sugars 3g • Protein 2g. DIETARY EXCHANGES: 1 Starch • 1 Carb Choice.

sun-dried tomato crescents

READY IN: 30 Minutes ✳ SERVINGS: 8 Crescents

- 1 can (8 oz.) Pillsbury® refrigerated crescent dinner rolls
- 8 teaspoons purchased sun-dried tomato sauce and spread (from 10-oz. jar)

- 4 teaspoons ricotta cheese
- 1 egg, beaten
- 1/2 to 1 teaspoon poppy seed

1 Heat oven to 375°F. Separate dough into 8 triangles. Place 1 teaspoon tomato sauce on shortest side of each triangle. Top each with 1/2 teaspoon ricotta cheese.

2 Roll up, starting at shortest side of triangle and rolling to opposite point. Place point side down on ungreased cookie sheet. Curve into crescent shape. Brush tops and sides with beaten egg. Sprinkle with poppy seed. Bake at 375°F for 10 to 13 minutes or until golden brown. Cool 5 minutes. Serve warm.

NUTRITION INFORMATION PER SERVING: Calories 110 • Total Fat 5g • Saturated Fat 1g • Cholesterol 0mg • Sodium 350mg • Total Carbohydrate 14g • Dietary Fiber 1g • Sugars 4g • Protein 2g. DIETARY EXCHANGES: 1 Starch • 1 Fat OR 1 Carbohydrate • 1 Fat • 1 Carb Choice.

cook's notes

No poppy seed in the kitchen? Sprinkle the dough with dried basil leaves, crushed fennel seed or coarse ground black pepper instead.

crispy onion biscuits

READY IN: 30 Minutes ✳ SERVINGS: 6 Biscuits

- 6 frozen buttermilk biscuits (from 25-oz. pkg.)
- 1 egg white, beaten
- 1/3 cup French-fried onions (from 2.8-oz. can), crushed

1 Heat oven to 375°F. Place frozen biscuits on ungreased cookie sheet, sides touching. Brush tops with beaten egg white. Top each with onions. Bake at 375°F for 20 to 24 minutes or until golden brown. Serve warm.

NUTRITION INFORMATION PER SERVING: Calories 210 • Total Fat 11g • Saturated Fat 3g • Cholesterol 0mg • Sodium 620mg • Total Carbohydrate 23g • Dietary Fiber 0g • Sugars 3g • Protein 5g. DIETARY EXCHANGES: 1-1/2 Starch • 2 Fat • 1-1/2 Carb Choices.

cook's notes

This recipe calls for frozen buttermilk biscuits, but other frozen biscuit varieties such as southern-style or Cheddar garlic are fun to try as well.

nutty orange-butterscotch biscuits

PREP TIME: 10 Minutes ✳ READY IN: 40 Minutes ✳ SERVINGS: 6 Biscuits

- 1 tablespoon margarine or butter, softened
- 1/2 cup butterscotch caramel ice cream topping
- 1/3 cup chopped pecans

- 2 teaspoons grated orange peel
- 6 Pillsbury® Home Baked Classics™ frozen buttermilk biscuits (from 25-oz. pkg.)

1 Heat oven to 375°F. With 1 tablespoon margarine, generously grease bottom and sides of 9-inch round cake pan. Spread ice cream topping in greased pan. Sprinkle with pecans and orange peel. Place frozen biscuits over pecans and orange peel.

2 Bake at 375°F for 25 to 28 minutes or until golden brown and biscuits are no longer doughy. Immediately invert biscuits on serving platter. Spread any topping remaining in pan over biscuits. Serve warm.

NUTRITION INFORMATION PER SERVING: Calories 330 • Total Fat 16g • Saturated Fat 3g • Cholesterol 0mg • Sodium 700mg • Total Carbohydrate 41g • Dietary Fiber 1g • Sugars 17g • Protein 5g. DIETARY EXCHANGES: 2 Starch • 1 Fruit • 2-1/2 Fat OR 3 Carbohydrate • 2-1/2 Fat • 3 Carb Choices.

special touch

For your holiday breakfast or brunch, garnish the serving platter with orange twists. To create the twists, cut a navel orange into thin slices. Make a slit in each slice from the edge to the center and twist the fruit, forming a semispiral.

STEVE GRIEGER
El Cajon, California
Bake-Off® Contest 40, 2002

cook's notes

Try sprinkling these rolls with

vanilla chips instead of the milk

chocolate ones.

sticky chewy chocolate pecan rolls

PREP TIME: 20 Minutes ✳ READY IN: 50 Minutes ✳ SERVINGS: 8 Rolls

1/4 cup packed brown sugar	1 can (8 oz.) Pillsbury® refrigerated crescent dinner rolls
1 teaspoon ground cinnamon	
1/4 cup butter or unsalted butter, softened	1 tablespoon butter or unsalted butter, melted
1/2 cup chopped pecans	1/2 cup milk chocolate chips
2 tablespoons granulated sugar	

1 Heat oven to 375°F. In small bowl, mix brown sugar, 1/2 teaspoon of the cinnamon and 1/4 cup butter. Spread mixture in bottom and up sides of 8 (2-3/4x3x1-1/4-inch) nonstick muffin cups. Sprinkle each cup with 1 tablespoon pecans.

2 In another small bowl, mix granulated sugar and remaining 1/2 teaspoon cinnamon; set aside. Unroll dough on work surface. Firmly press perforations to seal. Press to form 12x8-inch rectangle. Brush dough with 1 tablespoon melted butter. Sprinkle with sugar mixture and chocolate chips.

3 Starting with one short side, roll up tightly; pinch edge to seal. With serrated knife, cut into 8 (1-inch) slices. Place each slice, cut side down, over pecans in muffin cup.

4 Bake 15 to 20 minutes or until deep golden brown. Immediately turn rolls upside down onto serving platter. Cool 10 minutes. Serve warm.

NUTRITION INFORMATION PER SERVING: Calories 320 • Total Fat 21g • Saturated Fat 8g • Cholesterol 20mg • Sodium 280mg • Total Carbohydrate 28g • Dietary Fiber 1g. DIETARY EXCHANGES: 1 Starch • 1 Other Carbohydrate • 4 Fat • 2 Carb Choices.

italian breadsticks

PREP TIME: 30 Minutes ✳ READY IN: 2 Hours ✳ SERVINGS: 24

1 package active dry yeast	1/4 cup shortening
2/3 cup warm water	1 tablespoon water
2 to 2-1/4 cups all-purpose flour	1 egg white
1-1/2 teaspoons sugar	Sesame or poppy seed
1 teaspoon garlic salt	

1 In large bowl, dissolve yeast in 2/3 cup warm water (105°F to 115°F). Add 1 cup flour, sugar, garlic salt and shortening; blend at low speed until moistened. Beat 3 minutes at medium speed. By hand, stir in an additional 1 to 1-1/4 cups flour to form a soft dough.

2 Place dough in greased bowl; cover loosely with greased plastic wrap and cloth towel. Let rise in warm place (80°F to 85°F) until light and doubled in size, 30 to 40 minutes.

3 Grease 15x10x1-inch baking pan. On lightly floured surface, knead dough about 10 times or until no longer sticky. Roll into 15x10-inch rectangle; place in greased pan. Starting with 10-inch side, cut dough into 12 strips. Cut strips in half crosswise, forming 24 sticks.

4 In small bowl, combine 1 tablespoon water and egg white; beat slightly. Brush over sticks. Sprinkle with sesame seed. Cover; let rise in warm place, 15 to 20 minutes.

5 Heat oven to 375°F. Uncover dough. Bake 18 to 22 minutes or until golden brown. Immediately remove from pan; cool on wire rack for 5 minutes. Serve warm.

NUTRITION INFORMATION PER SERVING: Calories 70 • Total Fat 3g • Saturated Fat 1g • Cholesterol 0mg • Sodium 80mg • Total Carbohydrate 9g • Dietary Fiber 0g • Sugars 0g • Protein 2g. DIETARY EXCHANGES: 1/2 Starch • 1/2 Fat OR 1/2 Carbohydrate • 1/2 Fat.

cook's notes

For softer breadsticks, bake the

dough in a greased 13x9-inch

pan. Cut into 20 breadsticks.

sticky chewy
chocolate pecan rolls

LINDA J. GREESON
Spring Valley, California
Bake-Off® Contest 37, 1996
Prize Winner

biscuit mini focaccia

PREP TIME: 30 Minutes ✳ READY IN: 40 Minutes ✳ SERVINGS: 10

1/2	cup fresh basil leaves	1/4	cup olive oil or vegetable oil
1/4	cup fresh thyme sprigs	1	can (12 oz.) refrigerated flaky biscuits
2	garlic cloves, chopped	1/4	cup pine nuts
1/4	teaspoon salt, if desired	1/3	cup grated Parmesan cheese
	Dash pepper		

1 Heat oven to 400°F. In blender or food processor, place basil, thyme, garlic, salt, pepper and oil. Cover; blend until finely chopped, scraping down sides of container if necessary.

2 Separate dough into 10 biscuits. On ungreased cookie sheets, press or roll each biscuit to a 3-inch round. Make several indentations in tops of biscuits. Spread about 1 teaspoon basil mixture evenly over each biscuit. Sprinkle each biscuit evenly with 1 teaspoon pine nuts; press gently. Sprinkle with cheese. Bake 10 to 12 minutes or until biscuits are golden brown. Serve warm.

NUTRITION INFORMATION PER SERVING: Calories 190 • Total Fat 13g • Saturated Fat 2.5g • Cholesterol 0mg • Sodium 410mg • Total Carbohydrate 15g • Dietary Fiber 0g. DIETARY EXCHANGES: 1 Starch • 2-1/2 Fat • 1 Carb Choice.

old-fashioned batter bread

PREP TIME: 25 Minutes ✳ READY IN: 2 Hours 55 Minutes ✳ SERVINGS: 16

2 to 2-1/2 cups all-purpose flour	1 cup water
3/4 cup rolled oats	1/4 cup light molasses
1 teaspoon salt	1/4 cup margarine or butter
1 package active dry yeast	1 egg

1 In large bowl, combine 1 cup flour, oats, salt and yeast; mix well. In small saucepan, heat water, molasses and margarine until very warm (120°F to 130°F). Add warm liquid and egg to flour mixture; blend at low speed until moistened. Beat 3 minutes at medium speed.

2 By hand, stir in remaining 1 to 1-1/2 cups flour to form a stiff batter. Cover loosely with greased plastic wrap and cloth towel. Let rise in warm place (80°F to 85°F) until light and almost doubled in size, 25 to 30 minutes.

3 Grease 1-1/2-quart casserole or 8x4-inch loaf pan. Stir down batter to remove all air bubbles. Turn batter into greased casserole. Cover; let rise in warm place until dough reaches top of casserole, 15 to 20 minutes.

4 Heat oven to 375°F. Uncover dough. Bake 35 to 40 minutes or until loaf sounds hollow when lightly tapped. Immediately remove from casserole; cool on wire rack for 1 hour or until completely cooled.

NUTRITION INFORMATION PER SERVING: Calories 130 • Total Fat 4g • Saturated Fat 1g • Cholesterol 15mg • Sodium 170mg • Total Carbohydrate 21g • Dietary Fiber 1g • Sugars 3g • Protein 3g. DIETARY EXCHANGES: 1 Starch • 1/2 Fruit • 1/2 Fat OR 1-1/2 Carbohydrate • 1/2 Fat.

kitchen tip

To prevent yeast dough from drying out during rising, cover the dough. Spray a length of plastic wrap with nonstick cooking spray and press the sprayed side of the plastic directly onto the surface of the dough.

cheesy twists

READY IN: 30 Minutes ✳ SERVINGS: 6 Twists

1/4 cup grated Parmesan cheese	1 can (8 oz.) Pillsbury® refrigerated crescent dinner rolls
1/2 teaspoon dried parsley flakes	
1/4 teaspoon garlic powder	1 egg white, beaten
Dash paprika	2 teaspoons sesame seed
2 teaspoons margarine or butter, melted	

1 Heat oven to 375°F. In small bowl, combine cheese, parsley, garlic powder, paprika and margarine; mix well.

2 Unroll dough; separate crosswise into 2 equal sections along center perforations. Press perforations to seal. Spoon cheese mixture evenly over 1 dough section. Top with remaining dough section; press edges to seal. Cut into 6 strips. Twist strips; place on ungreased cookie sheet.

3 Brush tops of strips lightly with egg white. Sprinkle with sesame seed. Bake at 375°F for 9 to 15 minutes or until golden brown. Serve warm.

NUTRITION INFORMATION PER SERVING: Calories 175 • Total Fat 9g • Saturated Fat 3g • Cholesterol 5mg • Sodium 560mg • Total Carbohydrate 18g • Dietary Fiber 1g • Sugars 5g • Protein 5g. DIETARY EXCHANGES: 1 Starch • 2 Fat OR 1 Carbohydrate • 2 Fat • 1 Carb Choice.

cook's notes

Both Parmesan cheese, made from cow's milk, and pecorino Romano, made from sheep's milk, are hard grating cheeses that are traditionally served with pasta. You can use either in this recipe.

GRACE M. KAIN
West Boothbay Harbor, Maine
Bake-Off® Contest 10, 1958

Baking at a high altitude, 3,500 feet above sea level or more, can be a challenge. For best results, be sure to follow the high-altitude directions when they are included in the recipe.

graham cracker brown bread

PREP TIME: 20 Minutes ✳ READY IN: 2 Hours 10 Minutes ✳ SERVINGS: 2 Loaves (16 slices each)

2 cups graham cracker crumbs or finely crushed graham crackers (30 squares)
1/2 cup shortening
1-3/4 cups buttermilk
3/4 cup molasses
2 eggs, slightly beaten

1-3/4 cups all-purpose flour
2 teaspoons baking soda
1 teaspoon salt
1/4 to 1/2 teaspoon ground nutmeg
1 cup raisins

1 Heat oven to 375°F. Grease and flour bottoms only of two 8x4-inch loaf pans. In large bowl, beat graham cracker crumbs and shortening with electric mixer on medium speed until well blended. Add buttermilk, molasses and eggs; beat well.

2 In small bowl, mix flour, baking soda, salt and nutmeg. Add to graham cracker mixture; beat at low speed until well blended. Fold in raisins. Pour batter into pans.

3 Bake 35 to 40 minutes or until toothpick inserted in center comes out clean. Cool 10 minutes. Remove from pans to cooling rack. Cool completely, about 1 hour.

HIGH ALTITUDE (3500–6500 FT): Decrease buttermilk to 1-1/2 cups, increase all-purpose flour to 2 cups. Add 1/4 cup water with buttermilk, molasses and eggs. Bake 40 to 45 minutes.

NUTRITION INFORMATION PER SERVING: Calories 120 • Total Fat 4.5g • Saturated Fat 1g • Cholesterol 15mg • Sodium 200mg • Total Carbohydrate 19g • Dietary Fiber 0g. DIETARY EXCHANGES: 1 Starch • 1 Fat • 1 Carb Choice.

kitchen tip

To braid yeast bread dough, start at the center of the ropes and braid them loosely to each end. To seal the ends, pinch them together and tuck them under the loaf.

french bread braids

PREP TIME: 40 Minutes ✳ READY IN: 3 Hours 40 Minutes ✳ SERVINGS: 2 Loaves (18 slices each)

4-3/4 to 5-3/4 cups all-purpose flour
1 tablespoon sugar
3 teaspoons salt
2 packages active dry yeast

2 cups water
2 tablespoons shortening
1 tablespoon water
1 egg white

1 In large bowl, combine 3 cups flour, sugar, salt and yeast; mix well. In small saucepan, heat 2 cups water and shortening until very warm (120°F to 130°F). Add warm liquid to flour mixture; blend at low speed until moistened. Beat 3 minutes at medium speed. By hand, stir in an additional 1-1/2 to 2-1/4 cups flour to form a stiff dough.

2 On floured surface, knead in 1/4 to 1/2 cup flour until dough is smooth and elastic, about 8 minutes. Place dough in greased bowl; cover loosely with greased plastic wrap and cloth towel. Let rise in warm place (80°F to 85°F) until light and doubled in size, 45 to 60 minutes.

3 Grease large cookie sheet. Punch down dough several times to remove all air bubbles. Divide dough in half; divide each half into 3 equal parts. Roll each part into 14-inch rope. Braid 3 ropes together; seal ends. Place on greased cookie sheet. Repeat with other half of dough.

4 In small bowl, combine 1 tablespoon water and egg white; beat slightly. Carefully brush over loaves. Cover; let rise in warm place until light and doubled in size, 20 to 30 minutes.

5 Heat oven to 375°F. Uncover dough; brush loaves again with egg white mixture. Bake at 375°F for 25 to 30 minutes or until golden brown. Immediately remove from cookie sheet; cool on wire racks for 1 hour or until completely cooled.

NUTRITION INFORMATION PER SERVING: Calories 80 • Total Fat 1g • Saturated Fat 0g • Cholesterol 0mg • Sodium 180mg • Total Carbohydrate 16g • Dietary Fiber 1g • Sugars 1g • Protein 2g. DIETARY EXCHANGES: 1 Starch OR 1 Carbohydrate.

graham cracker brown bread

holiday stollen

holiday stollen

PREP TIME: 30 Minutes ✳ READY IN: 5 Hours 50 Minutes ✳ SERVINGS: 14

FRUIT MIXTURE
- 1/2 cup golden raisins
- 1/2 cup mixed candied fruit
- 1/2 cup coarsely chopped candied cherries
- 1/2 cup blanched slivered almonds
- 1/4 cup rum

DOUGH
- 3-1/2 to 4 cups all-purpose flour
- 1/4 cup granulated sugar
- 1 teaspoon salt

- 1 package active dry yeast
- 3/4 cup milk
- 1/4 cup water
- 1/4 cup shortening or margarine
- 1 egg

FROSTING AND GARNISH
- 1 cup powdered sugar
- 1 to 2 tablespoons milk
- Whole almonds
- Candied cherries

1 In small bowl, mix fruit mixture ingredients. Let stand at room temperature at least 1 hour, stirring occasionally.

2 In large bowl, mix 1 cup flour, the granulated sugar, salt and yeast. In 1-quart saucepan, heat 3/4 cup milk, the water and shortening until very warm (120°F to 130°F). Add warm liquid and egg to flour mixture; beat with electric mixer at low speed until moistened. Beat 3 minutes at medium speed.

3 By hand, stir in an additional 2 cups flour and fruit mixture until dough pulls cleanly away from side of bowl. On floured surface, knead in 1/2 to 1 cup flour about 5 minutes or until dough is elastic. (Dough will be sticky.)

4 Place dough in greased bowl; turn to grease all sides of dough. Cover dough loosely with plastic wrap and cloth towel. Let rise in warm place (80°F to 85°F) about 1-1/2 hours or until doubled in size.

5 Punch down dough several times to remove all air bubbles. Cover; let rise in warm place about 30 minutes or until almost doubled in size.

6 Grease cookie sheet. Punch down dough several times to remove all air bubbles. On lightly floured surface, roll to 12x8-inch oval. Fold in half lengthwise; form into crescent shape. Press folded edge firmly, and pinch open edges together to prevent dough from springing open during baking. Place on cookie sheet. Cover; let rise in warm place 35 to 45 minutes or until doubled in size.

7 Heat oven to 375°F. Uncover dough. Bake 25 to 35 minutes or until golden brown. Immediately remove from cookie sheet; cool completely on cooling rack, about 1 hour.

8 In small bowl, mix powdered sugar and enough milk for spreading consistency; blend until smooth. Spread over cooled loaf. Garnish with almonds and candied cherries.

NUTRITION INFORMATION PER SERVING: Calories 320 • Total Fat 7g • Saturated Fat 1g • Cholesterol 15mg • Sodium 200mg • Total Carbohydrate 56g • Dietary Fiber 2g • Sugars 24g • Protein 6g. DIETARY EXCHANGES: 2 Starch • 1-1/2 Fruit • 3-1/2 Other Carbohydrate • 1-1/2 Fat.

cook's notes

To make the stollen ahead, bake and cool it completely; do not frost or decorate it. Wrap the bread well in foil and freeze it. Loosen the foil and thaw the bread at room temperature for two to three hours before frosting and decorating it.

cook's notes

To jump-start preparation of these cheesy snacks, assemble the rolls up to 2 hours in advance and refrigerate them, covered, until baking time.

three-cheese crescent twirls

READY IN: 30 Minutes ✳ SERVINGS: 16

1/2 cup crumbled blue cheese (2 oz.)	1 tablespoon mayonnaise
1/4 cup shredded hot pepper Monterey Jack cheese (1 oz.)	1 can (8 oz.) Pillsbury® refrigerated crescent dinner rolls
2 tablespoons cream cheese, softened	2 teaspoons chopped fresh parsley

1 Heat oven to 375°F. Lightly spray cookie sheet with nonstick cooking spray. In small bowl, combine all cheeses and mayonnaise; mix until well blended and soft.

2 Separate dough into 2 long rectangles. Firmly press perforations to seal. Spread cheese mixture evenly over rectangles. Starting at short side, roll up each; pinch edges to seal. Cut each roll into 8 slices. Place cut side down on sprayed cookie sheet. Sprinkle with parsley.

3 Bake at 375°F for 12 to 15 minutes or until golden brown. Immediately remove from cookie sheet. Cool 3 minutes. Serve warm.

NUTRITION INFORMATION PER SERVING: Calories 80 • Total Fat 5g • Saturated Fat 2g • Cholesterol 5mg • Sodium 240mg • Total Carbohydrate 7g • Dietary Fiber 0g • Sugars 2g • Protein 2g. DIETARY EXCHANGES: 1/2 Starch • 1 Fat OR 1/2 Carbohydrate • 1 Fat • 1/2 Carb Choice.

cook's notes

These simple spirals are great as part of an Italian dinner, and they also make terrific appetizers.

sun-dried tomato and parmesan pinwheels

READY IN: 35 minutes ✳ SERVINGS: 32

1 can (8 oz.) Pillsbury® refrigerated crescent dinner rolls	1/3 cup chopped drained sun-dried tomatoes packed in oil
1/2 cup grated Parmesan cheese	

1 Heat oven to 375°F. Line cookie sheets with parchment paper or spray with nonstick cooking spray. Unroll dough; separate crosswise into 2 sections. Sprinkle 2 tablespoons of the cheese onto 1 section; pat into dough. Turn section over; sprinkle other side with 2 tablespoons cheese. Pat and press dough to form 8-inch square, sealing perforations. Repeat with second section of dough.

2 Cut each section into 16 squares. In each square, make diagonal slash in each corner almost to center of square. Fold tips of alternate slashed corners toward center, forming a pinwheel. Place on paper-lined cookie sheet. In center of each pinwheel, place 1/4 to 1/2 teaspoon sun-dried tomatoes.

3 Bake at 375°F for 8 to 10 minutes or until golden brown. Immediately remove from cookie sheet. Serve warm.

NUTRITION INFORMATION PER SERVING: Calories 35 • Total Fat 2g • Saturated Fat 1g • Cholesterol 0mg • Sodium 85mg • Total Carbohydrate 3g • Dietary Fiber 0g • Sugars 1g • Protein 1g. DIETARY EXCHANGE: 1/2 Fat.

special touch

Look like a professional baker! To create shiny golden tops on these rolls, beat 1 egg white with 1 tablespoon water and brush it on the tops of the rolls before baking.

pesto angel wing rolls

PREP TIME: 5 Minutes ✳ READY IN: 25 Minutes ✳ SERVINGS: 8 Rolls

1/4 cup 1/3-less-fat cream cheese (Neufchâtel), softened	1 can (11 oz.) refrigerated original breadsticks
2 tablespoons basil pesto	

1 Heat oven to 350°F. In small bowl, mix cream cheese and pesto. Remove dough from can. Unroll but do not separate dough. Spread cream cheese mixture evenly over dough.

2 Reroll dough; seal well. Cut into 8 rolls at perforations. Place on ungreased cookie sheet. With kitchen scissors or knife, make 1-inch-long cut (almost to the center) on two opposite sides of each roll. Bake 16 to 20 minutes or until golden brown.

NUTRITION INFORMATION PER SERVING: Calories 140 • Total Fat 6g • Saturated Fat 2g • Cholesterol 5mg • Sodium 340mg • Total Carbohydrate 19g • Dietary Fiber 0g • Sugars 2g • Protein 4g. DIETARY EXCHANGES: 1 Starch • 1 Fat • 1 Carb Choice.

jalapeño jack corn muffins

READY IN: 30 Minutes ✳ SERVINGS: 12 Muffins

3/4 cup milk	1 tablespoon sugar
1/2 cup buttermilk	2 teaspoons baking powder
2 tablespoons margarine or butter, melted	1/2 teaspoon baking soda
1 egg	1/2 teaspoon salt
1-1/2 cups all-purpose flour	3 oz. jalapeño Monterey Jack cheese, cut into 12 (3/4-inch) cubes
1/2 cup yellow cornmeal	

1 Heat oven to 425°F. Spray 12 regular-size muffin cups with cooking spray, or line with paper baking cups and spray paper cups.

2 In medium bowl, mix milk, buttermilk, margarine and egg; blend well. In large bowl, mix flour, cornmeal, sugar, baking powder, baking soda and salt.

3 Push dry ingredients aside to form well in center. Add milk mixture; stir just until dry ingredients are moistened. Spoon batter evenly into muffin cups, filling each 2/3 to 3/4 full. Press 1 cheese cube into center of each.

4 Bake 10 to 15 minutes or until golden brown and firm to the touch. Immediately remove muffins from pan. Cool slightly. Serve warm.

NUTRITION INFORMATION PER SERVING: Calories 140 • Total Fat 5g • Saturated Fat 3g • Cholesterol 30mg • Sodium 320mg • Total Carbohydrate 20g • Dietary Fiber 0g • Sugars 3g • Protein 5g. DIETARY EXCHANGES: 1 Starch • 1/2 Other Carbohydrate • 1 Fat • 1 Carb Choice.

kitchen tip

For each teaspoon of baking powder, you may substitute 1/2 teaspoon baking soda plus 1/2 teaspoon cream of tartar.

Special Soups, Salads & Sides

A holiday menu just isn't complete without exceptional dishes to complement the main course. Round out Yuletide feasts with the wonderful accompaniments here.

p. 95.

p. 91.

p. 83.

p. 99.

p. 96.

italian roasted vegetables p. 84

almond baby carrots

almond baby carrots

READY IN: 15 Minutes ✴ SERVINGS: 6

1 package (16 oz.) fresh baby carrots	2 tablespoons amaretto
2 tablespoons slivered almonds	Dash salt
2 tablespoons butter	1 tablespoon chopped fresh parsley

1 In 1-1/2-quart microwavable casserole, combine carrots and 1/4 cup water; cover. Microwave on High for 7 to 10 minutes or until tender, stirring once halfway through cooking. Drain.

2 Meanwhile, cook almonds in medium saucepan over medium heat for 3 to 5 minutes or until toasted, stirring frequently.

3 Add butter, amaretto, salt and cooked carrots to saucepan; mix well. Cook 2 to 3 minutes or until most of liquid is evaporated, stirring occasionally. Sprinkle with parsley.

NUTRITION INFORMATION PER SERVING: Calories 90 • Total Fat 5g • Saturated Fat 3g • Cholesterol 10mg • Sodium 75mg • Total Carbohydrate 10g • Dietary Fiber 2g • Sugars 6g • Protein 1g. DIETARY EXCHANGES: 1 Vegetable • 1 Fat.

cook's notes

If you'd prefer to leave out the amaretto, use 2 tablespoons water and 1/8 teaspoon almond extract instead.

spicy raisin sauce

READY IN: 10 Minutes ✴ SERVINGS: 16

1/2 cup firmly packed brown sugar	1 tablespoon margarine or butter
1 tablespoon cornstarch	1 cup water
1/4 teaspoon cinnamon	2 tablespoons lemon juice
1/4 cup raisins	

1 In small saucepan, combine brown sugar, cornstarch and cinnamon; blend well. Add all remaining ingredients; stir to combine. Bring mixture to a boil over medium-high heat, stirring occasionally. Boil and stir 1 minute. Reduce heat; simmer 8 to 10 minutes to blend flavors.

NUTRITION INFORMATION PER SERVING: Calories 45 • Total Fat 1g • Saturated Fat 0g • Cholesterol 0mg • Sodium 10mg • Total Carbohydrate 9g • Dietary Fiber 0g • Sugars 8g • Protein 0g. DIETARY EXCHANGES: 1/2 Fruit OR 1/2 Carbohydrate.

kitchen tip

Cornstarch comes in handy as a thickener for many recipes. In a pinch, use 1-1/2 teaspoons cornstarch as a thickener in place of 1 tablespoon flour.

molded cranberry orange salad

PREP TIME: 15 Minutes ✴ READY IN: 5 Hours 15 Minutes ✴ SERVINGS: 10

3-1/2 cups cranberry juice cocktail	1/2 cup chopped walnuts
1 package (6 oz.) orange flavor gelatin	1 can (11 oz.) mandarin orange segments, drained
1-1/2 cups chopped fresh or frozen cranberries	Lettuce leaves

1 In small saucepan, bring 1-1/2 cups of the cranberry juice cocktail to a boil. In large bowl, dissolve gelatin in hot cranberry cocktail. Stir in remaining 2 cups cranberry cocktail. Refrigerate until thickened but not set, about 1 hour.

2 Lightly oil 6-cup ring or other mold. Stir cranberries, walnuts and orange segments into thickened gelatin. Spoon into oiled mold. Refrigerate until firm, about 4 hours.

3 To serve gelatin, line serving plate with lettuce leaves. Unmold gelatin onto lettuce leaves on serving plate.

NUTRITION INFORMATION PER SERVING: Calories 180 • Total Fat 4g • Saturated Fat 0g • Cholesterol 0mg • Sodium 45mg • Total Carbohydrate 34g • Dietary Fiber 2g • Sugars 31g • Protein 2g. DIETARY EXCHANGES: 2-1/2 Fruit • 1/2 Fat OR 2-1/2 Carbohydrate • 1/2 Fat.

kitchen tip

Feel free to change up the fruits or other fillers in gelatin molds. But do not use fresh or frozen pineapple, kiwifruit, guava, gingerroot, papaya or figs—they contain an enzyme that prevents gelatin from setting properly. Canned pineapple may be used.

baked potato soup

READY IN: 45 Minutes ✳ SERVINGS: 7

4 large baking potatoes	1-1/4 cups shredded sharp Cheddar cheese (5 oz.)
4 slices bacon	3/4 teaspoon salt
6 cups milk	1/4 teaspoon pepper
1/2 cup all-purpose flour	1 container (8 oz.) sour cream
4 green onions, sliced	

1 Pierce potatoes with fork; place on microwavable paper towel or roasting rack in microwave. Microwave on High for 15 to 20 minutes or until tender, turning once halfway through cooking. Cool slightly.

2 Meanwhile, cook bacon in Dutch oven over medium heat until crisp. Remove from skillet; drain on paper towels. Crumble; set aside.

3 In same Dutch oven, combine milk and flour; blend well. Cook over medium heat for about 15 minutes or until bubbly and thickened, stirring frequently.

4 Cut cooked potatoes in half. Scoop out cooked potato from skins; place in medium bowl. Discard skins. Mash potatoes well.

5 Add potatoes, bacon, 2 tablespoons of the onions, 1 cup of the cheese, salt and pepper to milk mixture. Cook and stir until cheese is melted.

6 Add sour cream; cook and stir until soup is thoroughly heated. To serve, ladle soup into bowls; sprinkle with remaining onions and 1/4 cup cheese.

NUTRITION INFORMATION PER SERVING: Calories 400 • Total Fat 20g • Saturated Fat 12g • Cholesterol 55mg • Sodium 540mg • Total Carbohydrate 38g • Dietary Fiber 2g • Sugars 13g • Protein 17g. DIETARY EXCHANGES: 2-1/2 Starch • 1-1/2 High-Fat Meat • 1 Fat OR 2-1/2 Carbohydrate • 1-1/2 High-Fat Meat • 1 Fat.

smoked turkey waldorf salad

READY IN: 10 Minutes ✳ SERVINGS: 4

- 2 medium red apples, chopped
- 1/2 cup chopped celery
- 1/2 lb. smoked turkey, cubed (1-1/2 cups)
- 1/3 cup light mayonnaise or salad dressing
- 4 cups torn Bibb or Boston lettuce
- 1/4 cup chopped walnuts, toasted if desired

1 In medium bowl, combine apples, celery, turkey and mayonnaise; mix well. Arrange lettuce on individual plates. Spoon apple mixture onto lettuce. Sprinkle with walnuts.

NUTRITION INFORMATION PER SERVING: Calories 230 • Total Fat 13g • Saturated Fat 2g • Cholesterol 25mg • Sodium 690mg • Total Carbohydrate 15g • Dietary Fiber 3g • Sugars 10g • Protein 12g. DIETARY EXCHANGES: 1/2 Fruit • 1 Vegetable • 1-1/2 Lean Meat • 2 Fat OR 1/2 Carbohydrate • 1 Vegetable • 1-1/2 Lean Meat • 2 Fat.

mashed potato casserole

PREP TIME: 20 Minutes ✳ READY IN: 45 Minutes ✳ SERVINGS: 14

3 cups water	1 cup shredded Cheddar cheese (4 oz.)
1/4 cup butter or margarine	1/3 cup cooked real bacon pieces (from 3-oz. jar)
1 cup milk	1 can (2.8 oz.) french-fried onions (about 1 cup)
3 cups plain mashed potato mix (dry)	
1 container (8 oz.) sour cream	

1 Heat oven to 350°F. In 3-quart saucepan, heat water and butter to boiling. Boil 1 minute, stirring constantly. Add milk; remove from heat.

2 Stir in mashed potato mix with fork until potatoes are desired consistency. Stir in sour cream and cheese. Spoon into ungreased 13x9-inch (3-quart) glass baking dish. Sprinkle bacon and onions over top. Bake 20 to 25 minutes or until hot.

HIGH ALTITUDE (3500-6500 FT): Heat oven to 375°F.

NUTRITION INFORMATION PER SERVING: Calories 190 • Total Fat 13g • Saturated Fat 6g • Cholesterol 30mg • Sodium 230mg • Total Carbohydrate 12g • Dietary Fiber 0g • Sugars 2g • Protein 5g. DIETARY EXCHANGES: 1 Starch • 2-1/2 Fat • 1 Carb Choice.

cook's notes

To make this casserole ahead, prepare as directed, reserving the bacon and onions. Cover and refrigerate the casserole for 6 to 24 hours. Just before baking, top with the bacon and onions; bake 30 to 35 minutes or until hot.

creamy parmesan broccoli

italian roasted vegetables

au gratin potatoes and onion

PREP TIME: 20 Minutes ✳ READY IN: 8 Hours 20 Minutes ✳ SERVINGS: 12

1 cup shredded Cheddar-American cheese blend (4 oz.)

1/2 cup coarsely chopped onion (1 medium)

1/2 teaspoon dried thyme leaves

1/2 cup milk

1 can (10-3/4 oz.) condensed cream of mushroom soup

6 cups sliced peeled red potatoes (6 medium)

1 In small bowl, mix shredded Cheddar-American cheese, onion, thyme, milk and cream of mushroom soup.

2 In 3- to 4-quart slow cooker, layer half each of the potatoes and cheese mixture; repeat layers. Cover; cook on Low setting 7 to 8 hours.

NUTRITION INFORMATION PER SERVING: Calories 130 • Total Fat 5g • Saturated 2.5g • Cholesterol 10mg • Sodium 280mg • Total Carbohydrate 17g • Dietary Fiber 1g • Sugars 2g • Protein 4g. DIETARY EXCHANGES: 1 Starch • 1 Fat • 1 Carb Choice.

cherry cream gelatin squares

PREP TIME: 15 Minutes ✳ READY IN: 4 Hours 15 Minutes ✳ SERVINGS: 15

GELATIN

- 1 package (6 oz.) cherry flavor gelatin
- 2 cups boiling water
- 1 cup cold water
- 2 tablespoons lemon juice
- 1/2 teaspoon almond extract
- 1 can (21 oz.) cherry pie filling

TOPPING

- 1/2 cup sugar
- 1/2 cup sour cream
- 1 package (8 oz.) cream cheese, softened

special touch

If you like, place each serving of gelatin on a lettuce-lined salad plate and garnish with a cherry.

1 In large bowl, dissolve gelatin in boiling water. Stir in cold water, lemon juice, almond extract and pie filling. Pour into ungreased 13x9-inch (3-quart) baking dish. Refrigerate until firm, about 4 hours.

2 In small bowl, combine all topping ingredients; beat until smooth. Carefully spread over firm gelatin. Refrigerate until serving time.

NUTRITION INFORMATION PER SERVING: Calories 190 • Total Fat 7g • Saturated Fat 4g • Cholesterol 20mg • Sodium 80mg • Total Carbohydrate 29g • Dietary Fiber 0g • Sugars 27g • Protein 2g. DIETARY EXCHANGES: 1 Starch • 1 Fruit • 1 Fat OR 2 Carbohydrate • 1 Fat.

creole gumbo

PREP TIME: 45 Minutes READY IN: 1 Hour SERVINGS: 4

GUMBO

- 3 tablespoons olive oil
- 3/4 cup chopped celery
- 1/3 cup chopped green bell pepper
- 1/3 cup chopped onion
- 2 garlic cloves, finely chopped
- 1/4 cup all-purpose flour
- 3 cups water
- 1 can (16 oz.) whole tomatoes, undrained, cut up
- 1 tablespoon chopped fresh parsley

- 1 teaspoon salt
- 1/8 teaspoon pepper
- 1 cup diced canned, frozen or fresh okra
- 1 can (6 oz.) crabmeat, drained

CROUTONS

- 1 can (12 oz.) Pillsbury® Golden Layers® refrigerated flaky biscuits
- 1 tablespoon butter or margarine, melted
- 2 tablespoons grated Parmesan cheese
  Paprika

ELAINE THORNTON
Long Beach, Mississippi
Bake-Off® Contest 6, 1954

1 In 4-quart saucepan, heat oil over medium heat until hot. Cook celery, bell pepper, onion and garlic in oil 5 minutes. Stir in flour; cook about 10 minutes, stirring constantly, until mixture browns. Gradually add water and tomatoes, stirring constantly. Stir in remaining gumbo ingredients. Heat to boiling. Reduce heat; cover and simmer 1 hour.

2 Meanwhile, heat oven to 400°F. Separate dough into 10 biscuits; cut each into 4 pieces. Place on ungreased cookie sheet. Brush with butter; sprinkle with Parmesan cheese and paprika. Bake 6 to 9 minutes or until golden brown. Remove from cookie sheet immediately; cool on cooling racks. Pour gumbo into individual serving bowls; top each serving with croutons.

NUTRITION INFORMATION PER SERVING: Calories 510 • Total Fat 26g • Saturated Fat 6g • Cholesterol 40mg • Sodium 1840mg • Total Carbohydrate 51g • Dietary Fiber 3g. DIETARY EXCHANGES: 2 Starch • 1 Other Carbohydrate • 1 Vegetable • 1 Very Lean Meat • 5 Fat • 3-1/2 Carb Choices.

kitchen tip

A Dutch oven holds 4-1/2 to 8 quarts, while a stockpot has a capacity ranging from 6 to 16 quarts. Both pots can come in handy for cooks who enjoy making soups and stews.

vegetable-split pea soup

PREP TIME: 15 Minutes ✳ READY IN: 3 Hours ✳ SERVINGS: 7

2 cups dried green split peas, sorted, rinsed	1/2 teaspoon pepper
5 cups water	2 cups coarsely chopped cabbage
2 cans (11.5 oz. each) tomato juice (3 cups)	1 cup chopped carrots
3 garlic cloves, minced	1 cup chopped peeled turnip or potato
1 teaspoon salt	1/3 cup grated or shredded Parmesan cheese, if desired

1 In Dutch oven or stockpot, combine split peas and 12 cups (3 quarts) water. Bring to a boil. Boil 2 minutes. Remove from heat, cover and let stand 1 hour.

2 Drain and discard liquid from split peas; return peas to Dutch oven. Add 5 cups water, tomato juice, garlic, salt and pepper. Bring to a boil. Reduce heat; cover and simmer 1 hour or until peas are tender.

3 Add cabbage, carrots and turnip; simmer 20 to 30 minutes or until vegetables are tender. To serve, ladle soup into bowls; top with cheese.

NUTRITION INFORMATION PER SERVING: Calories 250 • Total Fat 2g • Saturated Fat 1g • Cholesterol 4mg • Sodium 760mg • Total Carbohydrate 42g • Dietary Fiber 16g • Sugars 7g • Protein 17g. DIETARY EXCHANGES: 2-1/2 Starch • 1 Vegetable • 1 Very Lean Meat OR 2-1/2 Carbohydrate • 1 Vegetable • 1 Very Lean Meat.

baked squash with pecan brittle

PREP TIME: 15 Minutes ✳ READY IN: 1 Hour 10 Minutes ✳ SERVINGS: 4

2 tablespoons chopped pecans	2 teaspoons margarine or butter, melted
1 tablespoon brown sugar	1/8 teaspoon cinnamon
1 tablespoon orange juice	1 acorn squash (1-1/2 lbs.)

1 Heat oven to 350°F. Line 8-inch square pan with foil; spray foil in pan with nonstick cooking spray.

2 In small bowl, combine all ingredients except acorn squash. Spread in sprayed foil-lined pan. Bake at 350°F for 8 to 10 minutes or until bubbly and deep golden brown, stirring once. Cool 15 minutes.

3 Meanwhile, quarter squash; remove seeds. Place squash, cut side up, in ungreased 13x9-inch pan. Add 1/2 cup water to pan; cover with foil. Bake at 350°F for 45 to 50 minutes or until tender.

4 Arrange baked squash pieces on serving platter. Crumble cooled pecan mixture; sprinkle over squash.

NUTRITION INFORMATION PER SERVING: Calories 120 • Total Fat 4g • Saturated Fat 1g • Cholesterol 0mg • Sodium 30mg • Total Carbohydrate 20g • Dietary Fiber 5g • Sugars 8g • Protein 2g. DIETARY EXCHANGES: 1 Starch • 1/2 Fruit • 1/2 Fat OR 1-1/2 Carbohydrate • 1/2 Fat.

cook's notes

Acorn and other varieties of winter squash have a hard skin and keep well. Try this easy recipe for a special autumn or winter dinner.

vegetable-split pea soup

pilgrim corn salad

MARGO SCOFIELD
Fair Oaks, California
Bake-Off® Contest 39, 2000

pilgrim corn salad

READY IN: 20 Minutes ✳ SERVINGS: 8

2 cans (11 oz. each) Green Giant® white shoepeg corn, drained

3/4 cup sweetened dried cranberries

1/4 cup chopped pecans

2 tablespoons balsamic vinegar

2 tablespoons olive oil

1 tablespoon apricot preserves

1 teaspoon Dijon mustard

1 teaspoon Worcestershire sauce

2 tablespoons finely chopped fresh basil leaves
   Fresh basil sprigs

8 pecan halves

1 In medium bowl, mix corn, cranberries and chopped pecans. In small bowl with wire whisk, mix vinegar, oil, preserves, mustard and Worcestershire sauce until smooth.

2 Add vinegar mixture and chopped basil to corn mixture; toss to coat well. Let stand at room temperature 10 minutes to blend flavors. Gently stir salad before serving; garnish with basil sprigs and pecan halves.

NUTRITION INFORMATION PER SERVING: Calories 170 • Total Fat 8g • Saturated Fat 1g • Cholesterol 0mg • Sodium 180mg • Total Carbohydrate 25g • Dietary Fiber 3g • Sugars 12g • Protein 2g. DIETARY EXCHANGES: 1/2 Starch • 1 Other Carbohydrate • 1-1/2 Fat • 1-1/2 Carb Choices.

cheesy rice casserole

PREP TIME: 30 Minutes ✳ READY IN: 1 Hour 30 Minutes ✳ SERVINGS: 4

1 tablespoon oil

1/4 cup chopped onion

1/4 cup chopped green bell pepper

1 garlic clove, minced

1 cup uncooked regular long-grain white rice

2 cups water

1-1/4 cups milk

3 eggs

1 tablespoon all-purpose flour

1 teaspoon salt

2 cups frozen mixed vegetables

2 cups shredded Italian blend cheese (8 oz.)

1 Heat oven to 350°F. Spray 2-quart casserole with nonstick cooking spray. Heat oil in large saucepan over medium heat until hot. Add onion, bell pepper and garlic; cook 2 to 3 minutes or until vegetables are tender, stirring occasionally.

2 Add rice and water; mix well. Bring to a boil. Reduce heat to low; cover and simmer 15 minutes or until rice is tender and liquid is absorbed.

3 Meanwhile, in medium bowl, combine milk, eggs, flour and salt; beat well. Add egg mixture, frozen vegetables and 1-1/2 cups of the cheese to cooked rice; mix well. Spoon mixture into sprayed casserole. Sprinkle with remaining 1/2 cup cheese.

4 Bake at 350°F for 55 to 60 minutes or until casserole is golden brown and knife inserted near center comes out clean.

NUTRITION INFORMATION PER SERVING: Calories 540 • Total Fat 24g • Saturated Fat 12g • Cholesterol 205mg • Sodium 1210mg • Total Carbohydrate 53g • Dietary Fiber 3g • Sugars 8g • Protein 27g. DIETARY EXCHANGES: 3-1/2 Starch • 2-1/2 High-Fat Meat • 1/2 Fat OR 3-1/2 Carbohydrate • 2-1/2 High-Fat Meat • 1/2 Fat.

kitchen tip

Rice makes a great side dish for many types of main courses. Store uncooked rice in an airtight container in a cool, dry place.

seasoned oven potatoes

PREP TIME: 10 Minutes ✳ READY IN: 1 Hour 10 Minutes ✳ SERVINGS: 4

1/2 teaspoon dried parsley flakes
1/2 teaspoon onion powder
1/2 teaspoon salt
  2 tablespoons oil
  3 to 4 medium baking potatoes, cut into 1 to
    1-1/2-inch cubes (3 cups)

1 Heat oven to 350°F. In ungreased 12x8-inch (2-quart) baking dish, combine parsley flakes, onion powder, salt and oil; blend well. Add potatoes; toss to coat well.

2 Bake at 350°F for 50 to 60 minutes or until tender, stirring once during baking. Drain potatoes on paper towels.

NUTRITION INFORMATION PER SERVING: Calories 200 • Total Fat 7g • Saturated Fat 1g • Cholesterol 0mg • Sodium 280mg • Total Carbohydrate 31g • Dietary Fiber 3g • Sugars 1g • Protein 3g. DIETARY EXCHANGES: 2 Starch • 1 Fat OR 2 Carbohydrate • 1 Fat.

kitchen tip

To cook potatoes in their skins, first scrub them, trim away soft spots or eyes and pare away any green coloration under the skin. Keep peeled or cut potatoes submerged in a bowl of cold water until cooking time to prevent discoloration.

winter fruit compote

PREP TIME: 10 Minutes ✳ READY IN: 5 Hours 10 Minutes ✳ SERVINGS: 10

  1 two-inch cinnamon stick
  2 small apples, peeled, sliced
1/3 cup sweetened dried cranberries
1/2 cup golden raisins
1/2 cup halved dried apricots

  1 can (8 oz.) pineapple tidbits in juice, undrained
1/4 cup sugar
3/4 cup orange juice
  1 can (21 oz.) peach pie filling

1 In 1-1/2- to 2-1/2-quart slow cooker, place cinnamon stick. Layer with apples, cranberries, raisins, apricots and pineapple with juice. Sprinkle with sugar. Pour orange juice over top. Cover; cook on Low heat setting 5 to 6 hours.

2 Just before serving, gently stir mixture. Remove and discard cinnamon stick. Gently stir in pie filling, cutting peach slices into smaller pieces as necessary.

NUTRITION INFORMATION PER SERVING: Calories 270 • Total Fat 0g • Saturated Fat 0g • Cholesterol 0mg • Sodium 20mg • Total Carbohydrate 67g • Dietary Fiber 2g. DIETARY EXCHANGES: 1 Fruit • 3-1/2 Other Carbohydrate • 4-1/2 Carb Choices.

cook's notes

Peach pie filling helps thicken this slow-cooked recipe. The filling is added shortly before serving to retain its attractive color and texture. If you like, use apple filling instead.

golden split pea soup

PREP TIME: 25 Minutes ✳ READY IN: 1 Hour 25 Minutes ✳ SERVINGS: 7

1 package (16 oz.) dried yellow split peas,
   sorted, rinsed

7 cups water

1 cup sliced carrots

1/2 cup chopped onion

1/2 cup chopped celery

1 tablespoon chicken-flavor instant bouillon

1 teaspoon salt

1/2 teaspoon hot pepper sauce

1 cup chopped cooked ham, if desired

1 In Dutch oven or large saucepan, combine all ingredients except ham. Bring to a boil over medium-high heat. Reduce heat to low; simmer 45 to 60 minutes or until peas and vegetables are very tender.

2 In blender container or food processor bowl with metal blade, blend half of soup until smooth. Return to Dutch oven; stir in ham. Cook over medium-low heat until thoroughly heated, stirring frequently.

NUTRITION INFORMATION PER SERVING: Calories 270 • Total Fat 2g • Saturated Fat 1g • Cholesterol 10mg • Sodium 1030mg • Total Carbohydrate 43g • Dietary Fiber 16g • Sugars 4g • Protein 20g. DIETARY EXCHANGES: 2-1/2 Starch • 1 Vegetable • 1-1/2 Very Lean Meat OR 2-1/2 Carbohydrate • 1 Vegetable • 1-1/2 Very Lean Meat.

cook's notes

Consider this recipe when you have an abundance of cooked ham left over from a holiday meal. The soup is a delicious way to use up your extra meat.

roasted tomato-corn chowder
with cilantro pesto

roasted tomato-corn chowder with cilantro pesto

PREP TIME: 15 Minutes ✳ READY IN: 30 Minutes ✳ SERVINGS: 4

CHOWDER

- 2 tablespoons extra-virgin olive oil
- 1 cup chopped white onions (2 medium)
- 1/4 cup chopped fresh poblano chile (about 1/2 chile)
- 1/2 teaspoon freshly ground black pepper
- 1/4 teaspoon salt
- 1-1/2 cups organic frozen whole kernel sweet corn (from 16-oz. bag)
- 1 can (14.5 oz.) organic fire-roasted diced tomatoes
- 1 can (14 oz.) fat-free chicken broth with 1/3 less sodium
- 1/2 cup half-and-half

PESTO

- 1 cup firmly packed fresh cilantro
- 2 tablespoons freshly grated Parmesan cheese
- 2 tablespoons salted roasted hulled pumpkin seeds (pepitas)
- 1/8 teaspoon salt
- 1/4 teaspoon freshly ground black pepper
- 2 tablespoons extra-virgin olive oil

1 In 3-quart saucepan, heat 2 tablespoons oil over medium-high heat. Add onions and chile; sprinkle with 1/2 teaspoon pepper and 1/4 teaspoon salt. Cook, stirring frequently, 5 minutes. Stir in frozen corn, tomatoes and broth. Heat to boiling over high heat, stirring occasionally. Reduce heat to low; cover and simmer 10 to 15 minutes.

2 Meanwhile, in small food processor, place all pesto ingredients except olive oil; process with on-and-off motions 2 or 3 times to mix. With processor running, slowly drizzle 2 tablespoons oil into mixture, processing about 30 seconds or until well blended. Set pesto aside.

3 In blender or with immersion blender, blend chowder in 2 batches, if necessary, about 30 to 60 seconds or until almost smooth. Stir in half-and-half. Heat just until warm.

4 Ladle chowder into individual bowls. Top each with 1 heaping tablespoon pesto to be swirled in before eating.

NUTRITION INFORMATION PER SERVING: Calories 320 • Total Fat 21g • Saturated Fat 5g • Cholesterol 15mg • Sodium 780mg • Total Carbohydrate 24g • Dietary Fiber 4g • Sugars 8g • Protein 9g. DIETARY EXCHANGES: 1 Starch • 1/2 Other Carbohydrate • 1 Vegetable • 1/2 High-Fat Meat • 3 Fat • 1-1/2 Carb Choices.

party caesar salad

READY IN: 25 Minutes ✳ SERVINGS: 12

DRESSING

- 1/2 cup refrigerated or frozen fat-free egg product, thawed
- 1/4 cup olive oil
- 2 tablespoons lemon juice
- 1 teaspoon Dijon mustard
- 1 teaspoon anchovy paste
- 2 garlic cloves, minced

SALAD

- 1 large head romaine lettuce, torn into bite-sized pieces (10 cups)
- 1 cup grated fresh Parmesan cheese (4 oz.)
- 1-1/2 cups croutons

1 In jar with tight-fitting lid, combine all dressing ingredients; shake well. (Dressing can be refrigerated for up to 3 days.)

2 In large salad bowl, combine all salad ingredients; toss gently. Pour dressing over salad; toss to coat.

NUTRITION INFORMATION PER SERVING: Calories 110 • Total Fat 7g • Saturated Fat 2g • Cholesterol 5mg • Sodium 230mg • Total Carbohydrate 5g • Dietary Fiber 1g • Sugars 1g • Protein 6g. DIETARY EXCHANGES: 1 Vegetable • 1/2 Lean Meat • 1 Fat.

JENNIFER MOHN
Austin, Texas
Bake-Off® Contest 42, 2006

kitchen tip

When handling chiles, wear rubber or plastic gloves to protect your hands from the oil or capsaicin in the chiles.

kitchen tip

If dressings made with olive oil thicken and appear cloudy in the refrigerator, set them out at room temperature for a while before dressing the salad. The oil will clarify and become thin again.

vegetable soup with barley

PREP TIME: 25 Minutes ✳ READY IN: 6 Hours 25 Minutes ✳ SERVINGS: 10

1 cup uncooked regular pearl barley	1 large dark-orange sweet potato, peeled, cubed
1 dried bay leaf	1-1/2 cups Green Giant® Niblets® frozen corn
1/2 teaspoon fennel seed	1-1/2 cups Green Giant® frozen cut green beans
1-1/2 cups ready-to-eat baby-cut carrots, halved crosswise	1-1/4 teaspoons salt
1 cup sliced celery (2 medium stalks)	1/4 teaspoon pepper
1 medium onion, chopped (about 1/2 cup)	2 cans (14 oz. each) vegetable broth
1/2 cup chopped green bell pepper (1/2 medium)	6 cups water
2 garlic cloves, finely chopped	1 can (14.5 oz.) diced tomatoes with basil, garlic and oregano, undrained

1 In 5- to 6-quart slow cooker, layer all ingredients except tomatoes; do not stir. Cover; cook on Low heat setting 6 to 8 hours.

2 About 10 minutes before serving, stir tomatoes into soup. Cover; cook on Low heat setting about 10 minutes longer or until tomatoes are hot. Remove and discard bay leaf before serving.

NUTRITION INFORMATION PER SERVING: Calories 140 • Total Fat 0.5g • Saturated Fat 0g • Cholesterol 0mg • Sodium 720mg • Total Carbohydrate 30g • Dietary Fiber 6g • Sugars 6g • Protein 4g. DIETARY EXCHANGES: 1 Starch • 1/2 Other Carbohydrate • 1 Vegetable • 2 Carb Choices.

wild rice and sausage dressing

PREP TIME: 10 Minutes ✳ READY IN: 1 Hour 5 Minutes ✳ SERVINGS: 16

5 cups water	1-1/2 cups uncooked regular long-grain white rice
2 teaspoons chicken-flavor instant bouillon or 2 chicken-flavor bouillon cubes	1 lb. bulk pork sausage
1-1/2 teaspoons salt	1-1/2 cups chopped celery
3/4 cup uncooked wild rice	3/4 cup chopped onions

1 In large saucepan, combine water, bouillon and salt; bring to a boil. Add wild rice. Reduce heat to low; cover and simmer 20 minutes.

2 Add long-grain rice. Cover; simmer an additional 25 minutes or until rice is tender and liquid is absorbed.

3 Meanwhile, in large skillet, combine pork sausage, celery and onions; cook until browned. Drain.

4 Stir in wild rice mixture. Serve rice and sausage dressing as a side dish or use to stuff turkey or Cornish game hens.

NUTRITION INFORMATION PER SERVING: Calories 150 • Total Fat 5g • Saturated Fat 2g • Cholesterol 10mg • Sodium 510mg • Total Carbohydrate 21g • Dietary Fiber 1g • Sugars 1g • Protein 5g. DIETARY EXCHANGES: 1 Starch • 1 Vegetable • 1 Fat OR 1 Carbohydrate • 1 Vegetable • 1 Fat.

vegetable soup with barley

easy corn chowder

french onion soup gratinée

kitchen tip

Broth (or stock) is the thin liquid left after simmering and straining ingredients such as vegetables, meat or poultry. It's easy to make your own, as long as you have time to wait for the slow simmering to bring out all the flavor.

french onion soup gratinée

PREP TIME: 25 Minutes ✳ READY IN: 50 Minutes ✳ SERVINGS: 6

3 tablespoons margarine or butter	1 teaspoon Worcestershire sauce
4 cups thinly sliced onions	Dash pepper
5 cups beef broth	1 cup shredded Swiss cheese (4 oz.)
1 beef-flavor bouillon cube or 1 teaspoon beef-flavor instant bouillon	1/4 cup grated Parmesan cheese
	6 slices French bread, toasted

1 Melt margarine in Dutch oven or large saucepan over low heat. Add onions; cook 15 minutes or until golden brown and tender, stirring occasionally.

2 Add broth, bouillon cube, Worcestershire sauce and pepper. Bring to a boil. Reduce heat to low; cover and simmer 20 to 25 minutes. Meanwhile, in medium bowl, combine Swiss and Parmesan cheeses.

3 To serve, place 6 ovenproof soup bowls on cookie sheet. Ladle onion soup into bowls. Top each with slice of toasted French bread; sprinkle each with about 2 tablespoons Swiss-Parmesan cheese mixture. Broil 4 to 6 inches from heat for 1 to 3 minutes or until cheese is bubbly.

NUTRITION INFORMATION PER SERVING: Calories 250 • Total Fat 13g • Saturated Fat 6g • Cholesterol 20mg • Sodium 1150mg • Total Carbohydrate 21g • Dietary Fiber 2g • Sugars 5g • Protein 13g. DIETARY EXCHANGES: 1 Starch • 1 Vegetable • 1 High-Fat Meat • 1 Fat OR 1 Carbohydrate • 1 Vegetable • 1 High-Fat Meat • 1 Fat.

easy corn chowder

READY IN: 30 Minutes ✳ SERVINGS: 3

- 1 can (11 oz.) vacuum-packed whole kernel corn, undrained
- 1/2 cup chopped onion
- 1/2 cup cubed peeled potatoes
- 1/3 cup water

- 2 teaspoons chicken-flavor instant bouillon
- 1-3/4 cups milk
- 1 tablespoon margarine or butter
- 2 tablespoons all-purpose flour

1 In large saucepan, combine corn, onion, potatoes, water and bouillon. Bring to a boil. Reduce heat to low; cover and simmer 10 minutes or until potatoes are tender, stirring occasionally.

2 Stir in 1-1/2 cups of the milk and margarine. In small bowl, combine remaining 1/4 cup milk and flour; beat with wire whisk until smooth. Add flour mixture to chowder; cook and stir until bubbly and thickened.

NUTRITION INFORMATION PER SERVING: Calories 260 • Total Fat 8g • Saturated Fat 3g • Cholesterol 10mg • Sodium 1080mg • Total Carbohydrate 39g • Dietary Fiber 3g • Sugars 15g • Protein 9g. DIETARY EXCHANGES: 2-1/2 Starch • 1-1/2 Fat OR 2-1/2 Carbohydrate • 1-1/2 Fat.

cook's notes

Store chopped onions and other veggies in the freezer for recipes such as this chowder. On busy days, you'll love the convenience of pulling out the already-chopped vegetables to add to the recipe.

corn and cheese-stuffed peppers

PREP TIME: 15 Minutes ✳ READY IN: 1 Hour 10 Minutes ✳ SERVINGS: 4

- 4 large red, green and/or yellow bell peppers, tops cut off, seeds and membranes removed
- 2 cups refrigerated polenta (from 1-lb. roll), cut into 1/4-inch pieces (12 oz.)
- 1 can (11 oz.) vacuum-packed whole kernel corn with red and green peppers, drained

- 3/4 cup shredded Monterey Jack cheese (3 oz.)
- 3/4 cup shredded provolone cheese (3 oz.)
- Salt and pepper to taste, if desired
- 1 cup light sour cream, if desired

1 Heat oven to 350°F. If necessary, cut thin slice off bottom of each bell pepper so peppers stand upright.

2 In medium bowl, mix polenta pieces, corn and half of each of the cheeses. Salt and pepper to taste. Spoon polenta mixture into bell peppers; sprinkle with remaining cheese.

3 Place filled peppers in ungreased 8-inch square (2-quart) glass baking dish. Fill dish halfway with water. Spray 12-inch square piece of foil with cooking spray; cover dish tightly. Bake 30 minutes.

4 Remove foil; bake 15 to 20 minutes or until bell peppers are crisp-tender and filling is hot. Cool 5 minutes. Carefully remove bell peppers from dish. Garnish with sour cream.

NUTRITION INFORMATION PER SERVING: Calories 330 • Total Fat 13g • Saturated Fat 8g • Cholesterol 35mg • Sodium 820mg • Total Carbohydrate 37g • Dietary Fiber 5g. DIETARY EXCHANGES: 2 Starch • 2 Vegetable • 1 High-Fat Meat • 1/2 Fat • 2-1/2 Carb Choices.

GLORIA RENDON
Murray, Utah
Bake-Off® Contest 41, 2004

cook's notes

One 14-1/2-ounce can of ready-to-serve chicken or beef broth equals 1-3/4 cups broth.

mom's chicken noodle soup

PREP TIME: 15 Minutes ✴ READY IN: 50 Minutes ✴ SERVINGS: 5

1-1/2 cups cubed cooked chicken	2 teaspoons chopped fresh parsley
1 cup sliced carrots	1 teaspoon chopped fresh dill
1/2 cup chopped celery	4 cans (14-1/2 oz. each) ready-to-serve chicken broth
1/2 cup chopped onion	
1 parsnip, peeled, cubed (3/4 cup)	2 cups uncooked wide egg noodles (3-1/2 oz.)

1 In Dutch oven or large saucepan, combine all ingredients except egg noodles; mix well. Cook over medium heat 20 minutes or until vegetables are tender, stirring occasionally. Add egg noodles; cook 15 minutes or until of desired doneness.

NUTRITION INFORMATION PER SERVING: Calories 230 • Total Fat 6g • Saturated Fat 2g • Cholesterol 55mg • Sodium 1110mg • Total Carbohydrate 23g • Dietary Fiber 3g • Sugars 4g • Protein 22g. DIETARY EXCHANGES: 1-1/2 Starch • 2-1/2 Very Lean Meat • 1/2 Fat OR 1-1/2 Carbohydrate • 2-1/2 Very Lean Meat • 1/2 Fat.

cook's notes

Wild rice has a nutty flavor when cooked. During cooking, the rice attains its attractive dark-and-light appearance.

wild rice and mushrooms

PREP TIME: 15 Minutes ✴ READY IN: 2 Hours ✴ SERVINGS: 8

3 tablespoons margarine or butter	1 cup uncooked wild rice
1 package (5 oz.) fresh brown mushrooms (such as crimini) or white button mushrooms, sliced	1/2 cup sliced green onions
	3 cups chicken broth
1/2 cup slivered almonds	

1 Heat oven to 350°F. Grease 1-1/2-quart casserole. Melt margarine in large skillet over medium heat. Add mushrooms and almonds; cook and stir 3 minutes or until mushrooms are tender and almonds begin to brown.

2 Add wild rice; cook 10 minutes, stirring frequently. Stir in onions and broth. Bring to a boil. Pour into greased casserole; cover.

3 Bake at 350°F for 45 minutes. Uncover; bake an additional 45 to 60 minutes or until rice is tender and liquid is absorbed.

NUTRITION INFORMATION PER SERVING: Calories 180 • Total Fat 9g • Saturated Fat 1g • Cholesterol 0mg • Sodium 350mg • Total Carbohydrate 18g • Dietary Fiber 2g • Sugars 1g • Protein 7g. DIETARY EXCHANGES: 1 Starch • 1 Vegetable • 1-1/2 Fat OR 1 Carbohydrate • 1 Vegetable • 1-1/2 Fat.

kitchen tip

Cleanup is easier when you coat the inside of the slow cooker with cooking spray before adding the food.

easy scalloped corn

PREP TIME: 15 Minutes ✴ READY IN: 3 Hours 15 Minutes ✴ SERVINGS: 8

2/3 cup all-purpose flour	2 teaspoons sugar
1/4 cup margarine or butter, melted	1 teaspoon salt
1 carton (8 oz.) refrigerated or frozen fat-free egg product, thawed (1 cup)	1/8 teaspoon pepper
	1 can (14.75 oz.) cream-style corn
3/4 cup evaporated milk	1 can (15.25 oz.) whole kernel corn, drained

1 Spray 2- to 4-quart slow cooker with nonstick cooking spray. In large bowl, combine all ingredients except whole kernel corn; mix well. Stir in whole kernel corn. Pour into sprayed slow cooker. Cover; cook on High setting for 2 to 3 hours.

NUTRITION INFORMATION PER SERVING: Calories 220 • Total Fat 8g • Saturated Fat 2g • Cholesterol 5mg • Sodium 670mg • Total Carbohydrate 32g • Dietary Fiber 3g • Sugars 7g • Protein 8g. DIETARY EXCHANGES: 2 Starch • 1/2 Fat OR 2 Carbohydrate • 1/2 Fat.

mom's chicken noodle soup

vegetarian navy bean soup

PREP TIME: 30 Minutes ✳ READY IN: 10 Hours 30 Minutes ✳ SERVINGS: 8

1 package (16 oz.) dried navy beans, sorted, rinsed

8 cups water (2 quarts)

1 cup finely chopped carrots

1 cup finely chopped celery, including leaves

1/2 cup finely chopped onion

1 cup vegetable juice cocktail

1 tablespoon chicken-flavor instant bouillon

1/8 teaspoon crushed red pepper flakes

1 In large saucepan or Dutch oven, combine beans and water. Bring to a boil. Boil 30 minutes. Remove from heat; let stand 1-1/2 hours or until beans are tender.

2 In 3-1/2- to 4-quart slow cooker, combine beans with water and all remaining ingredients; mix well. Cover and cook on Low setting for 6 to 8 hours or until beans and vegetables are very tender.

3 If desired, in blender container or food processor bowl with metal blade, puree part or all of soup until smooth.

NUTRITION INFORMATION PER SERVING: Calories 210 • Total Fat 1g • Saturated Fat 0g • Cholesterol 0mg • Sodium 470mg • Total Carbohydrate 39g • Dietary Fiber 9g • Sugars 6g • Protein 12g. DIETARY EXCHANGES: 2-1/2 Starch • 1/2 Very Lean Meat OR 2-1/2 Carbohydrate • 1/2 Very Lean Meat.

minute minestrone

READY IN: 30 Minutes ✳ SERVINGS: 5

2 tablespoons margarine or butter	1 cup water
1/4 cup chopped onion	1/2 cup uncooked vermicelli, broken into pieces (2 oz.)
1 medium zucchini, sliced	1 tablespoon grated Parmesan cheese
1 package (10 oz.) frozen baby lima beans in a pouch with butter sauce	1/4 teaspoon dried basil leaves
2 cans (10-1/2 oz. each) condensed beef broth	1/4 teaspoon pepper
1 can (14.5 or 16 oz.) whole tomatoes, undrained, cut up	1/8 teaspoon garlic salt
	Dash ground red pepper (cayenne)

1 Melt margarine in large saucepan over medium heat. Add onion and zucchini; cook and stir until vegetables are crisp-tender.

2 Remove frozen lima beans from pouch; add to cooked vegetables. Stir in all remaining ingredients. Simmer about 15 minutes or until vermicelli is tender, stirring occasionally.

NUTRITION INFORMATION PER SERVING: Calories 220 • Total Fat 7g • Saturated Fat 2g • Cholesterol 3mg • Sodium 1040mg • Total Carbohydrate 26g • Dietary Fiber 5g • Sugars 4g • Protein 12g. DIETARY EXCHANGES: 1-1/2 Starch • 1 Vegetable • 1 Very Lean Meat • 1 Fat OR 1-1/2 Carbohydrate • 1 Vegetable • 1 Very Lean Meat • 1 Fat.

cook's notes

If you don't have vermicelli on hand, try substituting a similar pasta such as thin spaghetti.

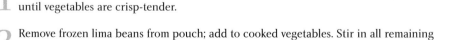

Memorable Main Courses

It's the star of any Christmastime feast—the entree. Turn to this chapter for impressive, mouth-watering dishes featuring turkey, chicken, beef, pork and more.

p. 122

p. 114

p. 111

p. 120

p. 106

oven-roasted chicken
with new potatoes p. 119

oven-roasted pork 'n vegetables

PREP TIME: 20 Minutes ✳ READY IN: 1 Hour ✳ SERVINGS: 6

 3 tablespoons olive or vegetable oil
 2 teaspoons dried rosemary leaves, crushed
 1 teaspoon dried sage leaves, crushed
1/2 teaspoon salt
1/4 teaspoon pepper
 16 to 20 small red potatoes (about 2 lb.), cut in half

 6 to 8 medium carrots (about 1 lb.), cut into 2-inch pieces
 2 small onions, cut into wedges
 2 pork tenderloins (about 3/4 lb. each)

1 Heat oven to 450°F. Generously spray 15x10x1-inch pan or shallow roasting pan with cooking spray.

2 In large bowl, mix oil, rosemary, sage, salt and pepper. Toss vegetables in mixture; remove with slotted spoon to pan (reserve remaining oil mixture). Bake vegetables 25 minutes. Stir vegetables and move to one side of pan. Roll pork in reserved oil mixture; place in pan.

3 Roast 30 to 35 minutes, stirring vegetables occasionally, until vegetables are tender, pork is no longer pink in center and meat thermometer inserted in center of pork reads 160°F.

NUTRITION INFORMATION PER SERVING: Calories 370 • Total Fat 12g • Saturated Fat 2.5g • Cholesterol 70mg • Sodium 310mg • Total Carbohydrate 37g • Dietary Fiber 6g • Sugars 6g • Protein 29g. DIETARY EXCHANGES: 2 Starch • 1 Vegetable • 3 Lean Meat • 1/2 Fat • 2-1/2 Carb Choices.

chicken wild rice amandine

PREP TIME: 35 Minutes ✻ READY IN: 1 Hour 50 Minutes ✻ SERVINGS: 8

1-1/2 cups uncooked wild rice	2 cans (14-1/2 oz.) ready-to-serve chicken broth
1 tablespoon oil	1/4 cup soy sauce
1-1/2 lbs. boneless skinless chicken breast halves, cubed	1/4 teaspoon hot pepper sauce
1/4 cup chopped onion	1/4 cup all-purpose flour
1 package (8 oz.) sliced fresh mushrooms (3 cups)	1 can (8 oz.) sliced water chestnuts, drained
	1/2 cup slivered almonds

1 Heat oven to 350°F. Spray 3-quart casserole with nonstick cooking spray. Rinse wild rice; place in large saucepan. Add enough water to cover. Bring to a boil over high heat. Reduce heat; cover and simmer 10 minutes.

2 Meanwhile, heat oil in Dutch oven over medium-high heat until hot. Add chicken; cook and stir 6 to 8 minutes or until lightly browned. Add onion and mushrooms; cook and stir 5 to 6 minutes or until onion and mushrooms are tender. Drain wild rice. Add to mixture in Dutch oven.

3 In large bowl, combine broth, soy sauce, hot pepper sauce and flour; blend well. Stir into chicken mixture in Dutch oven. Add water chestnuts; cook and stir until mixture is bubbly and slightly thickened. Remove from heat. Pour into sprayed casserole.

4 Bake at 350°F for 30 minutes. Stir in almonds; cover and bake an additional 30 to 45 minutes or until rice is tender and liquid is absorbed.

NUTRITION INFORMATION PER SERVING: Calories 330 • Total Fat 9g • Saturated Fat 1g • Cholesterol 50mg • Sodium 890mg • Total Carbohydrate 34g • Dietary Fiber 4g • Sugars 3g • Protein 28g. DIETARY EXCHANGES: 2 Starch • 1 Vegetable • 2-1/2 Very Lean Meat • 1 Fat OR 2 Carbohydrate • 1 Vegetable • 2-1/2 Very Lean Meat • 1 Fat.

kitchen tip

Keep food safety in mind when handling raw poultry—do not let it touch other foods or anything that will be used to touch other foods. Use hot, soapy water to wash surfaces that come into contact with raw poultry.

braised pork chops with cream gravy

PREP TIME: 15 Minutes ✻ READY IN: 55 Minutes ✻ SERVINGS: 4

4 pork loin chops (1/2 inch thick)	1/4 teaspoon dried thyme leaves
1/2 cup water	1/4 teaspoon Worcestershire sauce
2 teaspoons dried parsley flakes	1/3 cup milk
1/4 teaspoon salt	2 tablespoons all-purpose flour
1/4 teaspoon onion powder	

1 In large skillet over medium-high heat, brown pork chops on both sides. Add water, parsley flakes, salt, onion powder, thyme and Worcestershire sauce. Cover; simmer 20 to 30 minutes or until pork chops are tender.

2 Remove pork chops from skillet; keep warm. In small bowl, combine milk and flour; blend until smooth. Gradually stir into hot mixture in skillet. Cook until mixture boils and thickens, stirring constantly. Serve gravy with pork chops.

NUTRITION INFORMATION PER SERVING: Calories 180 • Total Fat 8g • Saturated Fat 3g • Cholesterol 65mg • Sodium 190mg • Total Carbohydrate 4g • Dietary Fiber 0g • Sugars 1g • Protein 24g. DIETARY EXCHANGE: 3-1/2 Lean Meat.

cook's notes

Try a side of mashed potatoes with these chops to soak up every mouth-watering drop of cream gravy.

beefeater's pepper-crusted roast

PREP TIME: 10 Minutes ✳ READY IN: 2 Hours 20 Minutes ✳ SERVINGS: 6

1 tablespoon butter, melted	3 tablespoons crushed multicolored peppercorns
1 tablespoon Worcestershire sauce	1 tablespoon chopped fresh thyme or
1 beef rib roast (4 lbs.)	1 teaspoon dried thyme leaves

1 Heat oven to 350°F. In small bowl, combine butter and Worcestershire sauce; mix well. Place roast in ungreased shallow roasting pan. Brush butter mixture over roast. Press peppercorns into top of roast; sprinkle with thyme. Insert meat thermometer so bulb reaches center of thickest part of meat but does not rest in fat or on bone.

2 Bake uncovered at 350°F for 1-1/2 to 2 hours or until meat thermometer registers 145°F for medium-rare or 160°F for medium doneness. Remove roast from oven. Cover with tent of foil. Let stand 10 to 15 minutes before carving.

NUTRITION INFORMATION PER SERVING: Calories 340 • Total Fat 19g • Saturated Fat 8g • Cholesterol 115mg • Sodium 150mg • Total Carbohydrate 3g • Dietary Fiber 1g • Sugars 0g • Protein 38g. DIETARY EXCHANGES: 5-1/2 Lean Meat • 1/2 Fat.

spinach and sausage phyllo bake

PREP TIME: 45 Minutes ✳ READY IN: 1 Hour 50 Minutes ✳ SERVINGS: 8

1 lb. bulk pork or Italian sausage	1 cup shredded Cheddar cheese (4 oz.)
1/2 cup thinly sliced purchased roasted red bell peppers (from 7.25-oz. jar)	1 cup ricotta cheese
1 can (2-1/4 oz.) sliced ripe olives, drained	1 package (9 oz.) frozen spinach in a pouch, thawed, drained
1 cup shredded mozzarella cheese (4 oz.)	16 sheets (17x12-inch) frozen phyllo (filo) pastry, thawed
5 eggs, beaten	1/2 cup butter, melted

1 Heat oven to 350°F. In large skillet over medium heat, brown sausage; drain. Cool slightly. Stir in roasted peppers, olives, mozzarella cheese and eggs; mix well.

2 In medium bowl, combine Cheddar cheese, ricotta cheese and spinach; mix well. Unroll phyllo pastry; cover with plastic wrap or towel. Place 1 sheet of phyllo in ungreased 13x9-inch (3-quart) baking dish, folding to fit. Brush lightly with melted butter. Continue layering and brushing with butter using 3 additional sheets of phyllo.

3 Spoon half of sausage mixture over phyllo. Layer and brush 4 more phyllo sheets with butter. Top with spinach mixture. Layer and brush 4 more phyllo sheets with butter. Top with remaining sausage mixture. Layer and brush 4 more phyllo sheets with butter. Score top of phyllo in diamond shapes.

4 Bake at 350°F for 50 to 60 minutes or until puffed and golden brown. Let stand 5 minutes before serving.

NUTRITION INFORMATION PER SERVING: Calories 550 • Total Fat 38g • Saturated Fat 18g • Cholesterol 230mg • Sodium 1070mg • Total Carbohydrate 25g • Dietary Fiber 2g • Sugars 2g • Protein 27g. DIETARY EXCHANGES: 1-1/2 Starch • 1 Vegetable • 3 High-Fat Meat • 2 Fat OR 1-1/2 Carbohydrate • 1 Vegetable • 3 High-Fat Meat • 2 Fat.

beefeater's pepper-crusted roast

three-cheese beef pasta shells

three-cheese beef pasta shells

PREP TIME: 25 Minutes ✳ READY IN: 1 Hour 20 Minutes ✳ SERVINGS: 8

24 uncooked jumbo pasta shells	1-1/2 cups shredded Italian cheese blend (6 oz.)
1 lb. lean (at least 80%) ground beef	1/2 cup grated Parmesan cheese
1 jar (26 oz.) chunky tomato pasta sauce	1 egg
1/4 cup water	1 to 2 tablespoons chopped fresh parsley, if desired
1 container (8 oz.) chive and onion cream cheese spread	

cook's notes

If you can't find chive and onion cream cheese spread, simply stir 1 tablespoon each of chives and onions, finely chopped, into plain cream cheese spread.

1 Heat oven to 350°F. Cook and drain pasta shells as directed on package. In 10-inch skillet, cook beef over medium-high heat 5 to 7 minutes, stirring occasionally, until thoroughly cooked; drain. Cool slightly, about 5 minutes.

2 In large bowl, mix pasta sauce and water. Pour 1 cup of the pasta sauce mixture in bottom of ungreased 13x9-inch (3-quart) glass baking dish. In medium bowl, mix cheese spread, 1 cup of the Italian cheese blend, the Parmesan cheese, egg and cooked beef. Spoon heaping tablespoon of mixture into each shell. Arrange stuffed shells over sauce in baking dish. Pour remaining sauce over top, covering shells completely. Cover with foil.

3 Bake 40 to 45 minutes or until bubbly and cheese filling is set. Sprinkle with remaining 1/2 cup Italian cheese. Bake about 10 minutes longer or until cheese is melted. Sprinkle with parsley.

HIGH ALTITUDE (3500-6500 FT): Heat oven to 375°F.

NUTRITION INFORMATION PER SERVING: Calories 490 • Total Fat 26g • Saturated Fat 13g • Cholesterol 110mg • Sodium 1170mg • Total Carbohydrate 39g • Dietary Fiber 3g • Sugars 11g • Protein 25g. DIETARY EXCHANGES: 2 Starch • 1/2 Other Carbohydrate • 2-1/2 Medium-Fat Meat • 2-1/2 Fat • 2-1/2 Carb Choices.

baked ham with orange-mustard glaze

PREP TIME: 20 Minutes ✳ READY IN: 3 Hours ✳ SERVINGS: 16

1 fully cooked bone-in ham half (6 to 8 lbs.)	2/3 cup orange marmalade
1 cup water	1/3 cup stone-ground mustard
1 cup dry sherry or orange juice	3 teaspoons dry mustard

1 Heat oven to 325°F. Place ham, fat side up, in disposable foil roasting pan on cookie sheet or on rack in shallow roasting pan. Pour water into pan. Bake at 325°F for 1 hour.

2 Remove ham from oven. Add sherry to roasting pan. If necessary, trim fat from ham. Score ham diagonally at 1-inch intervals, cutting about 1/4 inch deep; score in opposite direction to form diamond shapes. Insert meat thermometer so bulb reaches center of thickest part of ham but does not rest in fat or on bone.

3 In small bowl, combine marmalade and mustards; mix well. Brush half of marmalade mixture over ham; baste with pan juices. Return to oven; bake 1 to 1-1/2 hours or until meat thermometer registers 140°F, basting frequently with pan juices and brushing with remaining marmalade mixture.

4 Let baked ham stand in roasting pan for 15 minutes before slicing, basting frequently with pan juices.

NUTRITION INFORMATION PER SERVING: Calories 200 • Total Fat 7g • Saturated Fat 2g • Cholesterol 70mg • Sodium 1770mg • Total Carbohydrate 3g • Dietary Fiber 0g • Sugars 2g • Protein 32g. DIETARY EXCHANGE: 4 Lean Meat.

italian vegetarian lasagna

PREP TIME: 40 Minutes ✳ READY IN: 1 Hour 20 Minutes ✳ SERVINGS: 8

12 uncooked lasagna noodles
1/2 cup dry sherry or unsweetened apple juice
1 medium onion, finely chopped (1/2 cup)
1 package (8 oz.) sliced fresh mushrooms (3 cups)
2 large zucchini, shredded (about 4 cups)
2 medium red or green bell peppers, chopped (1 cup)
1/2 teaspoon salt

2 cups chopped fresh spinach
1 teaspoon dried basil leaves
1/2 teaspoon dried oregano leaves
1 container (15 oz.) light ricotta cheese
1 cup fat-free or low-fat cottage cheese
1/4 cup grated Parmesan cheese
1 can (8 oz.) tomato sauce
1 cup shredded mozzarella cheese (4 oz.)

1 Heat oven to 425°F. Spray 13x9-inch (3-quart) glass baking dish and sheet of foil (large enough to cover dish) with cooking spray. Cook lasagna noodles as directed on package; drain.

2 Meanwhile, in 12-inch nonstick skillet or Dutch oven, heat sherry to boiling over medium-high heat. Add onion; cook 3 minutes, stirring frequently. Stir in mushrooms, zucchini, bell peppers and salt. Cook 5 minutes, stirring occasionally. Stir in spinach, basil and oregano. Cook 2 minutes. Remove from heat; drain well.

3 In medium bowl, mix ricotta cheese, cottage cheese and Parmesan cheese.

4 Place 3 cooked noodles in bottom of baking dish. Top with 1/3 of ricotta mixture and 1/3 of vegetable mixture. Repeat layers 2 more times. Top with remaining 3 lasagna noodles, tomato sauce and mozzarella cheese. Cover tightly with foil, sprayed side down.

5 Bake 25 to 30 minutes or until bubbly around edges. Uncover baking dish; bake 5 minutes longer or until top is light golden brown. Let stand 5 minutes before serving. Cut into squares.

HIGH ALTITUDE (3500-6000 FT): Bake at 425°F 30 to 35 minutes. Uncover; bake 5 to 10 minutes longer or until top is light golden brown.

NUTRITION INFORMATION PER SERVING: Calories 300 • Total Fat 8g • Saturated 5g • Cholesterol 30mg • Sodium 720mg • Total Carbohydrate 36g • Dietary Fiber 3g • Sugars 8g • Protein 21g.

lemon-poached salmon

READY IN: 20 Minutes ✳ SERVINGS: 4

3 cups water
2 tablespoons sliced green onions
1/2 lemon, sliced
1/8 teaspoon salt
Dash pepper
4 salmon steaks (4 oz.)
Fresh dill, if desired

1 In large skillet, combine all ingredients except salmon. Bring to a boil. Reduce heat to low; simmer 5 minutes to blend flavors.

2 Add salmon; cover and simmer 6 to 9 minutes or until salmon flakes easily with fork. With slotted spoon, remove salmon from liquid; place on serving platter. If desired, garnish with dill and additional lemon slices.

NUTRITION INFORMATION PER SERVING: Calories 200 • Total Fat 11g • Saturated Fat 2g • Cholesterol 85mg • Sodium 65mg • Total Carbohydrate 0g • Dietary Fiber 0g • Sugars 0g • Protein 26g. DIETARY EXCHANGE: 3-1/2 Lean Meat.

italian vegetarian lasagna

cook's notes

For this recipe, you can use

leftover cooked turkey. Or look

for packages of diced cooked

turkey near the lunch meat

products at the supermarket.

creamy turkey and broccoli cobbler

PREP TIME: 20 Minutes ✳ READY IN: 50 Minutes ✳ SERVINGS: 6

1 can (10-3/4 oz.) condensed cream of chicken soup

1 cup milk

6 cups Green Giant Select® frozen broccoli florets (from two 14-oz. bags), thawed

3-1/2 cups cubed cooked turkey breast (about 1 lb.)

2 cups shredded sharp Cheddar cheese (8 oz.)

1 can (12 oz.) Pillsbury® Golden Layers® refrigerated buttermilk biscuits

1　Heat oven to 375°F. Spray 13x9-inch (3-quart) glass baking dish with cooking spray. In 12-inch skillet, mix soup and milk until well blended. Stir in thawed broccoli, turkey and cheese. Cook, stirring occasionally, until mixture is hot and bubbly. Pour into baking dish.

2　Separate dough into 10 biscuits; arrange on hot turkey mixture. Bake uncovered 20 to 28 minutes or until biscuits are deep golden brown.

HIGH ALTITUDE (3500-6500 FT): Add 1/4 cup water to skillet with soup and milk.

NUTRITION INFORMATION PER SERVING: Calories 550 • From Fat 230 • Total Fat 25g • Saturated 11g • Cholesterol 115mg • Sodium 1280mg • Total Carbohydrate 38g • Dietary Fiber 4g • Sugars 8g • Protein 43g.

stuffed apple-glazed pork chops

PREP TIME: 30 Minutes ✳ READY IN: 1 Hour 35 Minutes ✳ SERVINGS: 4

PORK CHOPS
- 4 pork loin chops (1 inch thick)

STUFFING
- 2 slices raisin bread, toasted, cut into cubes (about 1 cup)
- 1/2 cup chopped apple
- 1/2 cup chopped pecans
- 1/2 teaspoon salt
- 1/4 teaspoon grated orange peel
- 1/8 teaspoon cinnamon
- Dash pepper
- 3 tablespoons orange juice

GLAZE
- 2 tablespoons sugar
- 1 tablespoon cornstarch
- 1 cup apple juice
- 2 tablespoons margarine or butter

1. Heat oven to 350°F. Cut deep horizontal pocket in each pork chop.

2. In medium bowl, combine all stuffing ingredients; mix well. Stuff each chop with 1/4 of stuffing mixture; place chops in ungreased 13x9-inch pan. Bake at 350°F for 30 minutes.

3. Meanwhile, in small saucepan, combine sugar and cornstarch; mix well. Stir in apple juice. Cook over medium-low heat until mixture boils and thickens, stirring frequently. Remove from heat; stir in margarine.

4. Remove pork chops from oven. Pour glaze evenly over chops. Return to oven; bake an additional 30 to 35 minutes or until pork chops are no longer pink in center.

NUTRITION INFORMATION PER SERVING: Calories 440 • Total Fat 24g • Saturated Fat 5g • Cholesterol 65mg • Sodium 440mg • Total Carbohydrate 29g • Dietary Fiber 3g • Sugars 19g • Protein 26g. DIETARY EXCHANGES: 1/2 Starch • 1-1/2 Fruit • 3-1/2 Medium-Fat Meat • 1 Fat OR 2 Carbohydrate • 3-1/2 Medium-Fat Meat • 1 Fat.

apricot-glazed lamb chops

PREP TIME: 30 Minutes ✳ READY IN: 1 Hour ✳ SERVINGS: 4

- 1 can (16 oz.) apricot halves, drained, reserving liquid
- 1/4 cup oil
- 2 tablespoons vinegar
- 1/4 teaspoon salt
- 4 lamb chops (1 inch thick)
- 2 tablespoons brown sugar
- 2 teaspoons cornstarch
- Dash allspice
- 2 tablespoons orange juice

1. In shallow baking dish, combine 1/2 cup of the reserved apricot liquid, oil, vinegar and salt. (Reserve remaining apricot liquid for sauce.) Place lamb chops in apricot mixture, turning to coat all sides. Refrigerate 30 minutes.

2. Remove chops from marinade, reserving marinade. Place lamb chops on broiler pan. Broil 4 to 6 inches from heat for 9 to 11 minutes or until browned and of desired doneness, turning chops and basting occasionally with reserved marinade.

3. Meanwhile, reserve 8 apricot halves for garnish. In blender container or food processor bowl with metal blade, combine remaining apricots and reserved apricot liquid, brown sugar, cornstarch, allspice and orange juice. Blend or process 1 minute or until smooth; pour into small saucepan. Cook and stir over medium heat until thickened.

4. To serve, arrange lamb chops on serving platter; garnish with reserved apricot halves. Serve with warm apricot sauce.

NUTRITION INFORMATION PER SERVING: Calories 330 • Total Fat 18g • Saturated Fat 3g • Cholesterol 40mg • Sodium 170mg • Total Carbohydrate 28g • Dietary Fiber 2g • Sugars 23g • Protein 13g. DIETARY EXCHANGES: 2 Fruit • 2 Lean Meat • 2 Fat OR 2 Carbohydrate • 2 Lean Meat • 2 Fat.

orange-glazed roast chicken breasts with sweet potatoes

PREP TIME: 15 Minutes ✳ READY IN: 1 Hour ✳ SERVINGS: 4

BASTING SAUCE

- 1/4 cup orange marmalade
- 2 tablespoons orange juice
- 1 tablespoon balsamic vinegar
- 1 teaspoon dried thyme leaves
- 1/4 teaspoon salt
- 1/8 teaspoon pepper

CHICKEN AND VEGETABLES

- 4 bone-in skinless chicken breasts
- 2 medium dark-orange sweet potatoes, peeled, cut into 1-inch cubes
- 1 medium onion, cut into 8 wedges
- 1 teaspoon olive oil
- 1/3 cup sweetened dried cranberries
- 1/4 cup orange juice

1 Heat oven to 375°F. In 1-quart saucepan, cook basting sauce ingredients over low heat 3 to 4 minutes, stirring occasionally, until marmalade is melted.

2 In 15x10x1-inch pan, place chicken breasts. Brush with half of the basting sauce. In medium bowl, toss potatoes and onion with oil; place around chicken. Bake 25 minutes. Meanwhile, in small bowl, soak cranberries in 1/4 cup orange juice.

3 Brush chicken again with remaining basting sauce. Stir gently to coat vegetables with pan juices. With slotted spoon, sprinkle cranberries over vegetables; drizzle with juice. Bake about 20 minutes longer or until juice of chicken is clear when thickest part is cut to bone (170°F), and vegetables are tender.

NUTRITION INFORMATION PER SERVING: Calories 340 • Total Fat 5g • Saturated Fat 1g • Cholesterol 75mg • Sodium 220mg • Total Carbohydrate 46g • Dietary Fiber 3g • Sugars 26g • Protein 28g. DIETARY EXCHANGES: 2 Starch • 1 Fruit • 3 Other Carbohydrate • 3 Very Lean Meat • 1/2 Fat • Carb Choices.

pan-broiled steak smothered in mushrooms

READY IN: 30 Minutes ✳ SERVINGS: 4

- 1 tablespoon olive or vegetable oil
- 4 beef tenderloin steaks (4 oz.)
- 1/4 teaspoon salt
- 1/4 teaspoon coarse ground black pepper
- 1 tablespoon butter

- 2 large shallots, minced
- 1 package (8 oz.) sliced fresh mushrooms (3 cups)
- 1/4 cup red wine
- 1/4 cup beef broth

1 Heat oil in large skillet over medium-high heat until hot. Add steaks; sprinkle with salt and pepper. Cook steaks until of desired doneness, turning once. Remove steaks from skillet; cover to keep warm.

2 Add butter and shallots to skillet; cook and stir until shallots are tender. Add mushrooms and wine; cook 3 to 5 minutes, stirring occasionally. Add broth; cook until thoroughly heated. Serve over steaks.

NUTRITION INFORMATION PER SERVING: Calories 230 • Total Fat 14g • Saturated Fat 5g • Cholesterol 60mg • Sodium 250mg • Total Carbohydrate 4g. DIETARY EXCHANGES: 1 Vegetable • 2 Medium-Fat Meat • 1 Fat.

turkey and stuffing with onion glaze

PREP TIME: 15 Minutes ✳ READY IN: 5 Hours 15 Minutes ✳ SERVINGS: 5

1 tablespoon margarine or butter	3/4 cup water
1/2 cup chopped onion	1 boneless skinless turkey breast half (2 to 2-1/2 lbs.)
1 tablespoon apple jelly	Salt
1 package (6 oz.) turkey-flavor one-step stuffing mix	Pepper

1 Melt margarine in medium skillet over medium heat. Add onion; cook 4 to 5 minutes or until tender and lightly browned, stirring occasionally. Stir jelly into onion mixture. Cook an additional 1 to 2 minutes or until golden brown, stirring occasionally.

2 Meanwhile, spray 4- to 6-quart slow cooker with nonstick cooking spray. Place stuffing mix in sprayed slow cooker. Drizzle with water; mix gently. Sprinkle turkey breast half with salt and pepper. Place over the stuffing mix. Spoon onion mixture over turkey; spread evenly.

3 Cover; cook on Low heat setting for 5 to 6 hours. Cut turkey into slices. Serve stuffing topped with the turkey.

NUTRITION INFORMATION PER SERVING: Calories 350 • Total Fat 5g • Saturated Fat 2.5g • Cholesterol 125mg • Sodium 760mg • Total Carbohydrate 30g • Dietary Fiber 1g • Sugars 5g • Protein 58g. DIETARY EXCHANGES: 1-1/2 Starch • 1/2 Other Carbohydrate • 6 Very Lean Meat.

cook's notes

Any leftover slices of turkey can be used to make hot turkey sandwiches the next day.

oven-roasted chicken
with new potatoes

oven-roasted chicken with new potatoes

PREP TIME: 20 Minutes ✳ READY IN: 1 Hour 30 Minutes ✳ SERVINGS: 4

2 tablespoons chopped fresh herbs (such as oregano, sage or rosemary) or 2 teaspoons dried herb leaves	1/2 teaspoon pepper
	3 tablespoons olive oil
1 teaspoon salt	1 whole roasting chicken (3-1/2 to 4 lbs.)
	1-1/2 to 2 lbs. small red potatoes, unpeeled, halved

1 Heat oven to 450°F. In small bowl, mix herbs, salt, pepper and oil. Place chicken, breast side down, in shallow roasting pan. Arrange potatoes around chicken in pan. Drizzle half of oil mixture over potatoes; stir to mix. Bake 20 minutes.

2 Remove pan from oven. Spoon some of remaining oil mixture over chicken and potatoes; stir potatoes. Turn chicken breast side up. Return to oven; bake 10 minutes longer.

3 Remove pan from oven. Reduce oven temperature to 325°F. Drizzle remaining oil mixture over chicken and potatoes; stir potatoes. Insert ovenproof meat thermometer so tip is in thickest part of inside thigh and does not touch bone. Return to oven; bake 40 to 50 minutes longer or until thermometer reads 180°F, legs move easily when lifted or twisted, and potatoes are tender.

NUTRITION INFORMATION PER SERVING: Calories 635 • Total Fat 33g • Saturated Fat 8g • Cholesterol 150mg • Sodium 740mg • Total Carbohydrate 35g • Dietary Fiber 3g • Sugars 2g • Protein 50g. DIETARY EXCHANGES: 2 Starch • 6-1/2 Lean Meat • 2-1/2 Fat • 2 Carb Choices.

linguine with seafood sauce

READY IN: 20 Minutes ✳ SERVINGS: 8

12 oz. uncooked linguine	2 tablespoons lemon juice
4 tablespoons margarine or butter	1/4 cup chopped fresh parsley
4 green onions, sliced	1 teaspoon dried basil leaves
1 garlic clove, minced	1 teaspoon dried oregano leaves
1 package (12 oz.) frozen shelled deveined uncooked medium shrimp, thawed, drained	1/4 teaspoon pepper
	2 tablespoons cornstarch
1 can (6-1/2 oz.) minced clams, undrained	2 tablespoons cold water
1 cup chicken broth	1/4 cup sour cream
1/2 cup dry white wine	

1 Cook linguine to desired doneness as directed on package. Drain; cover linguine to keep warm.

2 Meanwhile, melt 2 tablespoons of the margarine in large skillet over medium heat. Add onions and garlic; cook and stir until onions are tender. Stir in shrimp, clams, broth, wine, lemon juice, parsley, basil, oregano and pepper. Bring to a boil. Reduce heat to low; simmer 5 minutes.

3 In small bowl, combine cornstarch and water; blend well. Gradually stir into seafood mixture. Cook until mixture boils and thickens, stirring constantly.

4 In large bowl, combine linguine, sour cream and remaining 2 tablespoons margarine; toss to coat. Serve seafood sauce over linguine.

NUTRITION INFORMATION PER SERVING: Calories 290 • Total Fat 10g • Saturated Fat 3g • Cholesterol 105mg • Sodium 380mg • Total Carbohydrate 35g • Dietary Fiber 2g • Sugars 3g • Protein 14g. DIETARY EXCHANGES: 2-1/2 Starch • 1 Very Lean Meat • 1-1/2 Fat OR 2-1/2 Carbohydrate • 1 Very Lean Meat • 1-1/2 Fat.

DOLLY CRAIG
Denver, Colorado
Bake-Off® Contest 41, 2004

turkey-sweet potato pot pies

PREP TIME: 15 Minutes ✳ READY IN: 55 Minutes ✳ SERVINGS: 4

1 can (15 oz.) sweet potatoes, drained, cut into bite-size pieces (2 cups)	3 teaspoons curry powder
	Salt and pepper to taste, if desired
1-1/2 cups cubed cooked turkey or chicken	1 can (18.6 oz.) Progresso® Rich & Hearty chicken pot pie style soup
1 cup Green Giant® frozen sweet peas (from 1-lb. bag), thawed, drained	1 Pillsbury® refrigerated pie crust (from 15-oz. box), softened as directed on box
3 tablespoons chopped sweet yellow onion	

1 Heat oven to 400°F. In large bowl, mix all ingredients except pie crust. Divide mixture evenly into 4 (1-1/4- to 2-cup) ungreased individual ramekins.

2 Remove pie crust from pouch; place crust flat on cutting board. Cut crust into 4 quarters. Top each filled ramekin with 1 quarter crust. With kitchen scissors or knife, trim crust edges. Pinch and flute edge, filling in areas with trimmed pie crust pieces where needed. With knife, cut several small slits in crusts for steam to escape. Place ramekins on cookie sheet.

3 Bake at 400°F for 25 to 33 minutes or until filling is bubbly and crust is deep golden brown, covering crust edge with foil during last 10 to 15 minutes of baking to prevent excessive browning. Cool 5 minutes before serving.

NUTRITION INFORMATION PER SERVING: Calories 490 • Total Fat 18g • Saturated 6g • Cholesterol 60mg • Sodium 800mg • Total Carbohydrate 61g • Dietary Fiber 5g • Sugars 16g • Protein 27g.

cranberry-glazed ham loaf

PREP TIME: 30 Minutes ✳ READY IN: 2 Hours ✳ SERVINGS: 2 Loaves (5 servings each)

LOAF	**GLAZE**
2 lbs. ground ham	1/2 cup cranberry juice cocktail
3/4 lb. extra-lean ground beef	1/3 cup firmly packed brown sugar
1 cup soft bread crumbs	1/2 teaspoon dry mustard
1 cup cranberry juice cocktail	
2 eggs, slightly beaten	

1 Heat oven to 350°F. In large bowl, combine all loaf ingredients; mix well. Shape into 2 loaves. Place side by side in ungreased 9-inch square pan. Bake at 350°F for 1 hour. Drain.

2 Meanwhile, in small saucepan, combine all glaze ingredients. Bring to a boil. Reduce heat to low; simmer 1 minute or until brown sugar is dissolved, stirring constantly.

3 Brush ham loaves with part of glaze. Bake an additional 25 to 30 minutes or until meat is firm, basting frequently. Let stand 5 minutes before serving.

NUTRITION INFORMATION PER SERVING: Calories 260 • Total Fat 10g • Saturated Fat 3g • Cholesterol 105mg • Sodium 1360mg • Total Carbohydrate 16g • Dietary Fiber 0g • Sugars 13g • Protein 26g. DIETARY EXCHANGES: 1 Fruit • 3-1/2 Lean Meat OR 1 Carbohydrate • 3-1/2 Lean Meat.

pot roast and gravy

Jolly Holiday Gatherings

Casual get-togethers at Christmastime call for menus that are flavorful, festive and fun. Thrill the whole gang with these can't-miss dishes full of seasonal spirit.

p. 132

p. 130

p. 150

p. 128

p. 138

tex-mex meatball pie p. 141

mexican chili dip

READY IN: 15 Minutes ✳ SERVINGS: 24

1/4 cup chopped onion (1/2 medium)
   1 garlic clove, minced
   2 tablespoons water
   1 can (14.5 oz.) stewed tomatoes, undrained
   1 can (4.5 oz.) Old El Paso® chopped green chiles, drained
1/2 teaspoon salt
1/2 teaspoon chili powder

Dash ground red pepper (cayenne) or red pepper sauce
1/2 cup shredded Monterey Jack cheese (2 oz.)
   1 package (8 oz.) 1/3-less-fat cream cheese (Neufchâtel), cut into small cubes
   Chili powder, if desired
   Assorted cut-up fresh vegetables or tortilla chips

1 In 2-quart saucepan, cook onion, garlic and water over medium heat 2 to 4 minutes, stirring occasionally, until onion is tender and water has evaporated.

2 Stir in tomatoes, chiles, salt, chili powder and ground red pepper. Cook about 2 minutes until hot, stirring occasionally.

3 Reduce heat to medium-low. Add cheeses; cook, stirring constantly, just until melted. Sprinkle with chili powder. Serve with cut-up fresh vegetables or tortilla chips.

NUTRITION INFORMATION PER SERVING: Calories 45 • Calories from Fat 25 • Total Fat 3g • Saturated Fat 2g • Cholesterol 10mg • Sodium 190mg • Total Carbohydrate 3g • Dietary Fiber 0g • Sugars 2g • Protein 2g. DIETARY EXCHANGES: 1 Fat • 0 Carb Choice.

sloppy joe pizza

PREP TIME: 20 Minutes ✳ READY IN: 45 Minutes ✳ SERVINGS: 8

1 lb. lean (at least 80%) ground beef

1 can (15.5 oz.) sloppy joe sauce

   Cornmeal

1 can (13.8 oz.) Pillsbury® refrigerated classic pizza crust

1/4 cup sliced green onions (4 medium)

1 cup shredded Cheddar cheese (4 oz.)

1 Heat oven to 425°F. In 10-inch skillet, cook beef over medium-high heat 5 to 7 minutes, stirring occasionally, until thoroughly cooked; drain. Stir in sloppy joe sauce. Reduce heat; simmer uncovered 5 minutes.

2 Meanwhile, sprinkle cornmeal on 14-inch pizza stone. Unroll dough; place on pizza stone. Starting at center, press out dough into 14-inch round, forming 1/2-inch rim.

3 Spoon hot beef mixture over dough. Top with onions and cheese. Bake 18 to 23 minutes or until crust is golden brown.

NUTRITION INFORMATION PER SERVING: Calories 300 • Total Fat 13g • Saturated Fat 6g • Trans Fat 0.5g • Cholesterol 50mg • Sodium 790mg • Total Carbohydrate 30g • Dietary Fiber 0g. DIETARY EXCHANGES: 1-1/2 Starch • 1/2 Other Carbohydrate • 2 Medium-Fat Meat • 2 Carb Choices.

kitchen tip

Use a pizza wheel to cut pizza into wedges. Start in the center and cut to the edge. This helps prevent pulling the toppings off of the wedges.

irish cream-topped brownie dessert

PREP TIME: 15 Minutes ✳ READY IN: 3 Hours 45 Minutes ✳ SERVINGS: 9

BROWNIE BASE
- 1 box (10.25 oz.) fudge brownie mix
- 1/4 cup vegetable oil
- 2 tablespoons Irish cream liqueur
- 2 eggs

IRISH CREAM TOPPING
- 1 carton (8 oz.) whipping cream (1 cup)
- 1/4 cup milk
- 1/4 cup instant vanilla pudding and pie filling mix (half of 3.4-oz. box)
- 3 tablespoons Irish cream liqueur
- 1 bar (1.4 oz.) chocolate-covered toffee candy, crushed

1 Heat oven to 350°F. Grease bottom only of 8-inch square pan with shortening. In large bowl, stir brownie mix, oil, 2 tablespoons liqueur and eggs with spoon about 50 strokes or until blended. Spread batter in pan.

2 Bake 23 to 26 minutes or until toothpick inserted in center comes out clean. Cool completely, about 1 hour.

3 In medium bowl, beat whipping cream, milk, pudding mix and 3 tablespoons liqueur with electric mixer on high speed 4 to 6 minutes or until soft peaks form. Spread mixture over cooled brownies. Sprinkle with crushed candy. Cover; refrigerate at least 2 hours before serving. Cut into squares. Store in refrigerator.

NUTRITION INFORMATION PER SERVING: Calories 330 • Total Fat 19g • Saturated Fat 8g • Cholesterol 85mg • Sodium 230mg • Total Carbohydrate 38g • Dietary Fiber 0g • Sugars 29g • Protein 4g.

WESTY GABANY
Olney, Maryland
Bake-Off® Contest 38, 1998

chicken salad focaccia sandwiches

READY IN: 30 Minutes ✳ SERVINGS: 4

FOCACCIA
- 1 can (13.8 oz.) Pillsbury® refrigerated classic pizza crust
- 2 to 3 tablespoons olive oil
- 2 garlic cloves, finely chopped
- 1/2 to 1-1/2 teaspoons kosher (coarse) salt
- 1-1/2 teaspoons dried rosemary leaves

SALAD
- 1-1/3 cups chopped cooked chicken
- 1/2 cup chopped celery
- 1/2 cup mayonnaise or salad dressing
- 2 medium green onions, chopped (1 tablespoon)
- 1 teaspoon dried tarragon leaves
- 1/2 teaspoon yellow mustard
- Dash garlic powder
- Dash onion powder

1 Heat oven to 350°F. Lightly spray cookie sheet with cooking spray. Unroll dough; place on cookie sheet. Starting at center, press out dough to form 12x10-inch rectangle. Starting with short end, fold dough in half; press lightly.

2 In small bowl, mix oil and chopped garlic. Spread over dough. Sprinkle with salt and rosemary. Bake 20 to 25 minutes or until edges are golden brown.

3 In medium bowl, mix salad ingredients. Refrigerate 15 minutes. Cut warm focaccia into 4 pieces. Split each piece to make 2 layers. Spread salad on bottom halves; cover with top halves.

NUTRITION INFORMATION PER SERVING: Calories 560 • Total Fat 32g • Saturated Fat 5g • Cholesterol 35mg • Sodium 1370mg • Total Carbohydrate 50g • Dietary Fiber 0g. DIETARY EXCHANGES: 2 Starch • 1-1/2 Other Carbohydrate • 1-1/2 Lean Meat • 5 Fat • 3 Carb Choices.

irish cream-topped brownie dessert

spanish chicken

PREP TIME: 10 Minutes ✳ READY IN: 6 Hours 30 Minutes ✳ SERVINGS: 6

1-3/4 lbs. boneless skinless chicken breasts, cut into 1-inch pieces	1/2 to 1 teaspoon crushed red pepper flakes
1 lb. Italian turkey sausage links, cut into 1-inch pieces	1 can (28 oz.) diced tomatoes, undrained
1 large red bell pepper, chopped (1-1/2 cups)	1 can (6 oz.) tomato paste
1 cup chopped onions	1 cup uncooked regular long-grain white rice
2 garlic cloves, finely chopped	2 cups water
1 teaspoon dried oregano leaves	1 can (14 oz.) quartered artichoke hearts, drained
	1 can (4 oz.) sliced ripe olives, drained

1   Spray 3-1/2- to 4-quart slow cooker with cooking spray. Mix chicken, sausage, bell pepper, onions, garlic, oregano, pepper flakes, tomatoes and tomato paste in slow cooker. Cover; cook on Low heat setting 6 to 8 hours.

2   About 25 minutes before serving, cook the white rice in 2 cups water as directed on the rice package.

3   Just before serving, stir artichoke hearts and olives into chicken mixture. Cover; cook until hot. Serve chicken mixture with rice.

NUTRITION INFORMATION PER SERVING: Calories 510 • Total Fat 14g • Saturated Fat 3.5g • Cholesterol 120mg • Sodium 1540mg • Total Carbohydrate 49g • Dietary Fiber 7g. DIETARY EXCHANGES: 2 Starch • 1/2 Other Carbohydrate • 2 Vegetable • 5 Very Lean Meat • 2 Fat • 3 Carb Choices.

one-pan crispy chicken and biscuits

PREP TIME: 5 Minutes ❋ READY IN: 40 Minutes ❋ SERVINGS: 4

2/3 cup cornflake crumbs	4 boneless skinless chicken breast halves
1 teaspoon seasoned salt	1 can (16.3 oz.) Pillsbury® Grands!® refrigerated buttermilk biscuits
1/4 cup milk	

1 Heat oven to 375°F. Line 15x10x1-inch baking pan with foil. In shallow dish, combine cornflake crumbs and seasoned salt; mix well. Place milk in another shallow dish. Dip chicken in milk; coat with crumb mixture. Arrange chicken in center of foil-lined pan.

2 Bake at 375°F for 15 minutes. Remove chicken from oven. Separate dough into 8 biscuits. Place biscuits in pan around chicken.

3 Return to oven; bake an additional 15 to 17 minutes or until biscuits are golden brown and chicken is fork-tender and juices run clear.

NUTRITION INFORMATION PER SERVING: Calories 605 • Total Fat 21g • Saturated Fat 6g • Cholesterol 75mg • Sodium 1960mg • Total Carbohydrate 68g • Dietary Fiber 2g • Sugars 18g • Protein 36g. DIETARY EXCHANGES: 4-1/2 Starch • 3 Medium-Fat Meat • 1 Fat OR 4-1/2 Carbohydrate • 3 Medium-Fat Meat • 1 Fat • 4-1/2 Carb Choices.

kitchen tip

It's easy to make your own cornflake crumbs. You'll need about 1-1/3 cups cornflake cereal to get 2/3 cup crumbs. Place the cereal in a resealable food storage plastic bag and crush it with a rolling pin, the bottom of a small saucepan or your hands. This is a job kids will love to help you with.

chocolate-peanut butter cookie pizza

PREP TIME: 15 Minutes ❋ READY IN: 1 Hour 30 Minutes ❋ SERVINGS: 12

1 roll (16.5 oz.) Pillsbury® Create 'n Bake® refrigerated chocolate chip cookies	1/4 cup milk
1 package (8 oz.) cream cheese, softened	1 cup frozen whipped topping, thawed
1/2 cup creamy peanut butter	3/4 cup hot fudge topping
1 cup powdered sugar	1/4 cup chopped peanuts

1 Heat oven to 350°F. In ungreased 12-inch pizza pan, break up cookie dough into pieces. With floured fingers, press out dough evenly in bottom of pan to form crust. Bake 15 to 20 minutes or until golden brown. Cool completely, about 30 minutes.

2 Meanwhile, in medium bowl, beat cream cheese, peanut butter, powdered sugar and milk until smooth. Fold in whipped topping.

3 Spread 1/2 cup of the fudge topping over cooled crust. Spread peanut butter mixture over top. Drizzle with remaining 1/4 cup fudge topping. Sprinkle with peanuts. Refrigerate at least 30 minutes or until serving time. Cut into wedges or squares.

NUTRITION INFORMATION PER SERVING: Calories 440 • Total Fat 23g • Saturated Fat 9g • Cholesterol 30mg • Sodium 300mg • Total Carbohydrate 51g • Dietary Fiber 1g. DIETARY EXCHANGES: 3-1/2 Other Carbohydrate • 1 High-Fat Meat • 3 Fat • 3-1/2 Carb Choices.

cook's notes

Prepare the cookie pizza crust up to a day ahead of time. After it's cooled, tightly wrap it in plastic wrap and store it at room temperature until you're ready to top it off.

three-pepper pizza

PREP TIME: 10 Minutes ✳ READY IN: 25 Minutes ✳ SERVINGS: 3

- 1 can (13.8 oz.) Pillsbury® refrigerated classic pizza crust
- 1-1/2 cups shredded mozzarella cheese (6 oz.)
- 1/2 teaspoon Italian seasoning
- 1 medium green bell pepper, chopped
- 1 medium red bell pepper, chopped
- 1 medium yellow bell pepper, chopped

1 Heat oven to 425°F. Lightly grease 12-inch pizza pan or 13x9-inch pan with shortening. Unroll dough; place in pan. Starting at center, press out dough to edge of pan. Bake 4 to 6 minutes or until crust just begins to brown.

2 Sprinkle 1/2 cup of the cheese evenly over partially baked crust. Sprinkle with Italian seasoning. Sprinkle peppers evenly over top. Sprinkle with remaining 1 cup cheese. Bake 8 to 12 minutes longer or until crust is deep golden brown and cheese is melted.

NUTRITION INFORMATION PER SERVING: Calories 530 • Total Fat 16g • Saturated Fat 8g • Cholesterol 30mg • Sodium 1240mg • Total Carbohydrate 71g • Dietary Fiber 2g. DIETARY EXCHANGES: 3-1/2 Starch • 1 Other Carbohydrate • 1 Vegetable • 2 Medium-Fat Meat • 1/2 Fat • 5 Carb Choices.

shredded chicken nachos

PREP TIME: 15 Minutes ✳ READY IN: 7 Hours 15 Minutes ✳ SERVINGS: 12

NACHOS
- 2 lbs. boneless skinless chicken thighs (about 10)
- 1 package (1.25 oz.) taco seasoning mix
- 1 can (15 oz.) pinto beans, drained
- 1 can (14.5 oz.) diced tomatoes, undrained
- 1 can (4.5 oz.) chopped green chiles
- 2 tablespoons lime juice
- 10 oz. restaurant-style tortilla chips (75 chips)

TOPPINGS
- 1 cup shredded Colby-Monterey Jack cheese blend (4 oz.)
- 3/4 cup sour cream
- 3/4 cup chunky-style salsa
- 4 medium green onions, sliced (1/4 cup)
- 1/4 cup sliced ripe or green olives
- 2 tablespoons chopped fresh cilantro
- 1 lime, cut into 12 wedges

1 In 3-1/2- to 4-quart slow cooker, place chicken thighs. Sprinkle with taco seasoning mix. Top with beans, tomatoes, chiles and lime juice. Cover; cook on Low heat setting 7 to 8 hours.

2 Just before serving, place topping ingredients in individual serving dishes. Remove chicken from slow cooker; place on cutting board. Mash beans in slow cooker. Shred chicken with 2 forks; return to slow cooker and mix well.

3 To serve, have guests place tortilla chips on serving plates; spoon 1/2 cup chicken mixture onto chips. Top nachos with desired toppings. Chicken mixture can be held on Low heat setting up to 2 hours.

NUTRITION INFORMATION PER SERVING: Calories 380 • Total Fat 18g • Saturated Fat 6g • Cholesterol 65mg • Sodium 710mg • Total Carbohydrate 29g • Dietary Fiber 5g. DIETARY EXCHANGES: 2 Starch • 2-1/2 Lean Meat, 2 Fat • 2 Carb Choices.

three-pepper pizza

double-crust pizza supreme

PREP TIME: 25 Minutes ✳ READY IN: 1 Hour 5 Minutes ✳ SERVINGS: 8

1 package (12 oz.) bulk pork sausage

2 cans (13.8 oz. each) Pillsbury® refrigerated
pizza crust

1 package (3.5 oz.) pepperoni slices

1 jar (14 oz.) pizza sauce

1 jar (4.5 oz.) sliced mushrooms, drained

1 medium green bell pepper, cut into
1/4-inch-thick rings, if desired

1 medium onion, chopped (1/2 cup), if desired

8 slices (3/4 oz. each) mozzarella cheese

2 tablespoons grated Parmesan cheese

1 Heat oven to 375°F. Lightly spray 12-inch pizza pan with cooking spray. Meanwhile, in 10-inch skillet, cook sausage over medium heat, stirring frequently, until no longer pink; drain well on paper towels.

2 Unroll 1 can of dough; place on pizza pan. Starting at center, press out dough to edge of pan. Layer sausage and pepperoni on dough. With back of spoon, carefully spread 1/2 cup of the pizza sauce evenly over pepperoni. Top with mushrooms, bell pepper, onion and slices of mozzarella cheese.

3 Unroll remaining can of dough; place on work surface. Starting at center, press out dough into 12-inch round. Fold dough in half; place over mozzarella cheese and unfold. Press edge to seal. Cut several slits in top crust for steam to escape. Sprinkle Parmesan cheese over top.

4 Bake 35 to 40 minutes or until crust is deep golden brown. Meanwhile, in 1-quart saucepan, heat remaining pizza sauce. Cut pizza into wedges; serve topped with warm pizza sauce.

NUTRITION INFORMATION PER SERVING: Calories 470 • Total Fat 18g • Saturated Fat 8g • Cholesterol 45mg • Sodium 1500mg • Total Carbohydrate 53g • Dietary Fiber 1g. DIETARY EXCHANGES: 2-1/2 Starch • 1 Other Carbohydrate • 2 High-Fat Meat • 3-1/2 Carb Choices.

hot reuben spread

PREP TIME: 10 Minutes ✻ READY IN: 1 Hour 40 Minutes ✻ SERVINGS: 32

- 2 cups shredded Swiss cheese (8 oz.)
- 3/4 cup Thousand Island dressing
- 1/2 lb. sliced cooked corned beef, coarsely chopped
- 1 can (16 oz.) sauerkraut, rinsed, well drained
- 1 package (3 oz.) cream cheese, cubed
- Cocktail rye bread slices, toasted, if desired

1 In 1-1/2- to 3-quart slow cooker, mix all ingredients except bread. Cover; cook on Low heat setting 1-1/2 to 2-1/2 hours. Stir spread before serving. Serve with toasted bread slices.

NUTRITION INFORMATION PER SERVING: Calories 80 • Total Fat 6g • Saturated Fat 2.5g • Cholesterol 15mg • Sodium 240mg • Total Carbohydrate 1g • Dietary Fiber 0g. DIETARY EXCHANGES: 1/2 High-Fat Meat • 1/2 Fat.

special touch

This tasty spread blends all the characteristic flavors of the Reuben Grill, a New York deli sandwich, into a warm dip. Garnish the finished dip with a bit of curly parsley.

banana split-brownie pizza

PREP TIME: 20 Minutes ✻ READY IN: 1 Hour 40 Minutes ✻ SERVINGS: 16

- 1 roll (16.5 oz.) Pillsbury® refrigerated traditional chocolate fudge brownies
- 1 package (8 oz.) cream cheese, softened
- 1 can (8 oz.) crushed pineapple, drained
- 2 bananas, sliced
- 1 cup sliced fresh strawberries
- 1/4 cup chocolate topping

1 Heat oven to 350°F. Line 12x3/4-inch pizza pan with foil; grease and flour foil. Spread brownie batter on foil in pan.

2 Bake 15 to 18 minutes or until toothpick inserted near center comes out clean. Cool completely, about 1 hour.

3 Meanwhile, in small bowl, beat cream cheese and pineapple on low speed until blended. Spread over brownie; top with fruit. Drizzle chocolate topping over fruit. Refrigerate until serving time. Cut into 16 wedges or squares. Cover and refrigerate any remaining pizza.

NUTRITION INFORMATION PER SERVING: Calories 210 • Total Fat 10g • Saturated Fat 4g • Cholesterol 15mg • Sodium 135mg • Total Carbohydrate 28g • Dietary Fiber 0g. DIETARY EXCHANGES: 2 Other Carbohydrate • 1/2 High-Fat Meat • 1 Fat • 2 Carb Choices.

cook's notes

If the chocolate topping is too thick to drizzle, microwave as directed on the container.

spicy southwest beef and bean chili

PREP TIME: 15 Minutes ✻ READY IN: 8 Hours 15 Minutes ✻ SERVINGS: 6

- 1-1/2 lbs. boneless beef round steak, 1/2 inch thick, cut into 3/4-inch pieces
- 1 medium onion, chopped (1/2 cup)
- 4 cans (8 oz. each) no-salt-added tomato sauce
- 1 can (15.25 oz.) whole kernel sweet corn, drained
- 1 can (15 oz.) black beans, drained, rinsed
- 1 can (4.5 oz.) chopped green chiles
- 2 tablespoons chili powder

1 In 4- to 5-quart slow cooker, mix all of the ingredients. Cover and cook on Low heat setting 8 to 9 hours.

NUTRITION INFORMATION PER SERVING: Calories 400 • Total Fat 6g • Saturated Fat 2g • Cholesterol 85mg • Sodium 370mg • Total Carbohydrate 44g • Dietary Fiber 11g. DIETARY EXCHANGES: 2 Starch • 1/2 Other Carbohydrate • 1 Vegetable • 5 Very Lean Meat • 3 Carb Choices.

cook's notes

You can substitute other kinds of canned beans, such as great northern, kidney or pinto, for the black beans.

kitchen tip

Only remove the slow cooker's lid to check for doneness at the minimum cook time. It is estimated that the temperature drops 10°F every time the lid is removed, and it takes about 20 minutes to get back to the right temperature.

white chili with chicken

PREP TIME: 15 Minutes ✳ READY IN: 8 Hours 15 Minutes ✳ SERVINGS: 6

1 lb. boneless skinless chicken thighs, cut into thin bite-sized strips

1 cup dried great northern beans, sorted, rinsed

1 medium onion, chopped (1/2 cup)

1 garlic clove, finely chopped

2 teaspoons dried oregano leaves

1/2 teaspoon salt

1 can (10-3/4 oz.) condensed cream of chicken soup

5 cups water

1 teaspoon ground cumin

1/4 teaspoon red pepper sauce

1 can (4.5 oz.) chopped green chiles

Sour cream, if desired

Chopped avocado, if desired

1 In 3-1/2- to 4-quart slow cooker, mix chicken, beans, onion, garlic, oregano, salt, soup and water. Cover; cook on Low heat setting 9 to 10 hours.

2 Just before serving, stir cumin, pepper sauce and chiles into chili. If desired, serve with additional pepper sauce, sour cream and chopped avocado.

NUTRITION INFORMATION PER SERVING: Calories 290 • Total Fat 10g • Saturated Fat 3g • Cholesterol 50mg • Sodium 700mg • Total Carbohydrate 27g • Dietary Fiber 6g. DIETARY EXCHANGES: 2 Starch • 2-1/2 Lean Meat • 2 Carb Choices.

deep-dish pizza pie bundle

PREP TIME: 10 Minutes ✳ READY IN: 35 Minutes ✳ SERVINGS: 4

1 can (13.8 oz.) Pillsbury® refrigerated classic pizza crust

2 cups shredded mozzarella cheese (8 oz.)

1/3 cup pizza sauce

25 slices pepperoni (from 3.5-oz. pkg.)

1 tablespoon grated Parmesan cheese

1 Heat oven to 400°F. Spray 8-inch round cake pan with cooking spray. Unroll pizza crust dough; place on work surface. Starting at center, press out dough to form 14x10-inch rectangle. Place in pan with sides of dough extending evenly over sides of pan. Lightly press dough in bottom and up sides of pan.

2 Sprinkle 1 cup of the mozzarella cheese over dough. Spread pizza sauce evenly over cheese. Top with pepperoni and remaining 1 cup mozzarella cheese.

3 With scissors, make 2-inch cut into each corner of dough. Bring all ends of dough together at center; twist to secure at top of pizza. Sprinkle with Parmesan cheese. Bake 20 to 25 minutes or until deep golden brown.

NUTRITION INFORMATION PER SERVING: Calories 480 • Total Fat 20g • Saturated Fat 10g • Cholesterol 45mg • Sodium 1340mg • Total Carbohydrate 51g • Dietary Fiber 0g. DIETARY EXCHANGES: 2-1/2 Starch • 1 Other Carbohydrate • 2-1/2 Medium-Fat Meat • 1 Fat • 3-1/2 Carb Choices.

white chili with chicken

tex-mex meatball pie

tex-mex meatball pie

PREP TIME: 10 Minutes ❊ READY IN: 55 Minutes ❊ SERVINGS: 6

1 Pillsbury® refrigerated pie crust (from 15-oz. box), softened as directed on box

18 frozen cooked meatballs (about 1 inch), thawed

1 cup Green Giant® Valley Fresh Steamers™ Niblets® frozen corn

3/4 cup Old El Paso® Thick 'n Chunky salsa

3/4 cup shredded Cheddar cheese (3 oz.)

1 cup shredded lettuce

1/4 cup sour cream

1 Heat oven to 375°F. On ungreased cookie sheet, unroll pie crust. Place meatballs on the center of crust.

2 In small bowl, mix corn and 1/2 cup of the salsa. Spoon corn mixture over meatballs. Fold edge of crust over filling (about 2 inches); ruffle decoratively.

3 Bake 35 to 40 minutes or until crust is deep golden brown. Sprinkle with cheese. Bake 3 to 5 minutes longer or until cheese is melted.

4 Top with shredded lettuce and sour cream. Drizzle with the remaining 1/4 cup salsa. Serve immediately.

NUTRITION INFORMATION PER SERVING: Calories 340 • Total Fat 20g • Saturated Fat 9g • Cholesterol 60mg • Sodium 640mg • Total Carbohydrate 29g • Dietary Fiber 0g • Sugars 3g • Protein 11g. DIETARY EXCHANGES: 1-1/2 Starch • 1/2 Other Carbohydrate • 1 High-Fat Meat • 2 Fat.

cook's notes

If your meatballs are large, cut them in half before placing them on the crust.

spicy oriental barbecued chicken drummettes

PREP TIME: 10 Minutes ❊ READY IN: 1 Hour 50 Minutes ❊ SERVINGS: 14

DRUMMETTES

1 package (3 lbs.) frozen chicken drummettes, thawed

2 tablespoons butter or margarine, melted

1/4 cup all-purpose flour

SAUCE

1/3 cup hoisin sauce

2 tablespoons oriental chili garlic sauce

1 tablespoon butter or margarine, melted

1 Heat oven to 450°F. With paper towels, pat excess moisture from thawed drummettes. In large bowl, place drummettes. Drizzle with 2 tablespoons melted butter. Sprinkle with flour; toss to mix. (Mixture will be crumbly.)

2 Transfer mixture to ungreased 15x10x1-inch baking pan, arranging drummettes in single layer. Bake for 40 to 45 minutes or until crisp and brown.

3 With slotted spoon, transfer browned drummettes to 4- to 6-quart slow cooker. In small bowl, combine all sauce ingredients; mix well. Pour sauce over drummettes; toss lightly to coat with sauce. Cover; cook on Low setting for 1 to 2 hours.

NUTRITION INFORMATION PER SERVING: Calories 140 • Total Fat 8g • Saturated Fat 2g • Cholesterol 40mg • Sodium 230mg • Total Carbohydrate 5g • Dietary Fiber 0g. DIETARY EXCHANGES: 1/2 Other Carbohydrate • 2 Lean Meat • 1/2 Carb Choice.

cook's notes

Oriental chili garlic sauce is much hotter and thicker than traditional chili sauce and can be found in a supermarket's Asian food section. If you'd prefer a milder flavor, use only one tablespoon of the sauce. Look in the Asian food section for hoisin sauce, too.

spanish sausage coins

READY IN: 30 Minutes ✳ SERVINGS: 20

1 tablespoon olive oil	1/2 teaspoon coriander
1/4 cup finely chopped onion	Dash ground red pepper (cayenne)
3 garlic cloves, minced	1 can (8 oz.) tomato sauce
1 lb. cooked Polish sausage or kielbasa links, cut into 1/2-inch-thick slices	1/4 cup dry red wine (such as Rioja, Bordeaux or Merlot)
1 teaspoon paprika	

1 Heat oil in large skillet over medium heat until hot. Add onion; cook 4 to 5 minutes or until softened, stirring occasionally.

2 Add garlic; cook and stir 30 to 60 seconds or until fragrant. Add sausage slices; cook 2 to 4 minutes or until lightly browned, turning once.

3 Stir in paprika, coriander and ground red pepper. Add tomato sauce and red wine; cook about 5 minutes to reduce slightly, stirring occasionally. Serve warm sausage mixture with cocktail toothpicks.

NUTRITION INFORMATION PER SERVING: Calories 85 • Total Fat 7g • Saturated Fat 2g • Cholesterol 15mg • Sodium 300mg • Total Carbohydrate 2g • Dietary Fiber 0g • Sugars 1g • Protein 3g. DIETARY EXCHANGES: 1/2 Medium-Fat Meat • 1 Fat.

cook's notes

Rioja is a dry red wine from the LaRioja province in Spain. The oak barrels in which it is aged impart a vanilla flavor.

buffalo chicken casserole

PREP TIME: 25 Minutes ✳ READY IN: 55 Minutes ✳ SERVINGS: 4

1/2 cup uncooked regular long-grain white rice	2 medium stalks celery, thinly sliced (1 cup)
1 cup water	1 can (14.5 oz.) stewed tomatoes, undrained
1 tablespoon olive or vegetable oil	1/2 cup buffalo wing sauce
1 lb. boneless skinless chicken breasts, cut into thin strips	1/4 cup blue cheese dressing

1 Cook rice in 1 cup water 20 minutes as directed on package. Meanwhile, heat oven to 350°F. In 12-inch skillet, heat oil over medium-high heat. Add chicken and celery; cook 5 to 7 minutes, stirring frequently, until chicken is no longer pink in center. Remove from heat. Open can of tomatoes; cut up tomatoes in can. Stir tomatoes and wing sauce into chicken mixture.

2 Spray 8-inch square baking dish with cooking spray. Spoon cooked rice into dish. Spread chicken mixture over rice (do not stir). Bake 25 to 30 minutes or until hot in center. Drizzle dressing over top.

HIGH ALTITUDE (3500-6500 FT): Bake 30 to 35 minutes.

NUTRITION INFORMATION PER SERVING: Calories 380 • Total Fat 16g • Saturated Fat 2.5g • Cholesterol 70mg • Sodium 1910mg • Total Carbohydrate 29g • Dietary Fiber 1g • Sugars 7g • Protein 28g. DIETARY EXCHANGES: 1/2 Starch • 1 Other Carbohydrate • 1 Vegetable • 3-1/2 Very Lean Meat • 3 Fat • 2 Carb Choices.

cook's notes

Turn up the heat by adding 1 teaspoon red pepper sauce to the buffalo wing sauce. You could also serve this casserole with a bowl of crumbled blue cheese so guests can sprinkle some on top if they like.

hot cheesy artichoke dip

READY IN: 15 Minutes ✳ SERVINGS: 22

1   cup milk

3/4   cup canned artichoke hearts, drained, chopped

1   slice bacon, crisply cooked, crumbled, or 1 tablespoon cooked real bacon pieces

4   teaspoons all-purpose flour

2   teaspoons Dijon mustard

1/4   teaspoon garlic powder

1/8   teaspoon pepper

1-1/2 cups shredded Cheddar cheese (6 oz.)

1   box (8 oz.) pasteurized prepared cheese product, cubed

Baguette French bread slices or Melba bagel chips

1 In 2-quart saucepan, mix milk, artichoke hearts, bacon, flour, mustard, garlic powder and pepper. Cook over medium-low heat 4 to 6 minutes, stirring constantly, until hot and thickened, but not boiling.

2 Gradually stir in cheeses. Cook about 2 minutes, stirring constantly, until cheeses are melted. Transfer mixture to fondue pot. Adjust flame or heat so mixture stays hot but does not boil. Serve warm with baguette bread slices.

NUTRITION INFORMATION PER SERVING: Calories 110 • Total Fat 6g • Saturated Fat 3g • Cholesterol 15mg • Sodium 320mg • Total Carbohydrate 10g • Dietary Fiber 0g • Sugars 2g • Protein 6g. DIETARY EXCHANGES: 1/2 Starch • 1/2 High-Fat Meat • 1/2 Fat • 1/2 Carb Choice.

cook's notes

Be sure to purchase plain, not marinated, artichoke hearts. Marinated varieties will give the dip a strong flavor.

biscuit-topped hamburger stew

PREP TIME: 30 Minutes ✹ READY IN: 50 Minutes ✹ SERVINGS: 4

cook's notes

Biscuit-topped casseroles must be assembled while the filling is hot so the biscuits cook from the bottom in addition to becoming brown on top. For this recipe, make sure the stew is piping hot before arranging the biscuits on it.

1   lb. lean (at least 80%) ground beef

1/2   cup coarsely chopped onion

1   can (14.5 oz.) diced tomatoes, undrained

1   jar (12 oz.) home-style beef gravy

1-1/2   cups diced peeled potatoes

1   cup carrot strips (1x1/4x1/4-inch)

1   cup Green Giant® Valley Fresh Steamers™ frozen cut green beans

1/4   teaspoon pepper

1   can (6 oz.) Pillsbury® Grands!® Jr. Golden Layers® refrigerated buttermilk flaky biscuits

1 Heat oven to 375°F. Spray 10-inch skillet with cooking spray. Heat over medium-high heat until hot. Add beef and onion; cook and stir until beef is thoroughly cooked; drain.

2 Add the remaining ingredients except the biscuits; mix well. Heat to boiling. Reduce the heat to medium-low; cover and cook 10 to 15 minutes, stirring occasionally, until vegetables are tender. Spoon into ungreased 8-inch square (2-quart) or oval (2-1/2-quart) glass baking dish.

3 Separate dough into 5 biscuits; cut each in half. Arrange, cut side down, around outside edges of hot mixture. Bake about 20 minutes or until casserole is bubbly and biscuits are deep golden brown.

NUTRITION INFORMATION PER SERVING: Calories 500 • Total Fat 23g • Saturated Fat 8g • Cholesterol 75mg • Sodium 1190mg • Total Carbohydrate 43g • Dietary Fiber 5g • Sugars 8g • Protein 29g. DIETARY EXCHANGES: 2-1/2 Starch • 2-1/2 Other Carbohydrate • 1 Vegetable • 3 Lean Meat • 2-1/2 Fat.

chicken breast club sandwiches

READY IN: 25 Minutes ✳ SERVINGS: 5

1 can (10.8 oz.) Pillsbury® Grands!® refrigerated flaky biscuits (5 biscuits)	1-1/2 cups shredded lettuce
10 slices bacon	10 thin tomato slices
1/3 cup mayonnaise	2 packages (6 oz. each) sliced chicken breast

1 Heat oven to 375°F. Separate dough into 5 biscuits. Split each into 2 rounds. Press or roll each round to form 4-inch round; place on ungreased cookie sheets. Bake at 375°F for 7 to 9 minutes or until golden brown. Meanwhile, cook bacon until crisp. Drain on paper towels.

2 To serve, spread bottom of each baked biscuit round evenly with mayonnaise. Top 5 biscuit rounds, mayonnaise side up, with lettuce, tomato, chicken and cooked bacon. Top each with biscuit round, mayonnaise side down. Cut each sandwich into quarters. If desired, insert toothpick into each quarter.

NUTRITION INFORMATION PER SERVING: Calories 460 • Total Fat 28g • Saturated Fat 7g • Cholesterol 55mg • Sodium 1400mg • Total Carbohydrate 28g • Dietary Fiber 2g • Sugars 5g • Protein 23g. DIETARY EXCHANGES: 2 Starch • 2-1/2 High-Fat Meat • 1 Fat OR 2 Carbohydrate • 2-1/2 High-Fat Meat • 1 Fat • 2 Carb Choices.

cook's notes

Iceberg lettuce is the green traditionally used in a club sandwich, but it's fun to try other salad leaves, too. Some possibilities are crisp romaine, tender green-leaf or Bibb, pleasantly bitter radicchio or crunchy endive.

baked crabmeat spread

PREP TIME: 20 Minutes ✳ READY IN: 35 Minutes ✳ SERVINGS: 12

2 tablespoons margarine or butter	1/4 teaspoon white pepper
1/2 cup chopped red bell pepper	1 cup milk
2 tablespoons sliced green onions	1/4 cup grated Parmesan cheese
1 garlic clove, minced	1/2 cup frozen or canned cooked crabmeat
2 tablespoons all-purpose flour	1/4 cup shredded Cheddar cheese (1 oz.)

1 Heat oven to 350°F. Grease 9-inch pie pan. Melt margarine in skillet over medium heat. Add bell pepper, onions and garlic; cook and stir 2 to 3 minutes or until vegetables are tender. Stir in flour and pepper; cook 1 minute.

2 Gradually add milk; cook until mixture boils, stirring constantly. Stir in Parmesan cheese. Remove from heat; fold in crabmeat. Pour into greased pan. Sprinkle with Cheddar cheese.

3 Bake at 350°F for 10 to 15 minutes or until thoroughly heated and cheese is melted. Serve with Melba toast rounds.

NUTRITION INFORMATION PER SERVING: Calories 60 • Total Fat 4g • Saturated Fat 2g • Cholesterol 10mg • Sodium 160mg • Total Carbohydrate 3g • Dietary Fiber 0g • Sugars 1g • Protein 4g. DIETARY EXCHANGES: 1/2 Lean Meat • 1/2 Fat.

cook's notes

Busy making preparations for a party? Save time preparing this yummy spread—use the minced garlic sold in jars at the grocery store.

LUPE CORTES
Forest, Virginia
Bake-Off® Contest 41, 2004

cook's notes

Running short on time? Look in your supermarket's frozen foods section for packages of cooked chicken.

jalapeño-chicken crescent pinwheels

PREP TIME: 20 Minutes ❋ READY IN: 40 Minutes ❋ SERVINGS: 32

4 oz. (half 8-oz. pkg.) cream cheese, softened

1/2 cup chopped cooked chicken

1/4 cup chopped fresh cilantro

2 to 3 tablespoons finely chopped sliced jalapeño chiles (from 12-oz. jar)

2 tablespoons finely chopped green onions (2 medium)

1/8 teaspoon salt

1 can (8 oz.) Pillsbury® refrigerated crescent dinner rolls

1 Heat oven to 375°F. In small bowl, mix all ingredients except crescent roll dough until well combined; set aside.

2 Unroll dough; separate into 2 long rectangles. Place 1 rectangle on cutting board; press perforations to seal. Spread half of cream cheese mixture on dough rectangle to within 1/2 inch of edges.

3 Starting with one long side, roll up rectangle; press seam to seal. With serrated knife, cut roll into 16 slices; place cut side down on ungreased cookie sheet. Repeat with remaining dough rectangle.

4 Bake 14 to 16 minutes or until light golden brown. Immediately remove from the cookie sheet. Serve warm.

NUTRITION INFORMATION PER SERVING: Calories 45 • Total Fat 3g • Saturated Fat 1.5g • Cholesterol 5mg • Sodium 85mg • Total Carbohydrate 3g • Dietary Fiber 0g • Sugars 0g • Protein 1g. DIETARY EXCHANGES: 1/2 Starch • 1/2 Fat • 0 Carb Choice.

cook's notes

This zesty main dish can be assembled the day before and refrigerated. A slightly longer bake time may be needed to heat it thoroughly. Top the casserole with dollops of sour cream if you like.

easy taco casserole

PREP TIME: 20 Minutes ❋ READY IN: 50 Minutes ❋ SERVINGS: 5

1 lb. lean (at least 80%) ground beef

1 can (15 to 16 oz.) chili beans in sauce, undrained

1 can (8 oz.) tomato sauce

1 package (1 oz.) Old El Paso® 40% less sodium taco seasoning mix

2 cups coarsely broken tortilla chips

8 medium green onions, sliced (1/2 cup)

1 medium tomato chopped (3/4 cup)

1 cup shredded Cheddar or Monterey Jack cheese (4 oz.)

1 Heat oven to 350°F. In 10-inch skillet, cook beef over medium-high heat 5-7 minutes, stirring occasionally, until thoroughly cooked; drain. Stir in beans, tomato sauce and taco seasoning mix. Reduce heat to medium; heat to boiling, stirring occasionally.

2 In ungreased 1-1/2 to 2-quart casserole, place tortilla chips. Top evenly with beef mixture. Sprinkle with onions, tomato and cheese.

3 Bake uncovered 20 to 30 minutes or until hot and bubbly. If desired, arrange additional tortilla chips around edge of casserole.

HIGH ALTITUDE (3500-6500 FT): Heat oven to 375°F. Bake without cheese 20 minutes. Add cheese, bake 5 to 10 minutes longer.

NUTRITION INFORMATION PER SERVING: Calories 480 • Total Fat 24g • Saturated Fat 9g • Cholesterol 80mg • Sodium 1550 mg • Total Carbohydrate 37g • Dietary Fiber 5g • Sugars 6g • Protein 28g.

jalapeño-chicken crescent pinwheels

four-cheese pasta

four-cheese pasta

PREP TIME: 25 Minutes ❋ READY IN: 50 Minutes ❋ SERVINGS: 6

- 5 cups uncooked penne pasta (16 oz.)
- 1/2 cup butter or margarine
- 2 garlic cloves, finely chopped
- 1/2 cup all-purpose flour
- 1 teaspoon salt
- 4-1/2 cups milk
- 1 cup shredded provolone cheese (4 oz.)

- 1 cup shredded mozzarella cheese (4 oz.)
- 1/2 cup shredded Parmesan cheese (2 oz.)
- 1/2 cup shredded fontina cheese (2 oz.)
- 1/3 cup chopped fresh parsley
- 1 tablespoon butter or margarine
- 1 cup panko bread crumbs

1 Heat oven to 350°F. Spray 13x9-inch (3-quart) glass baking dish with cooking spray. Cook and drain pasta as directed on package.

2 Meanwhile, in 4-quart saucepan or Dutch oven, melt 1/2 cup butter over low heat. Add garlic; cook 30 seconds, stirring frequently. With wire whisk, stir in flour and salt until smooth. Increase heat to medium; cook, stirring constantly, until mixture is smooth and bubbly. Gradually stir in milk. Heat to boiling, stirring constantly. Boil and stir 1 minute. Stir in cheeses. Cook until melted, stirring occasionally. Stir pasta and parsley into cheese sauce. Pour mixture into baking dish.

3 In 6-inch skillet, melt 1 tablespoon butter over medium-high heat; stir in bread crumbs. Cook and stir until crumbs are golden brown. Sprinkle over pasta mixture. Bake uncovered 20 to 25 minutes or until bubbly.

HIGH ALTITUDE (3500-6500 FT): Heat oven to 375°F. Bake 25 to 30 minutes.

NUTRITION INFORMATION PER SERVING: Calories 850 • Total Fat 39g • Saturated Fat 23g • Cholesterol 100mg • Sodium 1390mg • Total Carbohydrate 91g • Dietary Fiber 4g • Sugars 12g • Protein 35g. DIETARY EXCHANGES: 5 Starch • 1 Other Carbohydrate • 3 High-Fat Meat • 2 Fat • 6 Carb Choices.

kitchen tip

Panko bread crumbs are Japanese-style bread crumbs. They have a coarser texture and make for a much lighter and crunchier casserole. In a pinch, regular bread crumbs will also work.

smoky ham and navy bean stew

PREP TIME: 15 Minutes ❋ READY IN: 10 Hours 15 Minutes ❋ SERVINGS: 4

- 1 lb. cooked ham, cut into 1/2-inch cubes (3 cups)
- 2 cups water
- 1 cup dried navy beans
- 2 medium stalks celery, sliced (1 cup)
- 2 medium carrots, sliced (1 cup)

- 1 small onion, chopped (1/4 cup)
- 1/4 teaspoon dried thyme leaves
- 1/4 teaspoon Liquid Smoke
- 1/4 cup chopped fresh parsley

1 In 3-1/2- to 4-quart slow cooker, mix all ingredients except parsley. Cover; cook on Low heat setting 10 to 12 hours. Just before serving, stir in parsley.

NUTRITION INFORMATION PER SERVING: Calories 390 • Total Fat 11g • Saturated Fat 3.5g • Cholesterol 65mg • Sodium 1740mg • Total Carbohydrate 36g • Dietary Fiber 14g. DIETARY EXCHANGES: 2 Starch • 1 Vegetable • 4 Very Lean Meat • 1-1/2 Fat • 2-1/2 Carb Choices.

cook's notes

Liquid Smoke is exactly that— liquid mixed with smoke. It lends a smoky, hickory flavor to this bean stew. Look for it in the condiment aisle of the grocery store. If you like, you can omit it and the stew will still be tasty.

cook's notes

Don't have the round steak this recipe calls for? Looking to beat the clock on a busy night? Try using 1 pound of cubed beef stew meat instead. You could also replace some of the vegetables with leftovers you may have in the refrigerator.

beef and barley stew

PREP TIME: 15 Minutes ✳ READY IN: 10 Hours 15 Minutes ✳ SERVINGS: 5

1 lb. boneless beef round steak (1/2 inch thick), trimmed of fat, cut into 3/4-inch pieces

2 cups frozen cut green beans

1 cup shredded carrots (1 to 2 medium)

1/2 cup uncooked regular pearl barley

1 jar (12 oz.) mushroom gravy

1 jar (4.5 oz.) sliced mushrooms, drained

2-1/2 cups water

2 teaspoons beef bouillon granules

1/2 teaspoon dried thyme leaves

1/4 teaspoon pepper

1 In 3-1/2 or 4-quart slow cooker, place beef, green beans, carrots, barley, gravy and mushrooms. Stir together remaining ingredients. Pour over beef and vegetables; stir until mixed. Cover; cook on Low heat setting for 10 to 12 hours.

NUTRITION INFORMATION PER SERVING: Calories 360 • Total Fat 13g • Saturated Fat 4.5g • Cholesterol 75mg • Sodium 940mg • Total Carbohydrate 27g • Dietary Fiber 6g. DIETARY EXCHANGES: 1 Starch • 1/2 Other Carbohydrate • 1 Vegetable • 4 Lean Meat • 2 Carb Choices.

italian chicken pizza

PREP TIME: 25 Minutes ✳ READY IN: 40 Minutes ✳ SERVINGS: 6

1 can (10 oz.) Pillsbury® refrigerated pizza crust

1 package (9 oz.) frozen spinach in a pouch

1 tablespoon oil

1/2 cup coarsely chopped onion

1 package (6 oz.) refrigerated cooked Italian-style chicken breast strips, chopped

2 cups shredded mozzarella cheese (8 oz.)

1 package (2.8 to 3 oz.) precooked bacon slices, cut into 1/2-inch pieces

cook's notes

This easy pizza makes a great main dish, but you'll also enjoy it as an appetizer. Just prepare it as directed, then cut small squares and arrange them on a festive platter.

1 Heat oven to 400°F. Grease 15x10x1-inch baking pan. Unroll dough; place in greased pan. Starting at center, press out dough to edge of pan. Bake at 400°F for 9 to 13 minutes or until edges are light golden brown.

2 Meanwhile, cook spinach as directed on package. Drain well; squeeze to remove liquid. Heat oil in small skillet over medium-high heat until hot. Add onion; cook 3 to 4 minutes or until tender, stirring frequently.

3 Remove partially baked crust from oven. Top crust with spinach, onion, chicken, cheese and bacon. Return to oven; bake an additional 9 to 12 minutes or until cheese is melted.

NUTRITION INFORMATION PER SERVING: Calories 385 • Total Fat 19g • Saturated Fat 7g • Cholesterol 55mg • Sodium 890mg • Total Carbohydrate 26g • Dietary Fiber 2g • Sugars 4g • Protein 28g. DIETARY EXCHANGES: 2 Starch • 3 Medium-Fat Meat OR 2 Carbohydrate • 3 Medium-Fat Meat • 2 Carb Choices.

beef and barley stew

barbecued shredded pork sandwiches

PREP TIME: 15 Minutes ✱ READY IN: 8 Hours 15 Minutes ✱ SERVINGS: 6

1/2 cup barbecue sauce
1/2 cup sweet-and-sour sauce
1 garlic clove, finely chopped
2 lbs. boneless country-style pork ribs, trimmed of fat, cut into 2-inch pieces
6 kaiser rolls, split

1 In 3-1/2- to 4-quart slow cooker, mix both sauces and the garlic. Stir in pork to coat. Cover; cook on Low heat setting 8 to 10 hours.

2 Remove pork from slow cooker; place on cutting board. Shred pork by pulling apart with 2 forks. Return pork to sauce in slow cooker; mix well. To serve, spoon about 1/2 cup pork mixture into each roll.

NUTRITION INFORMATION PER SERVING: Calories 490 • Total Fat 20g • Saturated Fat 7g • Cholesterol 95mg • Sodium 630mg • Total Carbohydrate 41g • Dietary Fiber 1g. DIETARY EXCHANGES: 1-1/2 Starch • 1 Other Carbohydrate • 4 Medium-Fat Meat • 3 Carb Choices.

kitchen tip

A slow cooker is the perfect appliance to take to potlucks, family gatherings or office events. Put the slow cooker in a box or other container that will stay flat in your car. Place rubber bands around the lid and handles to secure the lid and prevent spills.

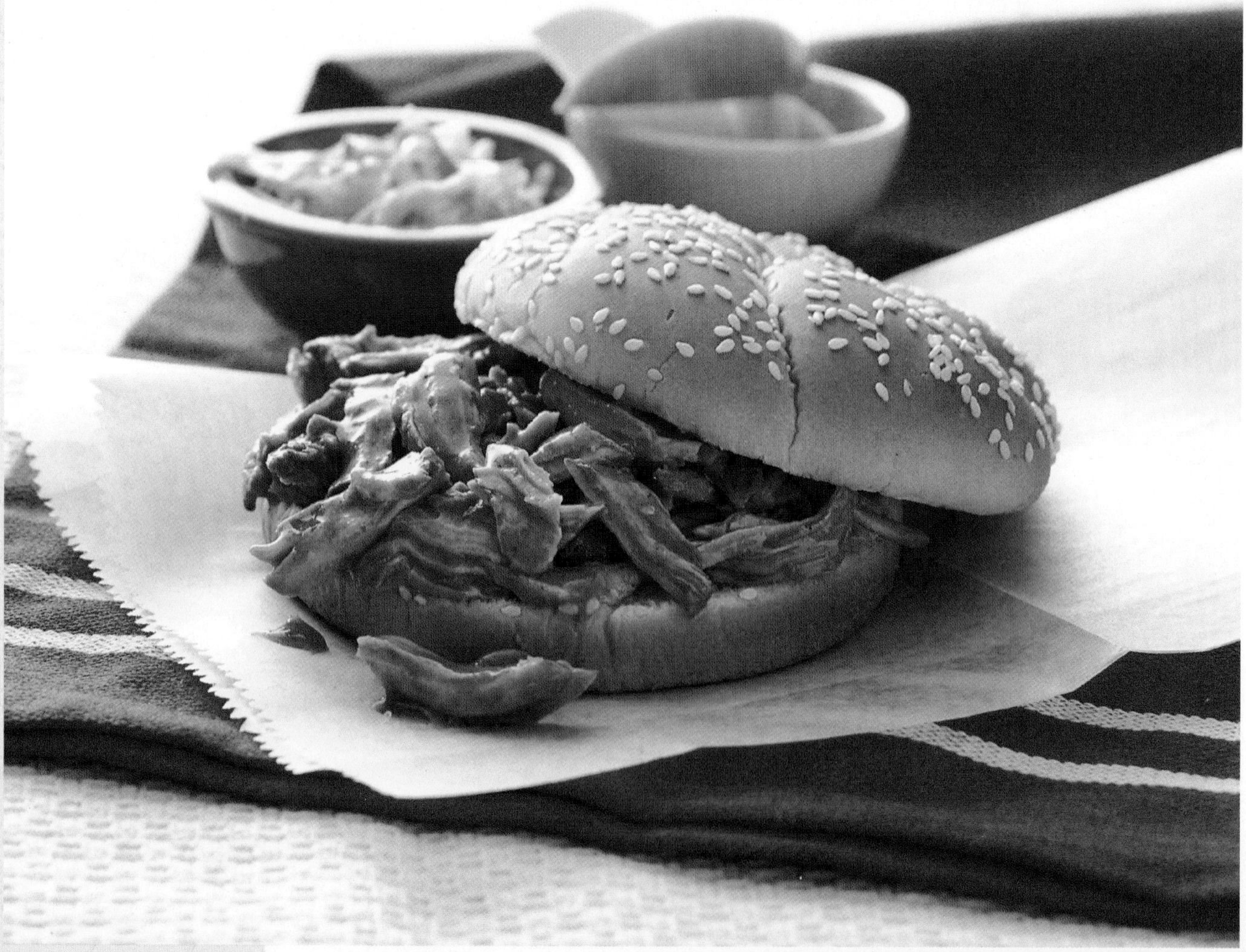

mini pizzas

PREP TIME: 30 Minutes ✳ READY IN: 30 Minutes ✳ SERVINGS: 18 Mini Pizzas

- 1 can (13.8 oz) Pillsbury® refrigerated classic pizza crust
- 1/4 cup basil pesto
- 18 slices plum (Roma) tomatoes
- 5 slices (1 oz. each) mozzarella cheese, cut into 18 (1-1/2-inch) squares

1 Heat oven to 425°F. Lightly spray cookie sheet with cooking spray. Unroll dough; place on cookie sheet. Press dough with fingers to form 15x10-inch rectangle. With 2-1/2-inch holiday-shaped metal cookie cutters, cut dough into shapes; remove excess dough. Bake 6 to 8 minutes or until set.

2 Remove partially baked crusts from oven; let cool 3 to 4 minutes. Spread each crust with pesto. Top each with 1 tomato slice and 1 cheese square. Bake 3 to 5 minutes longer or until cheese is melted and edges are browned.

NUTRITION INFORMATION PER SERVING: Calories 100 • Total Fat 4g • Saturated Fat 1.5g • Trans Fat 0g • Cholesterol 0mg • Sodium 230mg • Total Carbohydrate 11g • Dietary Fiber 0g • Sugars 2g • Protein 4g. DIETARY EXCHANGES: 1 Starch • 1/2 Fat.

cook's notes

For Mini Fruit Pizzas, spread the baked crusts with sweet cream cheese or frosting, then garnish them with fruit. Sliced kiwifruit and star fruit, diced mango and papaya, and whole berries always look attractive. Warm a bit of apricot jam until it is thin enough to brush over the fruit.

ROSEMARY LEICHT
Bethel, Ohio
Bake-Off® Contest 38, 1998

fruity almond dessert pizza

PREP TIME: 15 Minutes ✳ READY IN: 45 Minutes ✳ SERVINGS: 8

1 can (13.8 oz.) Pillsbury® refrigerated classic pizza crust

1/3 cup cream cheese or light cream cheese, softened

1/4 cup apricot preserves

1 large apple, peeled, thinly sliced

1/4 cup all-purpose or unbleached flour

1/4 cup packed brown sugar

2 tablespoons butter or margarine

1/4 cup blanched almonds, coarsely chopped

1 Heat oven to 425°F. Grease 12-inch pizza pan or 13x9-inch pan with shortening, or spray with cooking spray. Unroll dough; place in pan. Starting at center, press out dough to edge of pan. Spread cream cheese evenly over dough. Spread with preserves. Arrange apple slices over preserves.

2 In small bowl, mix flour and brown sugar. With pastry blender or fork, cut in butter until mixture resembles coarse crumbs. Stir in almonds. Sprinkle mixture evenly over apples.

3 Bake 15 to 20 minutes or until edges are golden brown. Cool 10 minutes. Cut into wedges. Serve warm.

NUTRITION INFORMATION PER SERVING: Calories 290 • Total Fat 10g • Saturated Fat 4.5g • Cholesterol 20mg • Sodium 410mg • Total Carbohydrate 44g • Dietary Fiber 0g. DIETARY EXCHANGES: 1 Starch • 2 Other Carbohydrate • 1/2 High-Fat Meat • 1 Fat • 3 Carb Choices.

grands!® grilled cheese sandwiches

READY IN: 20 Minutes ✳ SERVINGS: 4

1 can (16.3 oz.) Pillsbury® Grands!® refrigerated buttermilk biscuits

2 teaspoons oil

8 slices (2/3 oz.) American cheese

special touch

Put thin tomato slices and a sprinkling of real bacon pieces or crumbled cooked bacon between the cheese slices before topping the sandwiches with the remaining biscuit rounds.

1 Separate buttermilk biscuit dough into 8 biscuits. Press or roll each biscuit to form a 5-1/2-inch round.

2 Heat oil in large skillet over medium heat until hot. Add biscuit rounds, a few at a time; cook 3 minutes. Turn; cook an additional 3 minutes or until light golden brown. Remove from skillet.

3 Place 2 slices of cheese on each of 4 biscuit rounds. Top with remaining biscuit rounds. Return sandwiches to skillet; cook 2 to 3 minutes. Turn; cook an additional 2 minutes or until cheese is melted.

NUTRITION INFORMATION PER SERVING: Calories 550 • Total Fat 32g • Saturated Fat 13g • Cholesterol 40mg • Sodium 1730mg • Total Carbohydrate 49g • Dietary Fiber 1g • Sugars 9g • Protein 16g. DIETARY EXCHANGES: 3 Starch • 1/2 Fruit • 1 High-Fat Meat • 4-1/2 Fat OR 3-1/2 Carbohydrate • 1 High-Fat Meat • 4-1/2 Fat • 3 Carb Choices.

fruity almond dessert pizza

cheeseburger bites

PREP TIME: 15 Minutes ✳ READY IN: 3 Hours 15 Minutes ✳ SERVINGS: 24

BITES

- 1 lb. lean (at least 80%) ground beef
- 2 tablespoons ketchup
- 2 teaspoons instant minced onion
- 1 teaspoon yellow mustard
- 8 oz. American cheese loaf, cut into 2-inch cubes (2 cups)
- 24 miniature burger buns, split

TOPPINGS, AS DESIRED

Dill pickle chips

Sliced plum (Roma) tomatoes

Shredded lettuce

Additional ketchup and mustard

1 In 10-inch skillet, cook beef over medium-high heat 5 to 7 minutes, stirring frequently, until thoroughly cooked; drain. Stir in 2 tablespoons ketchup, the onion and 1 teaspoon mustard.

2 Spray 3-1/2- to 4-quart slow cooker with cooking spray. Spoon beef mixture into slow cooker. Top with cheese. Cover; cook on Low heat setting 3 to 4 hours.

3 Just before serving, stir beef mixture. Spoon 1 rounded tablespoon mixture into each bun. Serve with desired toppings.

NUTRITION INFORMATION PER SERVING: Calories 140 • Total Fat 6g • Saturated Fat 3g • Cholesterol 20mg • Sodium 290mg • Total Carbohydrate 13g • Dietary Fiber 0g. DIETARY EXCHANGES: 1 Starch • 1/2 Medium-Fat Meat • 1/2 Fat • 1 Carb Choices.

shortcut sausage-stuffed manicotti with sun-dried tomato sauce

PREP TIME: 20 Minutes ✳ READY IN: 2 Hours ✳ SERVINGS: 7

1 jar (26 oz.) sun-dried tomato pasta sauce	14 uncooked manicotti pasta shells (8 oz.)
1/2 cup water	2 cups shredded mozzarella cheese (8 oz.)
1-1/2 lbs. uncooked Italian sausage links (7 links)	1/4 cup shredded Parmesan cheese (1 oz.)

1 Heat oven to 350°F. Spray 13x9-inch (3-quart) glass baking dish with cooking spray. Spread 1 cup of the pasta sauce in dish. To remaining sauce in jar, add water and mix well.

2 Cut sausage links in half lengthwise; remove casings. Shape each piece of sausage into roll; stuff into uncooked pasta shell. Place stuffed shells on sauce in dish. Pour remaining pasta sauce mixture over shells.

3 Cover tightly with foil; bake 1 hour 20 minutes. Sprinkle with mozzarella and Parmesan cheeses; bake uncovered about 10 minutes longer or until cheeses are melted and pasta is tender. Let stand 10 minutes before serving.

NUTRITION INFORMATION PER SERVING: Calories 550 • Total Fat 29g • Saturated Fat 12g • Cholesterol 60mg • Sodium 1440mg • Total Carbohydrate 42g • Dietary Fiber 3g • Sugars 6g • Protein 30g. DIETARY EXCHANGES: 1-1/2 Starch • 1 Other Carbohydrate • 1 Vegetable • 3-1/2 High-Fat Meat.

grilled salami sandwiches

READY IN: 30 Minutes ✱ SERVINGS: 4

8 slices bakery-style Italian bread	8 slices hard salami (about 1/4 lb.)
3 tablespoons Caesar ranch or creamy Dijon gourmet light mayonnaise	1 small tomato, cut into 8 thin slices
2 tablespoons butter or margarine, softened	4 slices (3/4 oz. each) mozzarella cheese

1 Heat 12-inch skillet over medium heat. Spread one side of each bread slice with gourmet mayonnaise and other side with butter.

2 Place 2 bread slices, butter side down, in skillet. Top each with 2 salami slices, 2 tomato slices, 1 cheese slice and 1 bread slice, butter side up.

3 Cook 2 to 3 minutes or until bottoms of sandwiches are golden brown. Turn sandwiches; cook 1 to 2 minutes or until bottoms are golden brown and cheese is melted. Repeat with remaining 2 sandwiches.

NUTRITION INFORMATION PER SERVING: Calories 400 • Total Fat 25g • Saturated Fat 10g • Cholesterol 55mg • Sodium 1030mg • Total Carbohydrate 26g • Dietary Fiber 1g • Sugars 2g • Protein 16g. DIETARY EXCHANGES: 1-1/2 Starch • 1-1/2 High-Fat Meat • 2-1/2 Fat • 2 Carb Choices.

cook's notes

If you don't have flavored mayonnaise, just stir together equal parts mayo and ranch dressing or Dijon mustard.

spinach and mushroom pizza pie

PREP TIME: 10 Minutes ✱ READY IN: 50 Minutes ✱ SERVINGS: 6

2 cans (10 oz. each) Pillsbury® refrigerated pizza crust	1-1/2 cups shredded mozzarella cheese
1 can (8 oz.) pizza sauce (1 cup)	2 packages (9 oz. each) frozen spinach in a pouch, thawed, squeezed to drain
1 jar (4.5 oz.) sliced mushrooms, drained	1 teaspoon olive or vegetable oil
1/4 cup sliced ripe olives	1 tablespoon grated Parmesan cheese

1 Heat oven to 400°F. Lightly grease 9-inch pie pan. Unroll 1 can of dough into greased pan. Press in bottom and up sides of pan to form crust.

2 In small bowl, combine pizza sauce and mushrooms; mix well. Spoon onto dough. Layer olives, 3/4 cup of the mozzarella cheese, spinach and remaining 3/4 cup mozzarella cheese over mushroom mixture.

3 Unroll remaining can of dough. Press dough to form 9-inch round; place over filling. Pinch edges of dough to seal; roll up edge of dough or flute to form rim. Cut several slits in top crust for steam to escape. Brush with oil. Sprinkle with Parmesan cheese. Bake at 400°F for 35 to 40 minutes or until crust is deep golden brown.

NUTRITION INFORMATION PER SERVING: Calories 460 • Total Fat 15g • Saturated Fat 5g • Cholesterol 15mg • Sodium 1000mg • Total Carbohydrate 63g • Dietary Fiber 5g • Sugars 0g • Protein 19g. DIETARY EXCHANGES: 3-1/2 Starch • 2 Vegetable • 1 High-Fat Meat OR 3-1/2 Carbohydrate • 2 Vegetable • 1 High-Fat Meat • 4 Carb Choices.

cook's notes

For a heartier pie, add about 1/2 pound cooked bulk Italian turkey sausage or ground beef along with the olives in Step 2, then continue with the recipe as directed.

grilled salami sandwiches

jerk chicken wings with creamy dipping sauce

PREP TIME: 10 Minutes ✳ READY IN: 1 Hour 55 Minutes ✳ SERVINGS: 12

CHICKEN WINGS

- 2 tablespoons dried thyme leaves
- 1 tablespoon packed brown sugar
- 1 tablespoon minced garlic (3 to 4 medium cloves)
- 3 teaspoons ground allspice
- 1 teaspoon salt
- 2 tablespoons cider vinegar
- 2 tablespoons hot pepper sauce
- 1 package (3 lbs.) frozen chicken wing drummettes, thawed

DIPPING SAUCE

- 1/2 cup chopped green onions (8 medium)
- 1/2 cup sour cream
- 1/2 cup mayonnaise

1   In large nonmetal bowl, mix thyme, brown sugar, garlic, allspice, salt, vinegar and hot pepper sauce. Add chicken drummettes; toss to coat evenly. Cover; refrigerate 1 hour to marinate.

2   Heat oven to 425°F. Line two 15x10x1-inch pans with foil; spray foil with cooking spray. Place chicken drummettes in pans; discard any remaining marinade.

3   Bake 45 minutes or until chicken is no longer pink next to bone. Meanwhile, in small bowl, mix all dipping sauce ingredients. Serve chicken wings with sauce.

NUTRITION INFORMATION PER SERVING: Calories 170 • Total Fat 13g • Saturated 3g • Cholesterol 50mg • Sodium 140mg • Total Carbohydrate 1g • Dietary Fiber 0g • Sugars 1g • Protein 13g.

cook's notes

To get a head start on fixing this appetizer, make and bake the drummettes following the recipe, then place in a covered container and refrigerate for up to 24 hours. To reheat, place in a foil-lined 15x10x1-inch pan; heat at 350°F until thoroughly heated, about 20 minutes.

layered pizza dip

PREP TIME: 10 Minutes ✳ READY IN: 25 Minutes ✳ SERVINGS: 16

1   container (8 oz.) chives-and-onion cream
    cheese spread

1/2 cup pizza sauce

1/2 cup chopped green bell pepper (1/2 medium)

1/3 cup finely chopped pepperoni (1-3/4 oz.)

1/2 cup shredded mozzarella cheese (2 oz.)

1/2 cup shredded Cheddar cheese (2 oz.)
    Bagel chips or crackers

1 Heat oven to 350°F. In ungreased 9-inch glass pie pan or 1-quart shallow baking dish, layer
   cream cheese spread, pizza sauce, bell pepper, pepperoni, mozzarella and Cheddar cheese.

2 Bake 10 to 15 minutes or until dip is hot and cheese is melted. Serve warm with bagel chips or
   crackers.

NUTRITION INFORMATION PER SERVING: Calories 120 • Total Fat 9g • Saturated Fat 5g • Cholesterol 25mg • Sodium 200mg • Total
Carbohydrate 5g • Dietary Fiber 0g • Sugars 1g • Protein 4g. DIETARY EXCHANGES: 1 High-Fat Meat • 0 Carb Choice.

cook's notes

*If you like, skip the oven and
layer the dip ingredients in a
microwavable dish. Microwave
on High for 1 to 2 minutes or
just until hot.*

Christmas Around the World

Celebrate your family's heritage with a taste of the "old country"…or add excitement to menus with something new, from saucy Italian pasta to German chocolate cake.

p. 180

p. 170

p. 186

p. 169

p. 174

quesadilla pie p. 182

Pillsbury

Bake-Off

BARBARA JANSKY
Estero, Florida
Bake-Off® Contest 41, 2004
Prize Winner

layered caribbean chicken salad

READY IN: 30 Minutes ✳ SERVINGS: 6

DRESSING

1 container (6 oz.) Yoplait® Original 99% fat free piña colada yogurt

1-1/2 to 2 tablespoons lime juice

1 teaspoon Caribbean jerk seasoning

SALAD

3 cups shredded romaine lettuce

2 cups cubed cooked chicken

1 cup shredded Monterey Jack cheese (4 oz.)

1 can (15 oz.) Progresso® black beans, drained, rinsed

1-1/2 cups diced peeled ripe fresh mango

1/2 cup chopped seeded Italian plum tomatoes (1 to 2 medium)

1 cup shredded Cheddar cheese (4 oz.)

1/2 cup thinly sliced green onions (8 medium)

1/2 cup cashews

Fresh edible flowers, if desired

1 In small bowl, mix all dressing ingredients until well blended. In 3- or 4-quart clear glass serving bowl, layer all salad ingredients in order listed, except cashews and flowers. Spoon dressing evenly over salad; sprinkle cashews over top. Garnish with flowers.

NUTRITION INFORMATION PER SERVING: Calories 450 • Total Fat 21g • Saturated Fat 10g • Cholesterol 80mg • Sodium 320mg • Total Carbohydrate 34g • Dietary Fiber 8g • Sugars 15g • Protein 33g.

thai curry chicken and vegetables

READY IN: 1 Hour ✷ SERVINGS: 5

MANIKA MISRA
North Miami Beach, Florida
Bake-Off® Contest 35, 1992
Prize Winner

1-3/4 cups uncooked regular long-grain white rice	1 tablespoon soy sauce
3-1/4 cups water	1-1/2 lbs. boneless skinless chicken breasts, cut into 1-inch pieces
2 tablespoons vegetable oil	1 cup chicken broth
1 teaspoon five-spice powder	3 teaspoons curry powder
1/2 to 1-1/2 teaspoons salt	2 tablespoons rice vinegar or vinegar
1/2 teaspoon monosodium glutamate, if desired	1 can (14 oz.) coconut milk (not cream of coconut)
1/2 teaspoon garlic powder	1 cup ready-to-eat baby-cut carrots
1/2 teaspoon ground ginger	2 cups frozen broccoli florets
1/2 teaspoon pepper	1 can (8 oz.) sliced water chestnuts, drained
1/2 teaspoon ground red pepper (cayenne)	

1 Cook rice in water as directed on package. Cover to keep warm. In 10-inch skillet or wok, heat oil over medium-high heat until hot. Stir in five-spice powder, salt, monosodium glutamate, garlic powder, ginger, pepper, ground red pepper and soy sauce. Add chicken; cook and stir 5 to 8 minutes or until coated with seasonings, lightly browned and no longer pink in center.

2 Stir in broth, curry powder, vinegar, coconut milk and carrots. Heat to boiling. Reduce heat; simmer uncovered 20 to 25 minutes, stirring occasionally, until carrots are tender.

3 Stir in broccoli and water chestnuts. Heat to boiling; cook 3 to 5 minutes or until vegetables are crisp-tender. Serve over rice.

NUTRITION INFORMATION PER SERVING: Calories 690 • Total Fat 25g • Saturated Fat 15g • Cholesterol 80mg • Sodium 1530mg • Total Carbohydrate 75g • Dietary Fiber 5g. DIETARY EXCHANGES: 3-1/2 Starch • 1 Other Carbohydrate • 1 Vegetable • 4 Very Lean Meat • 4 Fat • 5 Carb Choices.

greek chicken pita folds

PREP TIME: 15 Minutes ✷ READY IN: 6 Hours 15 Minutes ✷ SERVINGS: 4 Sandwiches

1 medium onion, halved, sliced	1/4 teaspoon ground allspice
1 garlic clove, finely chopped	4 pita (pocket) breads
1 lb. boneless skinless chicken thighs	1/2 cup plain yogurt
1-1/2 teaspoons lemon-pepper seasoning	1 plum (Roma) tomato, sliced
1/2 teaspoon dried oregano leaves	1/2 medium cucumber, chopped (about 1/2 cup)

1 In 4- to 6-quart slow cooker, mix onion, garlic, chicken thighs, lemon-pepper seasoning, oregano and allspice; mix to coat chicken with seasoning. Cover; cook on Low heat setting 6 to 8 hours.

2 Heat pita breads as directed on package. Meanwhile, remove chicken from slow cooker; place on cutting board. Shred chicken with 2 forks.

3 To serve, stir yogurt into onion mixture in slow cooker. Spoon chicken onto warm pita breads. With slotted spoon, transfer onion mixture onto chicken; top with tomato and cucumber. Fold each pita bread in half.

NUTRITION INFORMATION PER SERVING: Calories 340 • Total Fat 10g • Saturated Fat 3g • Cholesterol 75mg • Sodium 460mg • Total Carbohydrate 32g • Dietary Fiber 2g. DIETARY EXCHANGES: 1 Starch • 1 Other Carbohydrate • 4 Very Lean Meat • 1-1/2 Fat • 2 Carb Choices.

cook's notes

If you don't have lemon-pepper seasoning, simply substitute 1 teaspoon grated lemon peel, 3/4 teaspoon salt and 1/4 teaspoon pepper.

penne provençal

READY IN: 30 Minutes ❋ SERVINGS: 6

2 cups uncooked penne (8 oz.) (tube-shaped pasta)	1 can (15 oz.) navy beans, drained, rinsed
3 cups diced peeled eggplant	3 garlic cloves, minced
2 cans (14.5 oz. each) diced tomatoes, undrained	2 teaspoons sugar
	Coarse ground black pepper, if desired
	2 tablespoons chopped fresh Italian parsley

1 Cook penne pasta to desired doneness as directed on package. Drain penne and cover to keep warm.

2 Meanwhile, in Dutch oven or large saucepan, combine eggplant, tomatoes, beans, garlic and sugar; mix well. Bring to a boil over medium-high heat. Reduce heat to low; simmer 10 to 15 minutes or until eggplant is tender. If desired, add coarse ground black pepper to taste.

3 Add warm penne pasta to eggplant mixture; toss gently to mix. Sprinkle with chopped fresh Italian parsley.

NUTRITION INFORMATION PER SERVING: Calories 270 • Total Fat 1g • Saturated Fat 0g • Cholesterol 0mg • Sodium 370mg • Total Carbohydrate 53g • Dietary Fiber 7g • Sugars 9g • Protein 12g. DIETARY EXCHANGES: 3 Starch • 1 Vegetable OR 3 Carbohydrate • 1 Vegetable.

quiche lorraine

PREP TIME: 30 Minutes ❋ READY IN: 1 Hour 15 Minutes ❋ SERVINGS: 6

1 refrigerated pie crust (from 15-oz. pkg.)	4 eggs
8 slices bacon	1-1/2 cups half-and-half
8 oz. Swiss cheese, cut into thin strips (2 cups)	1/4 cup chopped onion
2 tablespoons all-purpose flour	Dash pepper

1 Heat oven to 350°F. Prepare pie crust for one-crust filled pie using 9-inch pie pan. Cook bacon in large skillet over medium heat until crisp. Remove from skillet; drain on paper towels. Crumble.

2 In medium bowl, combine cheese and flour; mix well. In large bowl, beat eggs slightly. Add half-and-half, onion, pepper, bacon and cheese mixture; mix well. Spoon into crust-lined pan.

3 Bake at 350°F for 40 to 45 minutes or until knife inserted near center comes out clean. Let stand 10 minutes before serving.

NUTRITION INFORMATION PER SERVING: Calories 490 • Total Fat 34g • Saturated Fat 17g • Cholesterol 215mg • Sodium 440mg • Total Carbohydrate 24g • Dietary Fiber 0g • Sugars 5g • Protein 21g. DIETARY EXCHANGES: 1-1/2 Starch • 2-1/2 High-Fat Meat • 2-1/2 Fat OR 1-1/2 Carbohydrate • 2-1/2 High-Fat Meat • 2-1/2 Fat.

fruit sangria

READY IN: 10 Minutes ❋ SERVINGS: 10

2 cups dry red wine, chilled	1/4 cup sugar
2 cups orange juice	1 cup club soda, chilled
2 tablespoons lime juice	

1 In large nonmetal container or bowl, combine wine, orange juice, lime juice and sugar; stir until sugar is dissolved. Just before serving, slowly add club soda, stirring gently to blend. Serve over ice.

NUTRITION INFORMATION PER SERVING: Calories 70 • Total Fat 0g • Saturated Fat 0g • Cholesterol 0mg • Sodium 10mg • Total Carbohydrate 11g • Dietary Fiber 0g • Sugars 11g • Protein 0g. DIETARY EXCHANGES: 1 Fruit OR 1 Carbohydrate.

penne provençal

beef and spinach enchiladas

beef and spinach enchiladas

PREP TIME: 25 Minutes ✳ READY IN: 50 Minutes ✳ SERVINGS: 8

1 lb. lean (at least 80%) ground beef	2 cups shredded Monterey Jack cheese (8 oz.)
2 garlic cloves, minced	1 package (11.5 oz.) Old El Paso® flour tortillas for burritos, 8 inch (8 tortillas)
1-1/2 cups Green Giant® frozen cut leaf spinach (from 1-lb. bag)	1 can (8 oz.) tomato sauce
4 oz. cream cheese, cut into 1-inch cubes	1 cup Old El Paso® Thick 'n Chunky salsa
1/2 teaspoon ground cumin	2 tablespoons chopped fresh cilantro, if desired
1 can (4.5 oz.) Old El Paso® chopped green chiles	

1 Heat oven to 350°F. Spray 13x9-inch (3-quart) glass baking dish with nonstick cooking spray. In 12-inch skillet, cook ground beef and garlic over medium-high heat 5 to 7 minutes, stirring occasionally, until beef is thoroughly cooked; drain.

2 Add spinach; cook 3 to 5 minutes or until spinach is thawed, stirring frequently. Reduce heat to medium; stir in cream cheese, cumin, chiles and 1-1/2 cups of the cheese until combined. Spoon about 1/3 cup beef mixture down center of each tortilla. Roll up; place seam side down in baking dish.

3 In medium bowl, mix tomato sauce and salsa. Spoon over tortillas; sprinkle with remaining 1/2 cup cheese. Bake 20 to 25 minutes or until thoroughly heated. Sprinkle with cilantro.

HIGH ALTITUDE (3500-6500 FT): In Step 3, spray piece of foil with nonstick cooking spray; cover baking dish with foil. Bake 40 to 45 minutes.

NUTRITION INFORMATION PER SERVING: Calories 410 • Total Fat 24g • Saturated Fat 12g • Cholesterol 75mg • Sodium 970mg • Total Carbohydrate 27g • Dietary Fiber 1g • Sugars 3g • Protein 22g.

caramel flan (crème caramel)

PREP TIME: 15 Minutes ✳ READY IN: 5 Hours 45 Minutes ✳ SERVINGS: 8

1 cup sugar	1 teaspoon vanilla
5 eggs	3 cups fresh fruit (sliced strawberries, sliced kiwifruit, seedless grapes and/or pineapple cubes)
2-1/2 cups milk	

1 Heat oven to 325°F. In heavy small skillet, heat 1/2 cup of the sugar over medium heat until sugar melts and turns a rich golden-brown color, stirring constantly. Immediately pour sugar into 8-inch ring mold. Holding ring mold with pot holders, swirl so sugar coats bottom and sides.

2 In large bowl, slightly beat eggs. Stir in milk, remaining 1/2 cup sugar and vanilla. Place sugar-coated ring mold in shallow baking pan; place in oven. Pour egg mixture over sugar in mold. Pour very hot water into pan around mold to a depth of 1 inch.

3 Bake at 325°F for 55 to 60 minutes or until knife inserted halfway between center and edge comes out clean. Remove mold from hot water; place on wire rack. Cool 1 hour or until completely cooled. Refrigerate at least 3-1/2 hours.

4 To unmold, run knife around edge of custard to loosen; invert onto serving platter. Spoon any caramel that remains in mold over custard. Serve with fruit. Store in refrigerator.

NUTRITION INFORMATION PER SERVING: Calories 210 • Total Fat 5g • Saturated Fat 2g • Cholesterol 140mg • Sodium 80mg • Total Carbohydrate 33g • Dietary Fiber 1g • Sugars 32g • Protein 7g. DIETARY EXCHANGES: 2 Starch • 1 Fat OR 2 Carbohydrate • 1 Fat.

rich tiramisu

PREP TIME: 25 Minutes ✳ READY IN: 4 Hours 55 Minutes ✳ SERVINGS: 15

CAKE

1/4	cup margarine or butter
1/4	cup milk
2	eggs
3/4	cup sugar
3/4	cup all-purpose flour
1	teaspoon baking powder
1/4	teaspoon salt
1/4	teaspoon vanilla
3/4	cup hot strong coffee
1	tablespoon sugar

TOPPING

1	package (8 oz.) cream cheese, softened
1	container (8 oz.) mascarpone cheese
1/3	cup powdered sugar
2	tablespoons Marsala wine or dark rum
1	pint (2 cups) whipping cream
	Grated semisweet chocolate (about 1/2 oz.)

1 Heat oven to 375°F. Spray 13x9-inch pan with nonstick cooking spray. In small saucepan or 2-cup microwave-safe measuring cup, heat margarine and milk until steaming hot (about 1 minute on High in microwave).

2 Meanwhile, in large bowl, beat eggs at high speed until light. Gradually beat in 3/4 cup sugar; beat an additional 2 minutes.

3 Add flour, baking powder, salt, vanilla and hot milk mixture; beat at low speed until smooth. Pour into sprayed pan.

4 Bake at 375°F for 14 to 16 minutes or until cake springs back when touched lightly in center. In 1-cup measuring cup, combine coffee and 1 tablespoon sugar; mix well. Drizzle over warm cake. Cool 30 minutes or until completely cooled.

5 In large bowl, combine cream cheese and mascarpone cheese; beat at medium speed until smooth and creamy. Beat in powdered sugar and wine.

6 In large bowl, beat whipping cream until stiff peaks form. Fold into cream cheese mixture until combined. Spread evenly on cake. Sprinkle grated chocolate over top of cake. Cover; refrigerate at least 4 hours or overnight. To serve, cut into squares. Store in refrigerator.

HIGH ALTITUDE (3500-6500 FT): Increase flour to 1 cup. Bake as directed above.

NUTRITION INFORMATION PER SERVING: Calories 350 • Total Fat 27g • Saturated Fat 15g • Cholesterol 110mg • Sodium 180mg • Total Carbohydrate 21g • Dietary Fiber 0g • Sugars 16g • Protein 4g. DIETARY EXCHANGES: 1-1/2 Starch • 5 Fat OR 1-1/2 Carbohydrate • 5 Fat.

kung pao shrimp

READY IN: 20 Minutes ✳ SERVINGS: 4

3	tablespoons hoisin sauce
1	tablespoon dry sherry
1	teaspoon sugar
1/2	to 1 teaspoon chili paste
1	egg white
1	tablespoon cornstarch
3/4	lb. shelled deveined uncooked medium shrimp
1	tablespoon oil
1/2	teaspoon grated gingerroot
1	garlic clove, minced
1/4	cup dry-roasted peanuts

1 In small bowl, combine hoisin sauce, sherry, sugar and chili paste; mix well. Set aside. In medium bowl, combine egg white and cornstarch; beat well. Add shrimp; mix well to coat. Set aside.

2 Heat oil in large skillet or wok over medium-high heat until hot. Add shrimp mixture, ginger and garlic; cook and stir 2 to 3 minutes or until shrimp turn pink. Add sauce mixture; cook and stir 1 to 2 minutes or until shrimp are well coated. Stir in peanuts.

NUTRITION INFORMATION PER SERVING: Calories 190 • Total Fat 9g • Saturated Fat 1g • Cholesterol 120mg • Sodium 530mg • Total Carbohydrate 12g • Dietary Fiber 1g • Sugars 8g • Protein 16g. DIETARY EXCHANGES: 1 Starch • 2 Lean Meat OR 1 Carbohydrate • 2 Lean Meat.

rich tiramisu

costa rican cream cake

costa rican cream cake

PREP TIME: 30 Minutes ✳ READY IN: 4 Hours 15 Minutes ✳ SERVINGS:15

CAKE
1 box (18.25 oz.) Pillsbury® Moist Supreme® classic yellow cake mix
1 cup water
1/3 cup vegetable oil
3 eggs

SAUCE
1 cup whipping cream
1/3 cup rum or 1 teaspoon rum extract plus 1/3 cup water

1 can (14 oz.) sweetened condensed milk (not evaporated)
1 can (12 oz.) evaporated milk

TOPPING
1 cup whipping cream
1/3 cup coconut, toasted
1/3 cup chopped macadamia nuts

1 Heat oven to 350°F. Grease 13x9-inch (3-quart) baking dish. In large bowl, beat cake ingredients with electric mixer on low speed until moistened; beat 2 minutes on high speed. Pour into baking dish.

2 Bake 25 to 35 minutes or until toothpick inserted in center comes out clean. Meanwhile, in large bowl, mix sauce ingredients. Cool cake 5 minutes. Using long-tined fork, pierce hot cake in pan every 1 to 2 inches. Slowly pour sauce mixture over cake. Do not cover cake; refrigerate at least 3 hours to chill. (Cake will absorb most of sauce mixture.)

3 Just before serving, in small bowl, beat 1 cup whipping cream until stiff peaks form. Spread over cold cake. Sprinkle with coconut and macadamia nuts. Cover and refrigerate any remaining cake.

HIGH ALTITUDE (3500-6500 FT): Add 1/3 cup all-purpose flour to dry cake mix; increase water to 1 cup plus 2 tablespoons.

NUTRITION INFORMATION PER SERVING: Calories 440 • Total Fat 25g • Saturated Fat 12g • Cholesterol 95mg • Sodium 310mg • Total Carbohydrate 47g • Dietary Fiber 0g. DIETARY EXCHANGES: 1 Starch • 2 Other Carbohydrate • 1/2 High-Fat Meat • 4 Fat • 3 Carb Choices.

JANICE WEINRICK
LaMesa, California
Bake-Off® Contest 34, 1990
Prize Winner

cook's notes

To toast coconut, spread it on a cookie sheet; bake at 350°F 7 to 8 minutes, stirring occasionally, until light golden brown. Or spread it in a thin layer in a microwavable pie plate and microwave on Low (10%) 4-1/2 to 8 minutes or until light golden brown, tossing with a fork after each minute.

tuscan panzanella salad

READY IN: 25 Minutes ✳ SERVINGS: 6

3 cups cubed dry (day-old) Italian bread
1/4 cup balsamic vinegar
2 teaspoons olive oil
1/8 teaspoon coarse ground black pepper
2 medium tomatoes, seeded, diced

2 medium cucumbers, halved, seeded and chopped
1 red bell pepper, chopped
1/4 cup sliced ripe olives
1/4 cup thinly sliced fresh basil leaves

1 Heat oven to 350°F. Place bread cubes on ungreased cookie sheet. Toast bread at 350°F for 5 to 10 minutes or until lightly browned.

2 Meanwhile, in small bowl, combine vinegar, oil and pepper; blend well. In large bowl, combine tomatoes, cucumbers, bell pepper, olives and toasted bread cubes. Pour vinegar mixture over salad; toss gently to coat. Sprinkle with basil.

NUTRITION INFORMATION PER SERVING: Calories 100 • Total Fat 3g • Saturated Fat 0g • Cholesterol 0mg • Sodium 160mg • Total Carbohydrate 14g • Dietary Fiber 2g • Sugars 4g • Protein 3g. DIETARY EXCHANGES: 1/2 Starch • 1 Vegetable • 1/2 Fat OR 1/2 Carbohydrate • 1 Vegetable • 1/2 Fat.

cook's notes

Extra phyllo pastry dough can be rolled up, sealed tightly in plastic wrap and stored in the freezer.

apple-cranberry strudel

PREP TIME: 35 Minutes ✳ READY IN: 1 Hour 15 Minutes ✳ SERVINGS: 8

2 apples, chopped (about 2 cups)	2 teaspoons lemon juice
1/2 cup fresh or frozen cranberries	8 sheets (17x12-inch) frozen phyllo (filo) pastry, thawed
1/2 cup sugar	1/3 to 1/2 cup butter, melted
1/2 cup finely chopped walnuts	4 tablespoons unseasoned dry bread crumbs
1 teaspoon grated lemon peel	

1 Heat oven to 375°F. Grease 15x10x1-inch baking pan. In medium bowl, combine apples, cranberries, sugar, walnuts, lemon peel and lemon juice; toss to coat.

2 Unroll phyllo sheets; cover with plastic wrap or towel. Place 1 phyllo sheet on piece of plastic wrap. Brush with butter; sprinkle with 1 tablespoon bread crumbs. Repeat layering with remaining phyllo sheets and butter, sprinkling 1 tablespoon bread crumbs on every other sheet. (Top phyllo sheet should be brushed with butter only.)

3 Spoon apple mixture over phyllo stack to within 2 inches of each edge; press lightly. Fold shorter sides of phyllo up over filling. Starting with longer side and using plastic wrap, lift phyllo and carefully roll up jelly-roll fashion. Place, seam side down, in greased pan. Make several crosswise cuts in top of roll. Brush top with any remaining butter.

4 Bake at 375°F for 20 to 25 minutes or until golden brown. Cool at least 15 minutes before serving. To serve, cut into slices.

NUTRITION INFORMATION PER SERVING: Calories 300 • Total Fat 18g • Saturated Fat 8g • Cholesterol 30mg • Sodium 230mg • Total Carbohydrate 32g • Dietary Fiber 2g • Sugars 18g • Protein 3g. DIETARY EXCHANGES: 1 Starch • 1 Fruit • 3-1/2 Fat OR 2 Carbohydrate • 3-1/2 Fat.

chicken-bean tacos

PREP TIME: 15 Minutes ✳ READY IN: 7 Hours 15 Minutes ✳ SERVINGS: 12 (2 tacos each)

1-1/4 lbs. boneless skinless chicken thighs	1 can (19 oz.) cannellini beans, drained
3 tablespoons taco seasoning mix (from 1.25-oz. pkg.)	2 boxes (4.6 oz. each) taco shells (24 shells total)
1 can (4.5 oz.) chopped green chiles	1-1/2 cups shredded Cheddar cheese (6 oz.)
1 can (8 oz.) tomato sauce	1-1/2 cups shredded lettuce
1 teaspoon ground cumin	1 container (8 oz.) sour cream
1 teaspoon coriander seed, crushed	1 cup chunky-style salsa

1 In 3-1/2- or 4-quart slow cooker, place chicken thighs. Sprinkle with taco seasoning mix. Top with chiles. In medium bowl, mix tomato sauce, cumin and coriander seed. Pour over top. Top with beans.

2 Cover; cook on Low heat setting 7 to 8 hours. Remove chicken from slow cooker; place on cutting board. Mash beans in slow cooker. Shred chicken with 2 forks; return to slow cooker, and mix well.

3 To serve, spoon about 3 tablespoons chicken mixture into each taco shell. Top each with 1 tablespoon cheese, 1 tablespoon lettuce, 2 teaspoons sour cream and 2 teaspoons salsa.

NUTRITION INFORMATION PER SERVING: Calories 350 • Total Fat 17g • Saturated Fat 8g • Cholesterol 55mg • Sodium 710mg • Total Carbohydrate 29g • Dietary Fiber 4g. DIETARY EXCHANGES: 1-1/2 Starch • 1/2 Other Carbohydrate • 2 Lean Meat • 2 Fat • 2 Carb Choices.

cook's notes

Complete these tacos with any toppings your family may like, such as shredded Mexican cheese blend or ripe olives.

apple-cranberry strudel

MIKKI GOTTWALT
New Brighton, Minnesota
Bake-Off® Contest 41, 2004

crescent walnut-raisin potica

PREP TIME: 15 Minutes ✷ READY IN: 55 Minutes ✷ SERVINGS: 16

BREAD

- 1 cup chopped walnuts
- 1/2 cup raisins
- 2 tablespoons packed brown sugar
- 1/2 teaspoon ground cinnamon
- 1 tablespoon butter or margarine, melted
- 1 tablespoon half-and-half
- 1 tablespoon honey

- 1 egg
- 1 can (8 oz.) Pillsbury® refrigerated crescent dinner rolls

ICING

- 1/2 cup powdered sugar
- 1/8 teaspoon almond extract
- 1-1/2 to 2 teaspoons milk or half-and-half

1 Heat oven to 375°F. Grease cookie sheet with shortening or spray with cooking spray. In food processor, grind all bread ingredients except dough; set aside.

2 On lightly floured surface, unroll dough into 1 large rectangle; press or roll into 14x10-inch rectangle, firmly pressing perforations to seal. Spread nut mixture evenly over dough to within 1/2 inch of long sides.

3 Starting with one long side of rectangle, tightly roll up dough, carefully stretching roll until 17 inches long; press edge and ends to seal. Place on greased cookie sheet; loosely coil into spiral shape.

4 Bake at 375°F for 28 to 33 minutes or until deep golden brown. Cover loosely with foil if bread is browning too quickly. Cool 10 minutes.

5 Meanwhile, in small bowl, blend powdered sugar, almond extract and enough milk for desired drizzling consistency until smooth. Drizzle icing over warm bread. Cut into wedges. Serve warm.

NUTRITION INFORMATION PER SERVING: Calories 160 • Total Fat 9g • Saturated Fat 2g • Cholesterol 15mg • Sodium 120mg • Total Carbohydrate 17g • Dietary Fiber 0g • Sugars 12g • Protein 3g. DIETARY EXCHANGES: 1/2 Starch • 1/2 Other Carbohydrate • 2 Fat • 1 Carb Choice.

double chocolate-orange biscotti

PREP TIME: 1 Hour 45 Minutes ❋ READY IN: 2 Hours ❋ SERVINGS: 6-1/2 Dozen

COOKIES

- 3 cups all-purpose flour
- 1/2 cup sugar
- 1/2 cup firmly packed brown sugar
- 3 teaspoons baking powder
- 1/2 teaspoon salt
- 4 oz. unsweetened chocolate, melted, cooled
- 1 tablespoon grated orange peel
- 1/3 cup olive or vegetable oil
- 1/4 cup orange juice
- 2 teaspoons vanilla
- 3 eggs
- 6 oz. white chocolate baking bar, chopped

TOPPING

- 4 oz. white chocolate baking bar, chopped
- 1 tablespoon shortening

1 Heat oven to 350°F. Lightly grease 2 cookie sheets. In large bowl, combine flour, sugar, brown sugar, baking powder and salt; mix well. Add melted chocolate, orange peel, oil, orange juice, vanilla and eggs; blend well. (Dough will be stiff.) Add 6 oz. chopped baking bar; gently knead into dough.

2 Divide dough into 4 equal parts; shape each part into roll 14 inches long. Place 2 rolls on each cookie sheet; flatten each roll to 2-1/2-inch width. Bake at 350°F for 18 to 20 minutes or until firm to the touch.

3 Remove cookie sheets from oven. Reduce oven temperature to 300°F. Cool rolls on cookie sheets for 10 minutes.

4 Cut rolls diagonally into 1/2-inch-thick slices. Place slices, cut side up, on same cookie sheets. Bake at 300°F for 7 to 9 minutes or until top surface is dry.

5 Turn cookies over; bake an additional 7 to 9 minutes. Remove from cookie sheets. Cool 15 minutes or until completely cooled.

6 In small saucepan, melt topping ingredients over low heat, stirring until smooth. Drizzle over cookies.

NUTRITION INFORMATION PER SERVING: Calories 70 • Total Fat 3g • Saturated Fat 1g • Cholesterol 10mg • Sodium 40mg • Total Carbohydrate 9g • Dietary Fiber 0g • Sugars 5g • Protein 1g. DIETARY EXCHANGES: 1/2 Vegetable • 1/2 Fat OR 1/2 Carbohydrate • 1/2 Fat.

cook's notes

Biscotti is a terrific cookie for dunking. Try giving a dozen or so in a holiday gift basket alongside a package of coffee or hot cocoa mix.

ratatouille bean stew

PREP TIME: 15 Minutes ❋ READY IN: 18 Hours 45 Minutes ❋ SERVINGS: 5

- 1 cup dried chickpeas or garbanzo beans, sorted, rinsed
- 1 medium onion, chopped (1/2 cup)
- 2 garlic cloves, finely chopped
- 1 can (14 oz.) chicken broth
- 1 jar (4.5 oz.) sliced mushrooms, drained
- 1/4 teaspoon salt
- 1 large zucchini, sliced
- 1 medium red or green bell pepper, cut into pieces
- 1 teaspoon Italian seasoning
- 1 can (14.5 oz.) diced tomatoes with Italian-style herbs, undrained

1 Soak dried chickpeas in enough water to cover for at least 8 hours. Drain chickpeas, discarding water.

2 In 3-1/2- to 4-quart slow cooker, mix chickpeas, onion, garlic, broth, mushrooms and salt. Cover; cook on Low heat setting 10 to 12 hours.

3 Stir zucchini, bell pepper, Italian seasoning and tomatoes into stew. Increase heat setting to High. Cover; cook 30 to 35 minutes longer or until vegetables are tender.

NUTRITION INFORMATION PER SERVING: Calories 210 • Total Fat 3g • Saturated Fat 0g • Cholesterol 0mg • Sodium 700mg • Total Carbohydrate 34g • Dietary Fiber 9g. DIETARY EXCHANGES: 1 Starch • 1/2 Other Carbohydrate • 2 Vegetable • 1/2 Very Lean Meat • 1/2 Fat • 2 Carb Choices.

cook's notes

Want to check the progress of your food during slow cooking? If your slow cooker is round, try spinning the glass lid during cooking so that moisture falls off and you can see inside.

bolognese sauce with spaghetti

PREP TIME: 15 Minutes ✳ READY IN: 6 Hours 15 Minutes ✳ SERVINGS: 6

6 Italian sausage links (about 1-1/2 lbs.), cut into 1-inch pieces	1/2 teaspoon salt
1 cup finely chopped onions (1 large)	2 garlic cloves, finely chopped
3 tablespoons sugar	1 can (28 oz.) crushed tomatoes, undrained
1 teaspoon dried basil leaves	1 can (15 oz.) tomato sauce
1 teaspoon dried oregano leaves	1 can (12 oz.) tomato paste
	12 oz. uncooked spaghetti

1 In 3-1/2- to 4-quart slow cooker, mix all ingredients except spaghetti. Cover; cook on Low heat setting 6 to 8 hours. Skim and discard fat, if desired.

2 About 30 minutes before serving, cook spaghetti to desired doneness as directed on package. Serve sauce over spaghetti.

NUTRITION INFORMATION PER SERVING: Calories 670 • Total Fat 25g • Saturated Fat 8g • Cholesterol 45mg • Sodium 2430mg • Total Carbohydrate 82g • Dietary Fiber 8g. DIETARY EXCHANGES: 2-1/2 Starch • 2 Other Carbohydrate • 2-1/2 Vegetable • 2-1/2 High-Fat Meat • 1/2 Fat • 5-1/2 Carb Choices.

black forest cake

PREP TIME: 30 Minutes ✳ READY IN: 2 Hours 30 Minutes ✳ SERVINGS: 12

CAKE

1 package (1 lb. 2.25 oz.) pudding-included dark chocolate cake mix

1-1/4 cups water

1/3 cup oil

3 eggs

FILLING

1 can (21 oz.) cherry pie filling

1/2 teaspoon almond extract

FROSTING

1 pint (2 cups) whipping cream

1/2 cup powdered sugar

2 tablespoons brandy

Chocolate curls, if desired

1 Heat oven to 350°F. Grease and flour two 8- or 9-inch round cake pans. In large bowl, combine all cake ingredients; beat at low speed until moistened. Beat 2 minutes at medium speed. Pour batter into greased and floured pans.

2 Bake at 350°F. Bake 8-inch pans 30 to 40 minutes; bake 9-inch pans 25 to 35 minutes or until cake springs back when touched lightly in center. Cool 15 minutes. Remove from pans. Cool 1 hour or until completely cooled.

3 In small bowl, combine filling ingredients; mix well. In medium bowl, beat whipping cream at high speed until soft peaks form. Gradually add powdered sugar, beating until stiff peaks form. Fold in brandy.

4 Place 1 cake layer, top side down, on serving plate. Spread 1 cup filling to within 1 inch of edge. Top with second cake layer, top side up. Frost sides and top with whipped cream. Spoon remaining filling in center of top of cake. Garnish with chocolate curls. Store in refrigerator.

HIGH ALTITUDE (3500-6500 FT): Add 1/4 cup flour to dry cake mix; increase water to 1-1/3 cups. Bake as directed above.

NUTRITION INFORMATION PER SERVING: Calories 480 • Total Fat 26g • Saturated Fat 11g • Cholesterol 110mg • Sodium 420mg • Total Carbohydrate 55g • Dietary Fiber 2g • Sugars 42g • Protein 5g. DIETARY EXCHANGES: 1 Starch • 2-1/2 Fruit • 5-1/2 Fat OR 3-1/2 Carbohydrate • 5-1/2 Fat.

bolognese sauce with spaghetti

hungarian stew

PREP TIME: 15 Minutes ✸ **READY IN:** 7 Hours 35 Minutes ✸ SERVINGS: 8

2 lbs. lean boneless beef chuck roast, cut into 3/4-inch pieces	1/4 teaspoon pepper
2 cups ready-to-eat baby-cut carrots	1/2 cup chili sauce
1 medium onion, sliced (1/2 cup)	1 can (14 oz.) beef broth
1 medium green bell pepper, sliced	2 cups sliced fresh mushrooms
1/3 cup all-purpose flour	1 bag (16 oz.) uncooked wide egg noodles (10 cups)
3 teaspoons paprika	1 container (8 oz.) sour cream
1/2 teaspoon salt	2 tablespoons chopped fresh parsley
1/2 teaspoon dried thyme leaves	

1 In 3-1/2- to 4-quart slow cooker, mix beef, carrots, onion and bell pepper. Add flour, paprika, salt, thyme and pepper; toss to coat. Stir in chili sauce and broth. Cover; cook on Low heat setting 7 to 8 hours.

2 Stir mushrooms into stew. Cover; cook on Low heat setting 20 to 30 minutes longer or until mushrooms are tender. Meanwhile, cook noodles to desired doneness as directed on package; drain.

3 At serving time, stir sour cream into stew until well mixed. Spoon noodles into individual shallow bowls. Top each with stew. Sprinkle with parsley.

NUTRITION INFORMATION PER SERVING: Calories 510 • Total Fat 21g • Saturated Fat 9g • Cholesterol 120mg • Sodium 920mg • Total Carbohydrate 52g • Dietary Fiber 5g. DIETARY EXCHANGES: 2 Starch • 1 Other Carbohydrate • 1 Vegetable • 3 Medium-Fat Meat • 1 Fat • 3-1/2 Carb Choices.

roasted chicken and vegetables provençal

PREP TIME: 30 Minutes ✳ READY IN: 1 Hour 35 Minutes ✳ SERVINGS: 4

8 small new red potatoes, quartered

1 small yellow summer squash, cut into 1-inch pieces

1 small zucchini, cut into 1-inch pieces

1 red bell pepper, cut into 1-inch pieces

1 medium red onion, cut into eighths

1 package (8 oz.) fresh whole mushrooms

1/4 cup olive oil

2 teaspoons dried basil leaves

2 teaspoons dried thyme leaves

1/2 teaspoon salt

1/2 teaspoon coarse ground black pepper

3 garlic cloves, minced

3 to 3-1/2 lbs. cut-up frying chicken, skin removed

1 Heat oven to 375°F. In ungreased 13x9-inch (3-quart) baking dish, combine potatoes, summer squash, zucchini, bell pepper, onion and mushrooms.

2 In small bowl, combine oil, basil, thyme, salt, pepper and garlic; mix well. Brush half of oil mixture on vegetables. Place chicken pieces, meaty side up, over vegetables. Brush chicken with remaining oil mixture.

3 Bake at 375°F for 45 minutes. Baste with pan juices; bake an additional 15 to 20 minutes or until chicken is fork-tender, juices run clear and vegetables are tender. Baste with pan juices before serving.

NUTRITION INFORMATION PER SERVING: Calories 550 • Total Fat 24g • Saturated Fat 5g • Cholesterol 115mg • Sodium 390mg • Total Carbohydrate 41g • Dietary Fiber 7g • Sugars 7g • Protein 43g. DIETARY EXCHANGES: 2-1/2 Starch • 1 Vegetable • 4-1/2 Lean Meat • 1-1/2 Fat OR 2-1/2 Carbohydrate • 1 Vegetable • 4-1/2 Lean Meat • 1-1/2 Fat.

cook's notes

To test pieces of chicken for doneness, cut into a piece with a small, sharp knife. The meat should still look moist, but any visible juices should be clear, not pink. The meat should not look pink, except for the dark meat nearest the bone.

cook's notes

Instead of green enchilada sauce, try red. Or substitute salsa verde.

quesadilla pie

PREP TIME: 20 Minutes ☀ READY IN: 50 Minutes ☀ SERVINGS: 6

1 can (4.5 oz.) Old El Paso® chopped green chiles

1 can (15 oz.) Progresso® black beans, drained, rinsed

5 medium green onions, chopped (about 1/3 cup)

1 medium plum (Roma) tomato, chopped

1 can (10 oz.) Old El Paso® green enchilada sauce

1-1/2 cups shredded pepper Jack cheese (6 oz.)

1/2 cup chopped fresh cilantro

1-1/2 cups shredded Cheddar cheese (6 oz.)

4 Old El Paso® flour tortillas for burritos (8 inch)

1 Heat oven to 400°F. Spray 9-inch glass pie plate with cooking spray. In medium bowl, mix chiles, beans, onions, tomato, 1/2 cup of the enchilada sauce, the pepper Jack cheese, 1/4 cup of the cilantro and 1/2 cup of the Cheddar cheese; set aside.

2 Spoon 1/4 cup enchilada sauce into pie plate. Top with 1 tortilla and 1/3 of the bean mixture. Repeat twice to make 3 layers. Top with remaining tortilla. Cover loosely with foil.

3 Bake 30 minutes. Uncover; sprinkle with remaining Cheddar cheese. Bake 5 to 7 minutes longer or until cheese is melted. Sprinkle with remaining 1/4 cup cilantro. Serve with salsa if desired.

HIGH ALTITUDE (3500-6500 FT): In Step 3, increase second bake time to 7 to 9 minutes.

NUTRITION INFORMATION PER SERVING: Calories 440 • Total Fat 19g • Saturated Fat 9g • Cholesterol 45mg • Sodium 1180mg • Total Carbohydrate 47g • Dietary Fiber 9g • Sugars 4g • Protein 20g. DIETARY EXCHANGES: 3 Starch • 1-1/2 Medium-Fat Meat • 2 Fat • 3 Carb Choices.

MARILOU ROBINSON
Portland, Oregon
Bake-Off® Contest 40, 2002

jamaican ham and bean soup

READY IN: 30 Minutes ☀ SERVINGS: 6

SOUP

1 tablespoon vegetable oil

1/3 cup frozen chopped onion

2 cans (16 oz. each) vegetarian refried beans

1 can (11 oz.) vacuum-packed whole kernel corn with red and green peppers, undrained

1 can (11 oz.) vacuum-packed white shoepeg corn, undrained

1 can (4.5 oz.) chopped green chiles

1/2 cup chunky-style salsa

1 can (14-1/2 oz.) chicken broth

1 teaspoon Jamaican jerk seasoning

1 lb. lean cooked ham, cut into 1/2-inch pieces

1 can (2-1/4 oz.) sliced ripe olives, drained

1/3 cup lime juice

GARNISH

6 tablespoons sour cream

6 lime slices

1 In 4-quart saucepan, heat oil over medium heat until hot. Cook onion in oil 3 to 4 minutes, stirring frequently, until tender.

2 Stir in refried beans, corn, chiles, salsa, broth and jerk seasoning. Heat to boiling. Reduce heat to low; simmer 5 minutes, stirring occasionally.

3 Stir in ham, olives and lime juice. Cook 3 to 4 minutes, stirring occasionally, until hot. Ladle soup into individual bowls. Top each serving with 1 tablespoon sour cream and lime slice.

NUTRITION INFORMATION PER SERVING: Calories 460 • Total Fat 16g • Saturated Fat 5g • Cholesterol 65mg • Sodium 2750mg • Total Carbohydrate 49g • Dietary Fiber 11g. DIETARY EXCHANGES: 2 Starch • 1 Other Carbohydrate • 3-1/2 Very Lean Meat • 2-1/2 Fat • 3 Carb Choices.

quesadilla pie

quick fried rice

READY IN: 20 Minutes ✳ SERVINGS: 4

1-1/2	cups uncooked instant white rice	1/2	cup frozen early June peas
1-1/2	cups water	1/3	cup sliced green onions
1	teaspoon oil	1	cup fresh bean sprouts
2	eggs, beaten	1/4	cup soy sauce
4	teaspoons dark sesame oil		

1 Cook rice in water as directed on package. Meanwhile, heat 1 teaspoon oil in large nonstick skillet over medium-high heat until hot. Add beaten eggs; tilt pan to form thin layer of egg. Lift edges of egg with small spatula to let uncooked egg flow to bottom of skillet. Cover; cook 1 minute or until set. Slide egg from skillet onto cutting board. Set aside.

2 In same skillet, heat 4 teaspoons sesame oil over medium-high heat until hot. Add peas and onions; cook and stir 1 to 2 minutes or until vegetables are crisp-tender.

3 Add cooked rice, bean sprouts and soy sauce to skillet; cook and stir until rice is thoroughly heated.

4 Roll up egg; cut into small strips. Cut strips into 2-inch lengths; fold into rice mixture. Heat thoroughly. If desired, serve with additional soy sauce.

NUTRITION INFORMATION PER SERVING: Calories 250 • Total Fat 8g • Saturated Fat 2g • Cholesterol 105mg • Sodium 1090mg • Total Carbohydrate 36g • Dietary Fiber 2g • Sugars 3g • Protein 9g. DIETARY EXCHANGES: 2 Starch • 1 Vegetable • 1-1/2 Fat OR 2 Carbohydrate • 1 Vegetable • 1-1/2 Fat.

hummus sandwiches

READY IN: 20 Minutes ✳ SERVINGS: 4

1 can (15 oz.) garbanzo beans, drained, rinsed	3 garlic cloves, minced
1/4 cup sesame seed	8 slices pumpernickel bread
1/8 teaspoon ground red pepper (cayenne)	1 large tomato, sliced
2 tablespoons lemon juice	1 cup alfalfa sprouts
2 tablespoons water	

1 In food processor bowl with metal blade, combine garbanzo beans, sesame seed, ground red pepper, lemon juice, water and garlic; process until smooth. Cover; refrigerate at least 10 minutes to blend flavors.

2 To make sandwiches, generously spread 4 bread slices with bean mixture. Top with tomatoes, sprouts and remaining bread slices.

NUTRITION INFORMATION PER SERVING: Calories 310 • Total Fat 8g • Saturated Fat 1g • Cholesterol 0mg • Sodium 540mg • Total Carbohydrate 47g • Dietary Fiber 10g • Sugars 4g • Protein 13g. DIETARY EXCHANGES: 3 Starch • 1/2 Very Lean Meat • 1 Fat OR 3 Carbohydrate • 1/2 Very Lean Meat • 1 Fat.

kitchen tip

After juicing lemons, freeze the extra juice in an ice cube tray. Defrost the cubes when you need lemon juice for a recipe.

german chocolate cake
with coconut-pecan frosting

PREP TIME: 30 Minutes ✳ READY IN: 2 Hours 50 Minutes ✳ SERVINGS: 16

CAKE

4 oz. sweet cooking chocolate, cut into pieces	
1/2 cup water	
2 cups sugar	
1 cup margarine or butter, softened	
4 eggs	
2-1/2 cups all-purpose flour	
1 teaspoon baking soda	
1/2 teaspoon salt	
1 cup buttermilk	
1 teaspoon vanilla	

FROSTING

1 cup sugar	
1 cup evaporated milk	
1/2 cup margarine or butter	
3 eggs, beaten	
1-1/3 cups flaked coconut	
1 cup chopped pecans or walnuts	
1 teaspoon vanilla	

1 Heat oven to 350°F. Grease and lightly flour three 9-inch round cake pans. In small saucepan, melt chocolate with water over low heat. Cool.

2 In large bowl, combine 2 cups sugar and 1 cup margarine; beat until light and fluffy. Add 4 eggs, one at a time, beating well after each addition. Stir in chocolate mixture. Add all remaining cake ingredients; beat at low speed until well combined. Pour batter into greased and floured pans.

3 Bake at 350°F for 35 to 45 minutes or until toothpick inserted in center comes out clean. Cool 5 minutes. Remove from pans. Cool 1 hour or until completely cooled.

4 In medium saucepan, combine 1 cup sugar, evaporated milk, 1/2 cup margarine and 3 eggs; mix well. Cook over medium heat until mixture begins to bubble, stirring constantly. Remove saucepan from heat. Stir in coconut, pecans and 1 teaspoon vanilla. Cool 30 minutes or until completely cooled.

5 Place 1 cake layer, top side down, on serving plate. Spread with 1/3 of frosting. Repeat with remaining cake layers and frosting, ending with frosting.

HIGH ALTITUDE (3500-6500 FT): Decrease sugar in cake to 1-3/4 cups; decrease baking soda to 3/4 teaspoon. Bake at 375°F for 25 to 30 minutes.

NUTRITION INFORMATION PER SERVING: Calories 560 • Total Fat 30g • Saturated Fat 8g • Cholesterol 100mg • Sodium 420mg • Total Carbohydrate 64g • Dietary Fiber 2g • Sugars 46g • Protein 8g. DIETARY EXCHANGES: 3 Starch • 1-1/2 Fruit • 5 Fat OR 4-1/2 Carbohydrate • 5 Fat.

kitchen tip

Arrange multiple cake pans on one or more racks on the oven for baking, making sure the pans do not touch each other or the oven sides.

chinese sweet-and-sour pork

READY IN: 40 Minutes ✳ SERVINGS: 4

1-1/3 cups uncooked regular long-grain white rice
2-2/3 cups water
1/4 cup cornstarch
2 tablespoons all-purpose flour
1 teaspoon sugar
1/4 teaspoon baking soda
3 tablespoons water
1 egg, beaten
1/2 lb. boneless pork loin chops, cut into 2x1/2x1/4-inch pieces
Oil for frying
3 tablespoons brown sugar

2 tablespoons cornstarch
1/2 teaspoon chicken-flavor instant bouillon
1/2 cup water
3 tablespoons rice vinegar
2 tablespoons ketchup
2 teaspoons soy sauce
1 can (20 oz.) pineapple chunks in unsweetened juice, drained, reserving 3 tablespoons liquid
1 garlic clove, minced
1 green bell pepper, cut into 3/4-inch pieces

1 Cook rice in 2-2/3 cups water as directed on package. Meanwhile, in medium bowl, combine 1/4 cup cornstarch, flour, sugar, baking soda, 3 tablespoons water and egg; mix well. Add pork; stir until well blended.

2 In deep fryer, heavy saucepan or wok, heat 2 to 3 inches of oil to 375°F. Fry battered pork pieces, 1/4 of total amount at a time, for 2 to 3 minutes or until golden brown and no longer pink in center, turning once. Drain on paper towels. Reserve 1 tablespoon oil from deep fryer.

3 In small saucepan, combine brown sugar, 2 tablespoons cornstarch, bouillon, 1/2 cup water, vinegar, ketchup, soy sauce and reserved 3 tablespoons pineapple liquid; blend well. Cook over medium-high heat until bubbly and thickened, stirring constantly. Keep warm.

4 Heat reserved 1 tablespoon oil in large skillet or wok until hot. Add garlic and bell pepper; cook and stir 2 to 3 minutes or until pepper is crisp-tender. Stir in pineapple chunks, pork and sauce. Cook until thoroughly heated. Serve immediately over rice.

NUTRITION INFORMATION PER SERVING: Calories 640 • Total Fat 24g • Saturated Fat 4g • Cholesterol 85mg • Sodium 510mg • Total Carbohydrate 86g • Dietary Fiber 2g • Sugars 25g • Protein 19g. DIETARY EXCHANGES: 2-1/2 Starch • 3 Fruit • 1-1/2 Medium-Fat Meat • 3 Fat OR 5-1/2 Carbohydrate • 1-1/2 Medium-Fat Meat • 3 Fat.

mushroom piroshki appetizers

PREP TIME: 50 Minutes ✳ READY IN: 1 Hour 5 Minutes ✳ SERVINGS: 30

1/4 cup butter or margarine
1/2 cup finely chopped onion (1 medium)
1 package (8 oz.) fresh mushrooms, finely chopped
1 hard-cooked egg yolk, chopped

1/2 to 3/4 teaspoon salt
1/4 teaspoon pepper
3 Pillsbury® refrigerated pie crusts (from two 15-oz. boxes), softened as directed on box
1 egg, beaten, if desired

1 In 10-inch skillet, melt butter over medium heat. Cook and stir onion in butter just until tender. Add mushrooms; cook 3 minutes, stirring frequently. Stir in egg yolk, salt and pepper. Cool 10 minutes.

2 Meanwhile, heat oven to 400°F. Unroll 3 pie crusts. With 2-3/4-inch round cutter, cut 10 rounds from each crust.

3 Spoon rounded teaspoon of cooled mushroom mixture onto half of each pie-crust round. Fold dough over filling; press edges with fork to seal. Place on ungreased large cookie sheet. Brush with beaten egg. Bake 12 to 15 minutes or until light golden brown. Serve warm.

NUTRITION INFORMATION PER SERVING: Calories 80 • Total Fat 5g • Saturated Fat 2.5g • Cholesterol 15mg • Sodium 110mg • Total Carbohydrate 7g • Dietary Fiber 0g. DIETARY EXCHANGES: 1/2 Starch • 1 Fat • 1/2 Carb Choice.

cook's notes

Follow the package directions for specifics about cooking rice. One variety of rice may be substituted for another, but adjustments must be made in the amount of liquid and the cooking time.

MARCIA L. GALLNER
Omaha, Nebraska
Bake-Off® Contest 29, 1980
Prize Winner

chinese sweet-and-sour pork

Seasonal Sunrise Specialties

Christmas morning shines even brighter when you fill the breakfast table or brunch buffet with these tasty delights, from oven-warm glazed rolls to hearty egg bakes.

p. 191

p. 197

p. 207

p. 202

p. 205

chicken fajita quiche p. 201

cinnamon french toast bake

cinnamon french toast bake

PREP TIME: 15 Minutes ✳ READY IN: 1 Hour ✳ SERVINGS: 12

WILL SPERRY
Bunker Hill, West Virginia
Bake-Off® Contest 41, 2004

FRENCH TOAST BAKE

- 1/4 cup butter or margarine, melted
- 2 cans (12.4 oz. each) Pillsbury® refrigerated cinnamon rolls with icing
- 6 eggs
- 1/2 cup heavy whipping cream
- 2 teaspoons ground cinnamon
- 2 teaspoons vanilla
- 1 cup chopped pecans
- 1 cup maple syrup

GARNISH

- Icing from cinnamon rolls
- Powdered sugar
- 1/2 cup maple syrup, if desired

1 Heat oven to 375°F. Pour melted butter into ungreased 13x9-inch (3-quart) glass baking dish. Separate both cans of dough into 16 rolls; set icing aside. Cut each roll into 8 pieces; place pieces over butter in dish.

2 In medium bowl, beat eggs. Beat in cream, cinnamon and vanilla until well blended; gently pour over roll pieces. Sprinkle with pecans; drizzle with 1 cup syrup.

3 Bake at 375°F for 20 to 28 minutes or until golden brown. Cool 15 minutes. Meanwhile, remove covers from icing; microwave on Medium (50%) for 10 to 15 seconds or until drizzling consistency.

4 Drizzle icing over top; sprinkle with powdered sugar. If desired, spoon syrup from dish over individual servings. Serve with the additional 1/2 cup maple syrup.

HIGH ALTITUDE (3500-6500 FT): Bake at 375°F for 25 to 30 minutes.

NUTRITION INFORMATION PER SERVING: Calories 440 • Total Fat 23g • Saturated 8g • Cholesterol 125mg • Sodium 520mg • Total Carbohydrate 57g • Dietary Fiber 1g • Sugars 26g • Protein 8g. DIETARY EXCHANGES: 1-1/2 Starch • 2 Other Carbohydrate • 4-1/2 Fat • 3-1/2 Carb Choices.

ham and chile brunch pizza

READY IN: 30 Minutes ✳ SERVINGS: 6

- 1 can (10 oz.) Pillsbury® refrigerated pizza crust
- 6 eggs
- 1/4 teaspoon salt
- 1/8 teaspoon pepper
- 1 tablespoon margarine or butter
- 1 cup julienne-cut strips or chopped cooked ham
- 1 can (4.5 oz.) chopped green chiles
- 1-1/2 cups shredded Monterey Jack cheese or hot pepper Monterey Jack cheese (6 oz.)
- 2 tablespoons chopped fresh cilantro, if desired

1 Heat oven to 425°F. Grease 14-inch pizza pan. Unroll dough; place in greased pan. Starting at center, press out dough to edge of pan. Bake at 425°F for 6 to 8 minutes or until crust begins to brown.

2 Meanwhile, in medium bowl, combine eggs, salt and pepper; beat well. Melt margarine in large skillet over medium heat. Add eggs; cook 1 to 2 minutes or until firm but still moist, stirring frequently.

3 Remove partially baked crust from oven. Spoon and spread eggs over crust. Top with ham, chiles and cheese.

4 Return to oven; bake an additional 8 to 12 minutes or until crust is deep golden brown. Sprinkle with cilantro. Cut into wedges.

NUTRITION INFORMATION PER SERVING: Calories 355 • Total Fat 19g • Saturated Fat 8g • Cholesterol 250mg • Sodium 1121mg • Total Carbohydrate 24g • Dietary Fiber 1g • Sugars 5g • Protein 22g. DIETARY EXCHANGES: 1-1/2 Starch • 3 Medium-Fat Meat OR 1-1/2 Carbohydrate • 3 Medium-Fat Meat • 1-1/2 Carb Choices.

cook's notes

It will be easier to press the pizza dough into the pan if it's kept cold until you are ready to use it. If refrigerated dough gets too warm, it becomes sticky and hard to work with.

RETA EBBINNK
Torrance, California
Bake-Off® Contest 28, 1978

cook's notes

Walnuts, macadamia nuts and

pecans would all work well in

this recipe.

maple cream coffee treat

PREP TIME: 15 Minutes ✳ READY IN: 50 Minutes ✳ SERVINGS: 20

1 cup packed brown sugar	1/4 cup powdered sugar
1/2 cup chopped nuts	2 tablespoons butter or margarine, softened
1/3 cup maple-flavored syrup or dark corn syrup	1/2 cup coconut
1/4 cup butter or margarine, melted	2 cans (12 oz. each) Pillsbury® Golden Layers® refrigerated buttermilk flaky biscuits
1 package (8 oz.) cream cheese, softened	

1 Heat oven to 350°F. In ungreased 13x9-inch pan, mix brown sugar, nuts, syrup and 1/4 cup butter; spread evenly in bottom of pan. In small bowl with spoon, beat cream cheese, powdered sugar and 2 tablespoons butter until smooth. Stir in coconut.

2 Separate dough into 20 biscuits; press or roll each into 4-inch round. Spoon 1 tablespoon cream cheese mixture down center of each biscuit round to within 1/4 inch of edge. Overlap sides of dough over filling, forming finger-shaped rolls; arrange seam side down in 2 rows of 10 rolls each over brown sugar mixture in pan.

3 Bake 25 to 30 minutes or until deep golden brown. Cool 5 minutes. Invert pan onto sheet of foil, waxed paper or serving platter; remove pan. Serve warm. Store in refrigerator.

HIGH ALTITUDE (3500-6500 FT): Bake at 350°F 30 to 35 minutes.

NUTRITION INFORMATION PER SERVING: Calories 270 • Total Fat 14g • Saturated Fat 6g • Cholesterol 20mg • Sodium 430mg • Total Carbohydrate 32g • Dietary Fiber 0g • Sugars 18g • Protein 3g. DIETARY EXCHANGES: 1 Starch • 1 Other Carbohydrate • 3 Fat • 2 Carb Choices.

hearty breakfast sandwiches

READY IN: 30 Minutes ✳ SERVINGS: 8

1 can (16.3 oz.) Pillsbury® Grands!® refrigerated buttermilk biscuits

1 package (12 oz.) breakfast pork sausage patties (8 patties)

4 eggs

1/4 teaspoon pepper

1 cup shredded mozzarella cheese (4 oz.)

cook's notes

You can change the flavor of

this easy sandwich simply by

substituting a different cheese.

Consider Cheddar, Swiss or a

combination of Monterey Jack

and Colby.

1 Heat oven to 350°F. Bake biscuits as directed on can. Keep warm. Meanwhile, cook sausage patties as directed on package. Keep warm.

2 In small bowl, beat eggs and pepper until well blended. Spray medium skillet with nonstick cooking spray. Heat over medium heat until hot. Pour egg mixture into skillet. Reduce heat to low; cook until eggs are almost set but still moist, stirring occasionally from outside edge to center, allowing uncooked egg to flow to bottom of skillet.

3 Sprinkle cheese over eggs. Cover; remove from heat. Let stand 1 minute or until cheese is melted.

4 Split warm biscuits. Place 1 sausage patty on bottom half of each biscuit. Top each with eggs and top half of biscuit.

NUTRITION INFORMATION PER SERVING: Calories 360 • Total Fat 22g • Saturated Fat 8g • Cholesterol 135mg • Sodium 1050mg • Total Carbohydrate 25g • Dietary Fiber 1g • Sugars 5g • Protein 16g. DIETARY EXCHANGES: 1-1/2 Starch • 1-1/2 High-Fat Meat • 2 Fat OR 1-1/2 Carbohydrate • 1-1/2 High-Fat Meat • 2 Fat • 1-1/2 Carb Choices.

maple cream coffee treat

cook's notes

If you don't have time the day before, make this bake early in the morning for a late-morning brunch.

overnight cranberry-orange french toast

PREP TIME: 15 Minutes ✳ READY IN: 4 Hours 45 Minutes ✳ SERVINGS: 8

3/4	cup sweetened dried cranberries		1	tablespoon grated orange peel
3	tablespoons finely chopped pecans		2	cups milk
16	slices (3x2-1/2 inches) soft French bread, 1 inch thick		1-1/2	cups orange juice
6	eggs		3	tablespoons butter or margarine, melted
			1	cup maple-flavored or real maple syrup

1   Grease 13x9-inch (3-quart) glass baking dish with shortening or spray with cooking spray. Sprinkle cranberries and pecans evenly into dish; arrange French bread slices tightly in single layer over top.

2   In large bowl with wire whisk, beat eggs. Stir in orange peel, milk, orange juice and butter until smooth. Pour egg mixture over bread. Cover tightly with foil; refrigerate at least 4 hours or overnight.

3   When ready to bake, heat oven to 425°F. Uncover baking dish; bake 25 to 30 minutes or until bread is puffy and edges are golden brown. Serve with syrup.

NUTRITION INFORMATION PER SERVING: Calories 520 • Total Fat 14g • Saturated Fat 5g • Cholesterol 175mg • Sodium 590mg • Total Carbohydrate 85g • Dietary Fiber 2g • Sugars 32g • Protein 14g. DIETARY EXCHANGES: 4-1/2 Starch • 1 Other Carbohydrate • 2-1/2 Fat • 5-1/2 Carb Choices.

cherry-cheese crescent braid

PREP TIME: 20 Minutes ✽ READY IN: 55 Minutes ✽ SERVINGS: 8

BRAID

- 1 can (8 oz.) refrigerated crescent dinner rolls
- 1/2 cup pineapple cream cheese spread (from 8-oz. container)
- 2 tablespoons granulated sugar
- 1 egg, separated
- 1/2 cup chopped red candied cherries
- 1 tablespoon water
- 1 teaspoon granulated sugar

GLAZE

- 1/3 cup powdered sugar
- 1/4 teaspoon almond extract
- 1 to 2 teaspoons milk

GARNISH

Red candied cherries, if desired

1 Heat oven to 375°F. Spray cookie sheet with cooking spray. Unroll dough onto cookie sheet, forming 13x7-inch rectangle. Firmly press perforations to seal.

2 In medium bowl, beat cream cheese and 2 tablespoons granulated sugar. Beat in egg yolk. Stir in chopped cherries. Spoon lengthwise down center of dough rectangle in 2-1/2-inch-wide strip. Cut 1-inch-wide strips on each side of cream cheese filling to within 1/2 inch of filling. Fold strips at an angle across filling mixture, alternating from side to side.

3 In small bowl, beat egg white and water. Brush egg white mixture over dough. (Discard any remaining egg white mixture.) Sprinkle with 1 teaspoon granulated sugar.

4 Bake 15 to 20 minutes or until deep golden brown. Immediately remove from cookie sheet; place on serving tray. Cool 5 minutes.

5 In small bowl, mix powdered sugar, almond extract and enough milk for desired glaze consistency. Drizzle glaze over warm braid. Garnish with candied cherries. Cool 15 minutes before slicing. Serve warm. Store in refrigerator.

HIGH ALTITUDE (3500-6500 FT): Bake at 375°F 15 to 18 minutes.

NUTRITION INFORMATION PER SERVING: Calories 230 • Total Fat 11g • Saturated Fat 5g • Cholesterol 40mg • Sodium 340mg • Total Carbohydrate 29g • Dietary Fiber 0g • Sugars 18g • Protein 4g. DIETARY EXCHANGES: 1 Starch • 1 Other Carbohydrate • 2 Fat • 2 Carb Choices.

cook's notes

This bread can be assembled through Step 2 up to 2 hours ahead of time and refrigerated, loosely covered (don't brush it with the egg white or sprinkle on the sugar at this point). When you're ready to bake, continue following the recipe at Step 3, adding a few more minutes to the baking time if necessary.

hot irish creme mocha

READY IN: 10 Minutes ✽ SERVINGS: 8

- 6 cups hot strong brewed coffee
- 4 envelopes (1.25 oz. each) Irish creme instant cocoa mix
- 1/4 cup powdered sugar

- 2 cups half-and-half
- 1/4 cup Irish creme-flavored syrup, if desired

  Sweetened whipped cream, if desired

  Chocolate shavings, if desired

1 In 3-quart saucepan, mix hot coffee, cocoa mix and powdered sugar until blended. Stir in half-and-half and syrup. Cook over medium heat about 5 minutes, stirring occasionally, until hot. Serve in mugs; top with whipped cream and chocolate shavings.

NUTRITION INFORMATION PER SERVING: Calories 170 • Total Fat 8g • Saturated Fat 4g • Cholesterol 20mg • Sodium 90mg • Total Carbohydrate 22g • Dietary Fiber 0g • Sugars 20g • Protein 2g. DIETARY EXCHANGES: 1-1/2 Other Carbohydrate • 1-1/2 Fat • 1-1/2 Carb Choices.

MRS. ROBERT H. LEVINE
Omaha, Nebraska
Bake-Off® Contest 20, 1969

cook's notes

Dry cottage cheese works best for this recipe, but creamed cottage cheese may be used if it is rinsed with water and well drained on a paper towel.

quick crescent blintzes

PREP TIME: 20 Minutes ✳ READY IN: 35 Minutes ✳ SERVINGS: 16

FILLING
- 1 egg
- 1 cup dry cottage cheese (8 oz.)
- 1 package (3 oz.) cream cheese, softened
- 1 tablespoon sugar
- 1/2 teaspoon vanilla

BLINTZES
- 2 cans (8 oz. each) Pillsbury® refrigerated crescent dinner rolls
- 2 tablespoons butter or margarine, melted

TOPPINGS, IF DESIRED
- Sour cream
- Choice of preserves or fruit toppings

1 Heat oven to 375°F. In small bowl, mix all filling ingredients; set aside. Separate crescent dough into 8 rectangles. Press perforations of each rectangle to seal into 1 piece. Cut each rectangle in half crosswise to form 16 squares. Place about 1 tablespoon of filling on each square; fold dough in half and seal edges of squares with fork. On ungreased cookie sheets, place about 2 inches apart. Brush blintzes with melted butter.

2 Bake 12 to 15 minutes until golden brown. Serve warm with sour cream and a choice of preserves or fruit toppings.

NUTRITION INFORMATION PER SERVING: Calories 160 • Total Fat 10g • Saturated Fat 4g • Cholesterol 25mg • Sodium 250mg • Total Carbohydrate 12g • Dietary Fiber 0g. DIETARY EXCHANGES: 1/2 Starch • 1/2 Other Carbohydrate • 1/2 High-Fat Meat • 1 Fat • 1 Carb Choice.

ERNEST CROW
Rockville, Maryland
Bake-Off® Contest 38, 1998

cook's notes

For a crispier crust, bake it 6 to 7 minutes or until it just begins to brown. Then add the toppings and bake the pizza 8 to 12 minutes longer.

easy breakfast pizza

PREP TIME: 15 Minutes ✳ READY IN: 30 Minutes ✳ SERVINGS: 8

- 1 can (13.8 oz.) Pillsbury® refrigerated classic pizza crust
- 8 eggs
- 1/4 cup half-and-half or milk
- 1/8 teaspoon salt
- 1/8 teaspoon pepper
- 2 tablespoons butter or margarine
- 1 container (8 oz.) chives-and-onion, garden vegetable or regular cream cheese spread
- 8 slices crisply cooked bacon
- Chopped green onions, if desired

1 Heat oven to 425°F. Grease 12-inch pizza pan with shortening or spray with cooking spray. Unroll dough; place in pan. Starting at center, press out dough to edge of pan.

2 Meanwhile, in medium bowl, beat eggs, half-and-half, salt and pepper with wire whisk until well blended. In 10-inch skillet, melt butter over medium heat. Add egg mixture; cook, stirring occasionally, until thoroughly cooked but still moist. Remove from heat.

3 Spoon cooked egg mixture over dough. Drop cream cheese spread by teaspoonfuls over eggs. Arrange bacon in spoke fashion on top of pizza.

4 Bake 12 to 15 minutes longer or until crust is deep golden brown and toppings are hot. Garnish with onions.

NUTRITION INFORMATION PER SERVING: Calories 360 • Total Fat 22g • Saturated Fat 11g • Cholesterol 255mg • Sodium 850mg • Total Carbohydrate 25g • Dietary Fiber 0g. DIETARY EXCHANGES: 1-1/2 Starch • 1-1/2 High-Fat Meat • 2 Fat • 1-1/2 Carb Choices.

ham and vegetable scrambled eggs

READY IN: 20 Minutes ✳ SERVINGS: 4

8 eggs	1/2 cup finely chopped cooked ham
2 tablespoons milk	1/4 cup chopped green bell pepper
1/2 teaspoon garlic salt	1/4 cup chopped onion
2 tablespoons margarine or butter	1/2 cup shredded Cheddar cheese (2 oz.)

1   In medium bowl, combine eggs, milk and garlic salt; beat well. Set aside. Melt margarine in large skillet over medium heat. Add ham, bell pepper and onion; cook and stir 2 to 4 minutes or until vegetables are crisp-tender.

2   Pour egg mixture over ham mixture in skillet. Cook until eggs are firm but still moist, stirring occasionally from outside edge to center of pan. Remove from heat. Sprinkle with cheese. Cover; let stand 1 minute or until cheese is melted.

NUTRITION INFORMATION PER SERVING: Calories 280 • Total Fat: 21g • Saturated Fat 8g • Cholesterol 450mg • Sodium 770mg • Total Carbohydrate 3g • Dietary Fiber 0g • Sugars 2g • Protein 20g. DIETARY EXCHANGES: 3 Medium-Fat Meat • 1 Fat.

Kitchen tip

When buying eggs, remember to open the carton and check that the eggs look clean and do not have cracked or broken shells. Move each egg slightly with your finger to make sure it is not stuck to the carton by a bit of leaking egg.

JENNY RIEGSECKER
Delta, Ohio
Bake-Off® Contest 41, 2004

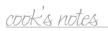

cook's notes

These cherry-topped breakfast treats are also good made with seedless raspberry jam or apricot preserves.

cherry-almond swirls

PREP TIME: 20 Minutes ✳ READY IN: 40 Minutes ✳ SERVINGS: 12

1/4 cup granulated sugar	1 egg yolk
1/2 cup slivered almonds	1 can (8 oz.) Pillsbury® refrigerated crescent dinner rolls
1 package (3 oz.) cream cheese, softened, cut into pieces	
1/4 teaspoon vanilla	1/4 cup cherry preserves
1/8 teaspoon almond extract	1/2 cup powdered sugar
	2 teaspoons water

1 Heat oven to 375°F. Spray 12 regular-size muffin cups with cooking spray. In food processor, process granulated sugar and almonds about 30 seconds or until almonds are finely ground. Add cream cheese, vanilla, almond extract and egg yolk; process about 10 seconds or until well blended.

2 On lightly floured surface, unroll dough into 1 large rectangle. With floured rolling pin or fingers, roll or press dough into 12x9-inch rectangle, firmly pressing perforations to seal.

3 Spread cream cheese mixture evenly over dough rectangle. Starting with 1 long side, roll up dough into log (filling will be soft). With serrated knife, cut log into 12 slices; place cut side up in muffin cups.

4 Bake 11 to 15 minutes or until light golden brown. Remove rolls from oven. With handle of wooden spoon, make indentation in center of each roll; spoon 1 teaspoon preserves into each.

5 Return to oven; bake 2 to 4 minutes longer or until golden brown. Run knife around edge of each muffin cup to loosen. Remove rolls from cups; place on wire racks.

6 In small bowl, blend powdered sugar and water until smooth; drizzle over warm rolls. Serve warm or cool. Store in refrigerator.

HIGH ALTITUDE (3500-6500 FT): In Step 4, bake at 375°F 13 to 17 minutes.

NUTRITION INFORMATION PER SERVING: Calories 190 • Total Fat 10g • Saturated Fat 3g • Cholesterol 25mg • Sodium 170mg • Total Carbohydrate 22g • Dietary Fiber 0g • Sugars 14g • Protein 3g. DIETARY EXCHANGES: 1 Starch • 1/2 Other Carbohydrate • 2 Fat • 1-1/2 Carb Choices.

skillet corn frittata

READY IN: 40 Minutes ✳ SERVINGS: 8

3 tablespoons margarine or butter	1/2 teaspoon salt
1 package (1 lb.) frozen whole kernel corn	1/8 teaspoon pepper
1/4 cup sliced green onions	2 tomatoes, peeled, sliced
10 eggs	1 green bell pepper, cut into rings
1/2 cup half-and-half	1 cup shredded Swiss cheese (4 oz.)
1 teaspoon dried basil leaves	

1 Melt margarine in large skillet over medium heat. Add frozen corn and onions; cook and stir about 5 minutes or until vegetables are crisp-tender. Reduce heat to low.

2 In large bowl, beat eggs well. Add half-and-half, basil, salt and pepper; blend well. Pour over vegetables. Cook over low heat 6 minutes.

3 As edges set, run spatula around edge of skillet, gently lifting vegetable mixture to allow uncooked egg to flow to bottom of skillet. Cover; cook an additional 6 minutes or until top is almost set. (Top will be moist.)

4 Arrange tomato slices and bell pepper rings around outer edge of frittata; sprinkle with cheese. Cover; cook an additional 5 minutes or until cheese is melted. Remove from heat; let stand 5 minutes. Cut into wedges to serve.

NUTRITION INFORMATION PER SERVING: Calories 270 • Total Fat 17g • Saturated Fat 6g • Cholesterol 285mg • Sodium 340mg • Total Carbohydrate 14g • Dietary Fiber 2g • Sugars 4g • Protein 14g. DIETARY EXCHANGES: 1 Starch • 1-1/2 Medium-Fat Meat • 1-1/2 Fat OR 1 Carbohydrate • 1-1/2 Medium-Fat Meat • 1-1/2 Fat.

carolina brunch-style grits

PREP TIME: 15 Minutes ✳ READY IN: 45 Minutes ✳ SERVINGS: 8

- 1 cup uncooked quick-cooking grits
- 4 cups water
- 1 can (11 oz.) vacuum-packed whole kernel corn with red and green peppers, drained
- 1 box (9 oz.) frozen spinach, thawed
- 1 package (1.25 oz.) taco seasoning mix
- 2 tablespoons chopped onion
- 2 tablespoons butter or margarine
- 2 cups shredded Cheddar cheese (8 oz.)

1 Heat oven to 350°F. Cook grits in water as directed on package. In ungreased 13x9-inch (3-quart) glass baking dish, mix cooked grits and remaining ingredients except 1 cup of the cheese. Sprinkle with remaining 1 cup cheese. Bake 22 to 27 minutes or until edges are bubbly and cheese is melted.

HIGH ALTITUDE (3500-6500 FT): Heat oven to 375°F.

NUTRITION INFORMATION PER SERVING: Calories 270 • Total Fat 13g • Saturated Fat 8g • Cholesterol 35mg • Sodium 770mg • Total Carbohydrate 27g • Dietary Fiber 2g. DIETARY EXCHANGES: 1-1/2 Starch • 1 High-Fat Meat • 1 Fat • 2 Carb Choices.

cook's notes

To make bell pepper rings, run a paring knife around the top of the pepper to detach the core and membrane (ribs). Then twist and pull out the stem. Using a spoon, scrape out any remaining seeds and membrane. With a chef's knife, slice the pepper crosswise to create rings.

Pillsbury Bake-Off®

INEZ DUKE
Mars Hill, North Carolina
Bake-Off® Contest 39, 2000
Prize Winner

cook's notes

You can quickly thaw spinach by cutting a small slit in the center of the spinach pouch and microwaving on High 2 to 3 minutes or until thawed. Remove it from the pouch and squeeze dry.

chicken fajita quiche

MARY BETH SCHULTZ
Valparaiso, Indiana
Bake-Off® Contest 42, 2006

chicken fajita quiche

PREP TIME: 20 Minutes ✳ READY IN: 1 Hour 25 Minutes ✳ SERVINGS: 8

1 tablespoon olive oil	1/4 teaspoon black pepper
1/2 teaspoon hot chili oil	1/8 teaspoon ground red pepper (cayenne)
1 small boneless skinless chicken breast (4 oz.), cut into thin bite-size strips	1 teaspoon fresh lime juice
1/4 medium green bell pepper, cut into julienne strips (2-1/4 inch)	4 eggs
1/4 medium red bell pepper, cut into julienne strips (2-1/4 inch)	1 cup whipping cream
1/4 medium yellow bell pepper, cut into julienne strips (2-1/4 inch)	1/2 teaspoon salt
1/4 teaspoon garlic salt	1 can (4.5 oz.) chopped green chiles
1/4 teaspoon ground cinnamon	1 cup shredded Cheddar cheese (4 oz.)
1/4 teaspoon chili powder	1 cup shredded Monterey Jack cheese (4 oz.)
	1 refrigerated pie crust (from 15-oz. box), softened as directed on box
	1 cup organic or chunky-style salsa

1 Heat oven to 375°F. In 10-inch skillet, heat olive and chili oil over medium-high heat. Add chicken; cook and stir 2 to 3 minutes or until lightly browned and no longer pink in center. Reserve several bell pepper strips of each color for garnish; add remaining strips to skillet. Cook about 1 minute, stirring frequently, until slightly softened. Sprinkle with garlic salt, cinnamon, chili powder, black pepper, ground red pepper and lime juice; stir to mix. Remove from heat; cool slightly.

2 In large bowl, beat eggs, whipping cream, salt and green chiles with wire whisk until blended. Gently stir in both cheeses. Stir chicken mixture into egg mixture.

3 Place pie crust in 10-inch quiche dish or 9-inch glass pie plate as directed on box for One-Crust Filled Pie. Pour chicken mixture into crust-lined pan. Arrange reserved bell pepper strips in pinwheel fashion over filling.

4 Bake 35 to 45 minutes or until knife inserted in center comes out clean and filling is golden brown. Let stand 15 to 20 minutes on wire rack before serving. Serve salsa over individual servings.

HIGH ALTITUDE (3500-6500 FT): In Step 2, stir 2 tablespoons flour into egg mixture. Bake 48 to 52 minutes.

NUTRITION INFORMATION PER SERVING: Calories 400 • Total Fat 30g • Saturated Fat 15g • Cholesterol 180mg • Sodium 700mg • Total Carbohydrate 18g • Dietary Fiber 0g • Sugars 3g • Protein 14g. DIETARY EXCHANGES: 1 Starch • 1-1/2 Medium-Fat Meat • 4-1/2 Fat • 1 Carb Choice.

caramel sticky buns

PREP TIME: 15 Minutes ✳ READY IN: 35 Minutes ✳ SERVINGS: 12

TOPPING	BUNS
1/4 cup butter or margarine, melted	1 tablespoon granulated sugar
1/4 cup packed brown sugar	1/2 teaspoon ground cinnamon
2 tablespoons light corn syrup	1 can (12 oz.) refrigerated flaky biscuits
1/4 cup chopped pecans	

1 Heat oven to 375°F. Grease 12 regular-size muffin cups with shortening. In small bowl, mix all topping ingredients. Spoon scant tablespoon topping into each muffin cup.

2 In plastic bag, mix sugar and cinnamon. Separate dough into 10 biscuits. Cut each biscuit into 6 pieces. Shake pieces in sugar mixture. Place 5 pieces of dough in each muffin cup.

3 Place pan on foil or cookie sheet to guard against spills. Bake 15 to 20 minutes or until golden brown. Cool 1 minute. Invert onto waxed paper. Serve warm.

NUTRITION INFORMATION PER SERVING: Calories 170 • Total Fat 9g • Saturated Fat 3.5g • Cholesterol 10mg • Sodium 330mg • Total Carbohydrate 20g • Dietary Fiber 0g • Sugars 9g • Protein 2g. DIETARY EXCHANGES: 1-1/2 Other Carbohydrate • 2 Fat • 1 Carb Choice.

cook's notes

Refrigerated biscuits are the key to these very quick and easy, ooey-gooey buns. For a deeper, richer flavor, substitute dark corn syrup for the light version.

LINDA MIRANDA
Wakefield, Rhode Island
Bake-Off® Contest 41, 2004

mushroom-crab-asparagus tart

PREP TIME: 20 Minutes * READY IN: 1 Hour 5 Minutes * SERVINGS: 8

1 box (9 oz.) Green Giant® frozen asparagus cuts	1/2 lb. lump crabmeat or 1 can (6 oz.) lump crabmeat, drained
1/4 cup butter or margarine	1 container (8 oz.) garlic-and-herb spreadable cheese
1 lb. fresh mushrooms, coarsely chopped	4 eggs
1/2 cup Progresso® Parmesan bread crumbs	2 tablespoons chopped fresh parsley
1/4 teaspoon pepper	
2 cups shredded sharp Cheddar or Swiss cheese (8 oz.)	

1 Heat oven to 375°F. Spray bottom and side of 12-inch tart pan with removable bottom or 13x9-inch (3-quart) glass baking dish with cooking spray. Cook asparagus as directed on box; drain and cool.

2 Meanwhile, in 12-inch skillet, melt butter over medium heat. Add mushrooms; cook about 5 minutes, stirring frequently, just until tender. Stir in bread crumbs and pepper. Press mushroom mixture evenly in bottom and up side of sprayed tart pan or in bottom of sprayed baking dish. Sprinkle shredded cheese over mushrooms. Top with asparagus and crabmeat.

3 In medium bowl or blender, place spreadable cheese, eggs and 1 tablespoon of the parsley. Beat with electric mixer on medium speed or cover and blend on low speed until smooth. Pour evenly over crabmeat.

4 Bake at 375°F for 30 to 35 minutes or until set in center and edges are golden brown. Sprinkle remaining tablespoon parsley over top. Let stand 10 minutes before serving. Carefully remove side of pan. Cut into wedges or squares.

NUTRITION INFORMATION PER SERVING: Calories 380 • Total Fat 29g • Saturated Fat 17g • Cholesterol 210mg • Sodium 630mg • Total Carbohydrate 9g • Dietary Fiber 1g • Sugars 3g • Protein 21g. DIETARY EXCHANGES: 1 Vegetable • 3 Medium-Fat Meat • 3 Fat • 1/2 Carb Choice.

breakfast calzones

PREP TIME: 15 Minutes * READY IN: 30 Minutes * SERVINGS: 4

4 eggs	1/2 cup shredded mozzarella cheese (2 oz.)
1/4 cup milk	16 slices pepperoni (from 3.5-oz. pkg.)
Dash pepper	4 teaspoons grated Parmesan cheese
2 teaspoons margarine or butter	
1 can (13.8 oz.) Pillsbury® refrigerated classic pizza crust	

1 Heat oven to 400°F. Spray large cookie sheet with cooking spray. In medium bowl, combine eggs, milk and pepper; beat until well blended. In medium nonstick skillet, melt margarine over medium heat. Add egg mixture; cook 3 to 5 minutes or until eggs are set but moist, stirring occasionally.

2 Unroll dough; place on work surface. Starting at center, press out dough to form 14x10-inch rectangle. Cut dough into four 7x5-inch rectangles. Divide mozzarella cheese evenly onto half of each rectangle to within 1/2 inch of edges. Top cheese with pepperoni, Parmesan cheese and eggs. Fold untopped dough over filling, turnover fashion; press edges firmly to seal.

3 Place calzones on sprayed cookie sheet. Bake at 400°F for 11 to 13 minutes or until golden brown.

NUTRITION INFORMATION PER SERVING: Calories 500 • Total Fat 23g • Saturated Fat 9g • Cholesterol 250mg • Sodium 1300mg • Total Carbohydrate 49g • Dietary Fiber 0g. DIETARY EXCHANGES: 2 Starch • 1 Other Carbohydrate • 2 Medium-Fat Meat • 2 Fat • 3 Carb Choices.

cook's notes

Try these tasty calzones in place of the usual sandwich for lunch.

mushroom-crab-asparagus tart

country apple coffee cake

country apple coffee cake

PREP TIME: 20 Minutes ✳ READY IN: 1 Hour 10 Minutes ✳ SERVINGS: 8

COFFEE CAKE
2 tablespoons margarine or butter, softened
1-1/2 cups chopped peeled apples
1 can (12 oz.) refrigerated flaky biscuits
1/3 cup firmly packed brown sugar
1/4 teaspoon cinnamon
1/3 cup light corn syrup

1-1/2 teaspoons whiskey, if desired
1 egg
1/2 cup pecan halves or pieces

GLAZE
1/3 cup powdered sugar
1/4 teaspoon vanilla
1 to 2 teaspoons milk

1 Heat oven to 350°F. Using 1 tablespoon of the margarine, generously grease 9-inch round cake pan or 8-inch square pan. Spread 1 cup of the apples in greased pan.

2 Separate dough into 10 biscuits; cut each into quarters. Arrange biscuit pieces, points up, over apples. Top with remaining 1/2 cup apples.

3 In small bowl, combine remaining 1 tablespoon margarine, brown sugar, cinnamon, corn syrup, whisky and egg; beat 2 to 3 minutes or until sugar is partially dissolved. Stir in pecans. Spoon over biscuit pieces and apples.

4 Bake at 350°F for 35 to 45 minutes or until deep golden brown. Cool 5 minutes. If desired, remove from pan.

5 In small bowl, blend all glaze ingredients, adding enough milk for desired drizzling consistency. Drizzle over warm cake. Serve warm or cool. Store in refrigerator.

NUTRITION INFORMATION PER SERVING: Calories 330 • Total Fat 14g • Saturated Fat 2g • Cholesterol 25mg • Sodium 510mg • Total Carbohydrate 47g • Dietary Fiber 2g • Sugars 24g • Protein 4g. DIETARY EXCHANGES: 1-1/2 Starch • 1-1/2 Fruit • 2-1/2 Fat OR 3 Carbohydrate • 2-1/2 Fat.

kitchen tip

To soften brown sugar, place a slice of bread or an apple wedge with the brown sugar in a covered container for a few days. If you're in a hurry, microwave on High for 20-30 seconds. Repeat if necessary, but watch carefully because the sugar will begin to melt. Always store brown sugar in an airtight container.

down-home creamed eggs on toasted english muffins

READY IN: 35 Minutes ✳ SERVINGS: 4

6 eggs
3 cups milk
3 tablespoons all-purpose flour

1/2 teaspoon salt
1/4 teaspoon pepper
4 English muffins, split, toasted

1 Place eggs in medium saucepan; cover with cold water. Bring to a boil. Reduce heat; simmer about 15 minutes. Immediately drain; run cold water over eggs to stop cooking. Peel eggs; slice thinly.

2 Pour milk into medium nonstick saucepan. Place saucepan over medium-high heat; stir in flour with wire whisk until well blended. Add salt and pepper. Cook and stir until bubbly and thickened. Remove from heat.

3 Place muffin halves, cut side up, on 4 individual plates. Arrange sliced eggs evenly over muffins, using 1-1/2 eggs per serving. Spoon sauce evenly over eggs.

NUTRITION INFORMATION PER SERVING: Calories 350 • Total Fat 12g • Saturated Fat 5g • Cholesterol 330mg • Sodium 720mg • Total Carbohydrate 40g • Dietary Fiber 2g • Sugars 17g • Protein 20g. DIETARY EXCHANGES: 2-1/2 Starch • 2 Medium-Fat Meat OR 2-1/2 Carbohydrate • 2 Medium-Fat Meat.

kitchen tip

When you have extra English muffins, use them to make mini pizzas for lunch or as a snack. Top the muffins with pizza sauce, mozzarella or any toppings you like.

lemon yogurt fruit dip

PREP TIME: 5 Minutes ✳ READY IN: 1 Hour 5 Minutes ✳ SERVINGS: 28

1 container (8 oz.) lemon yogurt	1/2 teaspoon grated lemon peel
1 container (8 oz.) sour cream	1/2 teaspoon lemon juice
1 teaspoon ginger	Assorted fresh fruit
1 tablespoon honey	

1 In small bowl, combine all ingredients; blend well. Cover; refrigerate 1 to 2 hours before serving to blend flavors. Serve dip with assorted fresh fruit.

NUTRITION INFORMATION PER SERVING: Calories 30 • Total Fat 2g • Saturated Fat 1g • Cholesterol 4mg • Sodium 10 mg • Total Carbohydrate 2g • Dietary Fiber 0g • Sugars 1g • Protein 1g. DIETARY EXCHANGE: 1/2 Fat.

glazed apples and canadian bacon

READY IN: 25 Minutes ✳ SERVINGS: 8

1/2 cup firmly packed brown sugar	2 large red and/or green cooking apples, cored, each cut into 16 wedges
1/8 teaspoon pepper	
1 tablespoon lemon juice	1 lb. sliced Canadian bacon

1 In large skillet, combine brown sugar, pepper and lemon juice; mix well. Cook and stir over medium heat until brown sugar is melted. Add apples; cook 5 to 6 minutes or until tender, stirring occasionally. With slotted spoon, place apples on serving platter.

2 Add Canadian bacon to same skillet; cook 1 to 2 minutes or until hot, turning once. Arrange on platter with apples. Spoon any remaining liquid in skillet over apples and Canadian bacon.

NUTRITION INFORMATION PER SERVING: Calories 180 • Total Fat 4g • Saturated Fat 1g • Cholesterol 30mg • Sodium 810mg • Total Carbohydrate 23g • Dietary Fiber 1g • Sugars 21g • Protein 12g. DIETARY EXCHANGES: 1-1/2 Fruit • 1-1/2 Lean Meat OR 1-1/2 Carbohydrate • 1-1/2 Lean Meat.

potato pancakes

READY IN: 45 Minutes ✳ SERVINGS: 16

6 cups shredded peeled potatoes	2 teaspoons salt
1 cup finely chopped onion	1/4 teaspoon pepper
1/4 cup all-purpose flour	Oil
6 eggs, beaten	Applesauce, if desired

1 Place shredded potatoes in clean cloth; squeeze to remove excess moisture. In medium bowl, combine potatoes and all remaining ingredients except oil.

2 Heat 1/4 inch oil in large, heavy skillet over medium heat until hot. Using about 1/3 cup potato mixture for each, form very thin pancake patties 3 to 4 inches in diameter. Fry 2 to 3 minutes on each side or until lightly browned. Drain on paper towels. If needed, add more oil to skillet to fry remaining pancakes. If desired, serve with applesauce.

NUTRITION INFORMATION PER SERVING: Calories 170 • Total Fat 12g • Saturated Fat 2g • Cholesterol 80mg • Sodium 290mg • Total Carbohydrate 12g • Dietary Fiber 1g • Sugars 1g • Protein 4g. DIETARY EXCHANGES: 1 Starch • 2 Fat OR 1 Carbohydrate • 2 Fat.

lemon poppy seed muffins

PREP TIME: 10 Minutes ✳ READY IN: 40 Minutes ✳ SERVINGS: 15

1 box (15.8 oz.) lemon-poppy seed premium muffin mix (with glaze)

3/4 cup milk

1/4 cup vegetable oil

2 eggs

1/3 cup lemon curd (from 10- or 11-1/4-oz. jar)

1 Heat oven to 425°F. Line 15 standard-size muffin cups with paper baking cups. In medium bowl, stir muffin mix, milk, oil and eggs with spoon just until blended (batter may be lumpy).

2 Spoon about 2 tablespoons batter into each muffin cup. Place about 1 teaspoon lemon curd on batter in each cup. Top with remaining batter, dividing evenly among cups.

3 Bake 14 to 17 minutes or until golden brown. Cool in pan on wire rack 10 minutes. Remove from pan.

4 Squeeze glaze packet from muffin mix about 10 seconds (do not microwave). With scissors, cut off tip of 1 corner of packet. Drizzle glaze over warm muffins. Serve warm or cool.

HIGH ALTITUDE (3500-6500 FT): Add 1 tablespoon flour to dry muffin mix. Bake at 425°F 12 to 15 minutes. Continue as directed above.

NUTRITION INFORMATION PER SERVING: Calories 180 • Total Fat 6g • Saturated Fat 5g • Cholesterol 30mg • Sodium 190mg • Total Carbohydrate 29g • Dietary Fiber 0g • Sugars 15g • Protein 3g. DIETARY EXCHANGES: 1 Starch • 1 Fat • 2 Carb Choices.

kitchen tip

Lemon curd is usually found alongside the jams and jellies in the supermarket. Lemon pie filling can be used instead of the lemon curd in this recipe.

ham and veggie strata

ham and veggie strata

PREP TIME: 30 Minutes ✳ READY IN: 7 Hours 30 Minutes ✳ SERVINGS: 10

2 tablespoons olive oil

3 medium onions, chopped (about 1-1/2 cups)

1 medium green bell pepper, chopped (1 cup)

1 tablespoon minced garlic

1 package (8 oz.) sliced cooked ham, cut into small pieces

3 medium tomatoes, seeded, chopped

12 slices day-old English muffin or sourdough bread (about 1-1/2 lbs.), torn into pieces

8 eggs

3 cups milk

1-1/2 teaspoons salt

1/4 teaspoon pepper

1 cup shredded Cheddar cheese (4 oz.)

1 In 12-inch nonstick skillet, heat oil over medium heat. Add onions, bell pepper and garlic; cook 6 to 8 minutes, stirring frequently, until tender. Stir in ham and tomatoes. Cook 2 minutes longer.

2 Meanwhile, spray 13x9-inch (3-quart) glass baking dish with cooking spray. Place torn bread in baking dish. In large bowl, beat eggs, milk, salt and pepper until well blended.

3 Spoon ham mixture over bread. Pour egg mixture over top. Cover; refrigerate at least 6 hours or overnight.

4 When ready to bake, heat oven to 350°F. Uncover baking dish; bake 30 minutes. Sprinkle with cheese; bake 30 minutes longer or until knife inserted in center comes out clean. Cut into squares.

HIGH ALTITUDE (3500-6500 FT): Prepare as directed. Bake covered at 350°F 50 minutes. Uncover; add cheese. Bake 20 minutes longer or until knife inserted in center comes out clean.

NUTRITION INFORMATION PER SERVING: Calories 380 • Total Fat 15g • Saturated Fat 6g • Cholesterol 200mg • Sodium 1070mg • Total Carbohydrate 39g • Dietary Fiber 3g • Sugars 9g • Protein 22g.

cook's notes

This make-ahead breakfast casserole can be toted in a cooler and baked at the home of a potluck gathering. Be sure to ask the hostess if her oven is available.

four-grain pancakes

READY IN: 40 Minutes ✳ SERVINGS: 4

3/4 cup whole wheat flour

1/2 cup all-purpose flour

1/2 cup cornmeal

1/3 cup quick-cooking rolled oats

2 teaspoons baking powder

1 teaspoon baking soda

1/2 teaspoon salt

2 cups buttermilk

1/3 cup margarine or butter, melted

3 tablespoons maple-flavored syrup

2 eggs, beaten

1 In large bowl, combine all ingredients; stir until large lumps disappear. (Batter will be thick. For thinner pancakes, thin batter with a small amount of water.)

2 Heat griddle or large skillet over medium-high heat (375°F) until hot. Lightly grease griddle with oil. For each pancake, pour about 1/4 cup batter onto hot griddle. Cook 2-1/2 to 3 minutes or until edges look cooked and bubbles begin to break on surface. Turn pancakes; cook 2 to 2-1/2 minutes or until golden brown. If desired, serve with additional syrup.

NUTRITION INFORMATION PER SERVING: Calories 480 • Total Fat 20g • Saturated Fat 5g • Cholesterol 110mg • Sodium 1190mg • Total Carbohydrate 61g • Dietary Fiber 5g • Sugars 12g • Protein 14g. DIETARY EXCHANGES: 4 Starch • 1/2 Medium-Fat Meat • 3 Fat OR 4 Carbohydrate • 1/2 Medium-Fat Meat • 3 Fat.

cook's notes

For waffles instead, heat a waffle iron. Spread the batter evenly in the hot waffle iron and bake 2 to 3 minutes or until steaming stops and the waffle is golden brown. Repeat with the remaining batter. The yield is 8 (5-inch) waffles (4 servings).

black bean and corn enchilada egg bake

PREP TIME: 20 Minutes ✳ READY IN: 5 Hours 20 Minutes ✳ SERVINGS: 12

10 corn tortillas (6 inches)
1 can (15 oz.) black beans, drained, rinsed
1 can (11 oz.) vacuum-packed whole kernel corn with red and green peppers, drained
1 can (10-3/4 oz.) condensed nacho cheese soup
6 eggs

2 cups milk
1 teaspoon cumin
1/2 cup shredded Cheddar cheese (2 oz.)
1/2 red bell pepper, if desired
3 sprigs fresh cilantro, if desired
Salsa and sour cream, if desired

1 Grease 13x9-inch (3-quart) baking dish. Arrange and overlap 6 tortillas on bottom of dish. Spoon beans and corn evenly over tortillas. Spoon cheese soup evenly over vegetables. Cut remaining tortillas into 1-inch strips; arrange over top.

2 In large bowl, combine eggs, milk and cumin; beat well. Pour over tortilla strips. Cover tightly; refrigerate 4 hours or overnight.

3 Heat oven to 325°F. Uncover dish; sprinkle with cheese. Bake at 325°F for 55 to 60 minutes or until eggs are set. Let stand 5 minutes before serving.

4 To garnish, cut five 1-inch pieces from bell pepper to resemble petals. Arrange petals in center of dish to resemble poinsettia; tuck 2 or 3 sprigs of cilantro between petals. Or chop bell pepper and cilantro; sprinkle over top. To serve, cut into squares. If desired, top with salsa and sour cream.

NUTRITION INFORMATION PER SERVING: Calories 190 • Total Fat 7g • Saturated Fat 3g • Cholesterol 115mg • Sodium 420mg • Total Carbohydrate 22g • Dietary Fiber 3g • Sugars 5g • Protein 10g. DIETARY EXCHANGES: 1-1/2 Starch • 1 Lean Meat • 1/2 Fat OR 1 Carbohydrate • 1 Lean Meat • 1/2 Fat.

queen's muffins

PREP TIME: 20 Minutes ✳ READY IN: 55 Minutes ✳ SERVINGS: 18

1 cup granulated sugar
1 cup butter or margarine, softened
3 eggs
1 teaspoon lemon extract
1 teaspoon orange extract

2 cups all-purpose flour
2 teaspoons baking powder
1/2 teaspoon ground cinnamon
1 box (10 oz.) dried currants
2 tablespoons powdered sugar

1 Heat oven to 325°F. Place paper baking cup in each of 18 regular-size muffin cups. In large bowl, beat granulated sugar and butter until light and fluffy. Beat in 1 egg at a time until well blended. Add lemon and orange extracts; beat well.

2 Gradually add flour, baking powder and cinnamon; mix well. Stir in currants. Pour batter into muffin cups, filling each 3/4 full.

3 Bake 25 to 30 minutes or until toothpick inserted in center comes out clean. Immediately remove from pan; cool 5 minutes. Sprinkle with powdered sugar.

HIGH ALTITUDE (3500-6500 FT): Increase flour to 2-1/4 cups.

NUTRITION INFORMATION PER SERVING: Calories 260 • Total Fat 11g • Saturated Fat 7g • Cholesterol 60mg • Sodium 140mg • Total Carbohydrate 35g • Dietary Fiber 2g • Sugars 23g • Protein 3g. DIETARY EXCHANGES: 1 Starch • 1-1/2 Other Carbohydrate • 2 Fat • 2 Carb Choices.

black bean and corn enchilada egg bake

celebration brunch strata

celebration brunch strata

PREP TIME: 30 Minutes ✳ READY IN: 1 Hour 50 Minutes ✳ SERVINGS: 12

1/2 cup margarine or butter, softened	8 eggs
12 slices white bread	2-1/2 cups milk
2 cups shredded Cheddar cheese (8 oz.)	3 tablespoons chopped fresh parsley or chervil
1 package (9 oz.) frozen asparagus cuts in a pouch, thawed, drained	1 teaspoon salt
6 oz. flaked cooked crabmeat	1 teaspoon paprika
	1/4 teaspoon pepper

1 Heat oven to 325°F. Spread margarine on one side of each slice of bread. Arrange 6 slices, margarine side down, in ungreased 13x9-inch (3-quart) baking dish. Layer cheese, asparagus and crabmeat over bread. Place remaining bread slices, margarine side up, over crabmeat.

2 In large bowl, combine all remaining ingredients; beat well. Pour egg mixture evenly over bread. Let stand 10 to 15 minutes. Bake at 325°F for 55 to 65 minutes or until knife inserted in center comes out clean.

NUTRITION INFORMATION PER SERVING: Calories 300 • Total Fat 19g • Saturated Fat 7g • Cholesterol 175mg • Sodium 760mg • Total Carbohydrate 17g • Dietary Fiber 1g • Sugars 4g • Protein 16g. DIETARY EXCHANGES: 1 Starch • 2 Medium-Fat Meat • 1-1/2 Fat OR 1 Carbohydrate • 2 Medium-Fat Meat • 1-1/2 Fat.

Kitchen tip

An egg's size has no relation to quality. You may purchase small, medium or extra-large to match the appetites in your household, but use eggs labeled "large" for preparing recipes.

sausage-mushroom biscuit casserole

PREP TIME: 40 Minutes ✳ READY IN: 1 Hour 5 Minutes ✳ SERVINGS: 12

1 package (12 oz.) pork sausage links	1/4 teaspoon pepper
8 tablespoons margarine or butter	12 eggs
1/2 cup all-purpose flour	1 can (5 oz.) evaporated milk (1/3 cup)
4 cups milk	1/2 teaspoon salt
1 jar (4.5 oz.) sliced mushrooms, drained	1 can (12 oz.) Pillsbury® Golden Layers™ refrigerated flaky biscuits
1 jar (2 oz.) real bacon pieces	

1 Heat oven to 350°F. Lightly spray 13x9-inch (3-quart) glass baking dish with nonstick cooking spray. Crumble sausage into large saucepan; cook over medium-high heat until sausage is browned and thoroughly cooked, stirring frequently. Remove sausage from saucepan; drain. Set aside.

2 In same large saucepan, melt 6 tablespoons of the margarine. Add flour; stir with wire whisk until smooth. Cook over low heat for 1 minute, stirring constantly. Gradually stir in milk. Cook until bubbly and thickened, stirring constantly. Add cooked sausage, mushrooms, bacon and pepper; mix well. Set aside.

3 In large bowl, combine eggs, evaporated milk and salt; beat with wire whisk until well blended. Melt remaining 2 tablespoons margarine in large skillet over medium heat. Add egg mixture; cook until firm but still moist, stirring occasionally.

4 Pour 1/3 of sauce into sprayed baking dish. Top with half of egg mixture. Repeat layers. Top with remaining sauce.

5 Separate dough into 10 biscuits; cut each into quarters. Arrange biscuit pieces, points up, over sauce. Bake at 350°F for 20 to 25 minutes or until mixture is thoroughly heated and biscuits are golden brown.

NUTRITION INFORMATION PER SERVING: Calories 390 • Total Fat 25g • Saturated Fat 8g • Cholesterol 240mg • Sodium 1010mg • Total Carbohydrate 24g • Dietary Fiber 1g • Sugars 10g • Protein 17g. DIETARY EXCHANGES: 1-1/2 Starch • 2 High-Fat Meat • 1-1/2 Fat OR 1-1/2 Carbohydrate • 2 High-Fat Meat • 1-1/2 Fat • 1-1/2 Carb Choices.

Gifts of Good Taste

A handmade touch makes edible Christmas presents something special. These merry mixes, snacks and other treats you can create at home are sure to warm hearts.

p. 229

p. 218

p. 217

p. 224

p. 221

peanut butter-brownie
cookies p. 222

oatmeal carmelitas

oatmeal carmelitas

PREP TIME: 30 Minutes ✳ READY IN: 2 Hours 55 Minutes ✳ SERVINGS: 36 Bars

BASE

2	cups all-purpose flour
2	cups quick-cooking oats
1-1/2	cups packed brown sugar
1	teaspoon baking soda
1/2	teaspoon salt
1-1/4	cups butter or margarine, softened

FILLING

1	jar (12.5 oz.) caramel topping (1 cup)
3	tablespoons all-purpose flour
1	cup semisweet chocolate chips (6 oz.)
1/2	cup chopped nuts

ERLYCE LARSON
Kennedy, Minnesota
Bake-Off® Contest 18, 1967

1 Heat oven to 350°F. Grease 13x9-inch pan with shortening or cooking spray. In large bowl, beat all base ingredients with electric mixer on low speed until crumbly. Reserve half of crumb mixture (about 3 cups) for topping. Press remaining crumb mixture in bottom of pan.

2 Bake crumb-mixture base 10 minutes. Meanwhile, in small bowl, mix caramel topping and 3 tablespoons flour.

3 Sprinkle chocolate chips and nuts over partially baked base. Drizzle evenly with caramel mixture; sprinkle with reserved crumb mixture.

4 Bake 18 to 22 minutes longer or until golden brown. Cool completely in pan on cooling rack, about 1 hour. Refrigerate until filling is set, 1 to 2 hours. For bars, cut into 6 rows by 6 rows. Store in tightly covered container.

NUTRITION INFORMATION PER SERVING: Calories 200 • Total Fat 9g • Saturated Fat 5g • Cholesterol 15mg • Sodium 150mg • Total Carbohydrate 27g • Dietary Fiber 1g • Sugars 16g • Protein 2g. DIETARY EXCHANGES: 1/2 Starch • 1-1/2 Other Carbohydrate • 1-1/2 Fat • 2 Carb Choices.

holiday fruitcake

PREP TIME: 30 Minutes ✳ READY IN: 11 Hours 30 Minutes ✳ SERVINGS: 36

2	cups water
1/4	cup oil
2	eggs
2	packages (1 lb. 0.6 or 15.4 oz. each) date or nut quick bread mix

2	cups pecans (halves or chopped)
2	cups raisins
2	cups (12 to 13 oz.) candied cherries, halved
1	cup cut-up candied pineapple
	Corn syrup, if desired

1 Heat oven to 350°F. Grease and flour bottom and sides of 12-cup Bundt® pan or 10-inch tube pan. In large bowl, combine water, oil and eggs; beat well. Add all remaining ingredients except corn syrup; stir by hand until combined. Pour into greased and floured pan.

2 Bake at 350°F for 80 to 90 minutes or until toothpick inserted in center comes out clean. Cool 30 minutes. Loosen edges of fruitcake; remove from pan. Cool 1 hour or until completely cooled.

3 Wrap tightly in plastic wrap or foil; refrigerate at least 8 hours. Store in refrigerator for up to 2 weeks or in freezer for up to 3 months.

4 Before serving, heat corn syrup until warm. Brush over fruitcake. If desired, decorate with additional candied fruits and nuts or as desired.

HIGH ALTITUDE (3500-6500 FT): Add 1/4 cup flour to dry quick bread mix. Bake as directed above.

NUTRITION INFORMATION PER SERVING: Calories 240 • Total Fat 7g • Saturated Fat 1g • Cholesterol 10mg • Sodium 140mg • Total Carbohydrate 42g • Dietary Fiber 2g • Sugars 26 g • Protein 2g. DIETARY EXCHANGES: 1 Starch • 2 Fruit • 1 Fat OR 3 Carbohydrate • 1 Fat.

cook's notes

The corn syrup glaze adds a beautiful shine to this cake. Topped with nuts and fruits as well, it makes a memorable holiday treat.

chocolate-pecan pie

PREP TIME: 25 Minutes ❋ READY IN: 2 Hours 30 Minutes ❋ SERVINGS: 10

1 Pillsbury® refrigerated pie crust (from 15-oz. box), softened as directed on box	3 eggs
1 cup light corn syrup	1 cup semisweet chocolate chips (6 oz.)
1/2 cup sugar	1-1/2 cups pecan halves
1/4 cup butter or margarine, melted	10 pecan halves
1 teaspoon vanilla	1/2 cup whipping cream, whipped

1 Heat oven to 325°F. Make pie crust as directed on box for One-Crust Filled Pie, using 9-inch glass pie plate.

2 In large bowl, beat corn syrup, sugar, butter, vanilla and eggs with electric mixer on medium speed until well blended. Reserve 2 tablespoons chocolate chips for topping. Stir in remaining chocolate chips and 1-1/2 cups pecans. Spread evenly in crust-lined pan.

3 Bake 55 to 65 minutes or until deep golden brown and filling is set. Cool completely, about 1 hour.

4 Line cookie sheet with waxed paper. In small microwavable bowl, microwave the reserved 2 tablespoons chocolate chips uncovered on Medium (50%) 1 to 1-1/2 minutes or until melted; stir. Dip each of 10 pecan halves in chocolate; place on lined cookie sheet. Refrigerate 15 to 20 minutes or until chocolate is set. Garnish pie with whipped cream and chocolate-dipped pecans. Store in refrigerator.

HIGH ALTITUDE (3500-6500 FT): Heat oven to 350°F. Bake 50 to 55 minutes.

NUTRITION INFORMATION PER SERVING: Calories 550 • Total Fat 32g • Saturated Fat 12g • Cholesterol 90mg • Sodium 170mg • Total Carbohydrate 60g • Dietary Fiber 2g • Sugars 33g • Protein 4g. DIETARY EXCHANGES: 1 Starch • 3 Other Carbohydrate • 6-1/2 Fat • 4 Carb Choices.

date and cherry cream scones

PREP TIME: 20 Minutes ❋ READY IN: 35 Minutes ❋ SERVINGS: 12

2 cups all-purpose flour	1/2 cup chopped dried cherries
3 tablespoons granulated sugar	1/2 cup white vanilla baking chips
3 teaspoons baking powder	1-1/3 cups whipping cream
2 teaspoons grated orange peel	1 cup powdered sugar
1/2 teaspoon salt	2 to 3 tablespoons orange juice
1/2 cup chopped dates	

1 Heat oven to 400°F. Lightly grease cookie sheet. In large bowl, mix flour, granulated sugar, baking powder, orange peel and salt until well blended. Stir in dates, cherries and baking chips. Add whipping cream all at once; stir just until dry ingredients are moistened.

2 On lightly floured surface, knead dough 6 or 7 times until smooth. Divide dough in half. Pat each half into 6-inch round; cut each into 6 wedges. Place 2 inches apart on cookie sheet.

3 Bake 10 to 13 minutes or until light golden brown. Cool 5 minutes. Meanwhile, in small bowl, mix powdered sugar and enough orange juice for desired drizzling consistency. Drizzle icing over warm scones. Serve warm.

HIGH ALTITUDE (3500-6500 FT): Increase flour to 2-1/4 cups; decrease whipping cream to 1 cup and add 1/3 cup water.

NUTRITION INFORMATION PER SERVING: Calories 270 • Total Fat 11g • Saturated Fat 7g • Cholesterol 30mg • Sodium 250mg • Total Carbohydrate 40g • Dietary Fiber 1g • Sugars 23g • Protein 4g. DIETARY EXCHANGES: 1 Starch • 1-1/2 Other Carbohydrate • 2 Fat • 2-1/2 Carb Choices.

chocolate-pecan pie

cook's notes

Cut and shape a bow from red

Fruit by the Foot® snack rolls.

Use this attractive wreath as

a centerpiece for a holiday

buffet. (But do invite your

guests to eat it!)

festive chex mix® wreath

PREP TIME: 15 Minutes ✳ READY IN: 1 Hour ✳ SERVINGS: 12

2 tablespoons butter or margarine	1/4 cup small green gumdrops, cut in half
25 regular marshmallows	1/4 cup small red gumdrops, cut in half
1 bag (8.75 oz.) Chex Mix® honey nut snack mix	

1 Spray large cookie sheet with cooking spray. In 4-quart saucepan, melt butter over low heat. Add marshmallows; cook, stirring constantly, until completely melted.

2 Stir in honey nut snack mix and red and green gumdrop pieces until well mixed; pour onto cookie sheet.

3 Spray sheet of waxed paper with cooking spray. With paper, sprayed side down, and hands, shape mixture into wreath shape with 4-inch hole in center. Cool completely, about 45 minutes. To serve, cut into slices.

NUTRITION INFORMATION PER SERVING: Calories 195 • Total Fat 5g • Saturated Fat 2g • Cholesterol 5mg • Sodium 185mg • Total Carbohydrate 35g • Dietary Fiber 0g • Sugars 18g • Protein 2g. DIETARY EXCHANGES: 1 Starch • 1 Other Carbohydrate • 1 Fat • 2 Carb Choices.

praline butter nuggets

READY IN: 1 Hour 20 Minutes ✳ SERVINGS: 24 Cookies

1/4 cup granulated sugar	1/3 cup butter or margarine, softened
1/4 cup pecan halves	1/3 cup shortening
1-1/2 cups all-purpose flour	1 teaspoon vanilla
1/4 cup packed brown sugar	1/2 cup powdered sugar
1/4 to 1/2 teaspoon salt	

RUTH MAXWELL
Fort Smith, Arizona
Bake-Off® Contest 1, 1949

1 Heat oven to 325°F. In 8-inch or 10-inch heavy skillet, melt granulated sugar over medium-low heat, without stirring, until golden brown. Stir in pecan halves until coated. Pour mixture onto sheet of foil. Cool 15 minutes or until hard. Finely chop pecan-sugar candy.

2 In small bowl, stir together flour, brown sugar and salt. In large bowl, beat butter, shortening and vanilla with electric mixer on medium speed until light and fluffy. Add flour mixture; beat until well combined. Stir in chopped pecan-sugar candy. (Dough will be crumbly.)

3 Shape dough into balls, using about 1 level measuring tablespoon dough for each; place on ungreased cookie sheets.

4 Bake 15 to 20 minutes or until set but not browned. Cool 5 minutes; remove from cookie sheets. Roll warm cookies in powdered sugar; place on cooling racks to cool.

HIGH ALTITUDE (3500-6500 FT): In Step 1, stir granulated sugar and 2 teaspoons water in 8-inch or 10-inch heavy skillet until well mixed. With pastry brush dipped in water, brush any sugar down from sides of skillet. Heat over medium heat, without stirring, 10 to 12 minutes or until golden brown.

NUTRITION INFORMATION PER SERVING: Calories 110 • Total Fat 6g • Saturated Fat 2.5g • Cholesterol 5mg • Sodium 45mg • Total Carbohydrate 13g • Dietary Fiber 0g • Sugars 7g • Protein 0g. DIETARY EXCHANGES: 1 Other Carbohydrate • 1 Fat • 1 Carb Choice.

hazelnut marble bark

PREP TIME: 20 Minutes ✳ READY IN: 1 Hour 20 Minutes ✳ SERVINGS: 24

1 box (6 oz.) white chocolate baking bars
6 oz. semisweet baking chocolate
3 oz. hazelnuts (filberts), toasted, finely chopped (1/2 cup)

1 Line cookie sheet with foil or waxed paper. In medium microwavable bowl, microwave white chocolate on High 1 minute, stirring once halfway through microwaving, until melted. If necessary, continue to microwave on High in 15-second increments, stirring until smooth.

2 In another medium microwavable bowl, microwave semisweet chocolate on High 1 minute, stirring once halfway through microwaving, until melted. If necessary, continue to microwave on High in 15-second increments, stirring until smooth.

3 Stir 1/4 cup of the hazelnuts into each bowl of chocolate. Alternately spoon white mixture and brown mixture in rows, side by side, onto cookie sheet; spread evenly to about 1/4-inch thickness. With knife or small metal spatula, cut through both mixtures to swirl for marbled design. Refrigerate until firm, about 1 hour. Break into pieces.

NUTRITION INFORMATION PER SERVING: Calories 105 • Total Fat 7g • Saturated Fat 3g • Cholesterol 0mg • Sodium 5mg • Total Carbohydrate 9g • Dietary Fiber 1g • Sugars 8g • Protein 1g. DIETARY EXCHANGES: 1/2 Other Carbohydrate • 1-1/2 Fat • 1/2 Carb Choice.

cook's notes

To toast hazelnuts, spread the whole nuts on a cookie sheet; bake at 350°F 8 to 10 minutes, stirring occasionally, until the skins begin to crack open and flake. If desired, to remove the skins, place the warm nuts on a cloth towel and fold the towel over the nuts; rub vigorously. Finely chop the nuts to make 1/2 cup.

DEB MCGOWAN
Louisville, Ohio
Bake-Off® Contest 41, 2004

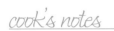

cook's notes

When cooling these cookies

on the cookie sheets, set the

entire pan on a wire cooling

rack for better air circulation.

peanut butter-brownie cookies

PREP TIME: 1 Hour ✷ READY IN: 1 Hour 30 Minutes ✷ SERVINGS: 24 Cookies

1 box (19.5 oz.) Pillsbury® traditional fudge brownie mix	1 cup powdered sugar
1/4 cup butter or margarine, melted	1 cup creamy peanut butter
4 oz. cream cheese (half of 8-oz. pkg.), softened	1/2 container (1-lb. size) Pillsbury® Creamy Supreme® chocolate fudge frosting (about 3/4 cup)
1 egg	

1 Heat oven to 350°F. In medium bowl, beat brownie mix, melted butter, cream cheese and egg 50 strokes with spoon until well blended (dough will be sticky).

2 Drop dough by rounded tablespoonfuls 2 inches apart onto ungreased cookie sheets to make 24 cookies; smooth edge of each to form round cookie.

3 In small bowl, mix powdered sugar and peanut butter with spoon until mixture forms a ball. With hands, roll rounded teaspoonfuls peanut butter mixture into 24 balls. Lightly press 1 ball into center of each ball of dough.

4 Bake 10 to 14 minutes or until edges are set. Cool cookies on cookie sheets at least 30 minutes. Remove cooled cookies from cookie sheets. Spread thin layer of frosting over peanut butter portion of each.

HIGH ALTITUDE (3500-6500 FT): Before baking, flatten cookies slightly. Bake 11 to 15 minutes.

NUTRITION INFORMATION PER SERVING: Calories 270 • Total Fat 13g • Saturated Fat 6g • Cholesterol 20mg • Sodium 140mg • Total Carbohydrate 32g • Dietary Fiber 1g • Sugars 24g • Protein 4g. DIETARY EXCHANGES: 1/2 Starch • 1-1/2 Other Carbohydrate • 1/2 High-Fat Meat • 2 Fat • 2 Carb Choices.

chocolate chip macadamia nut muffins

PREP TIME: 15 Minutes ✷ READY IN: 35 Minutes ✷ SERVINGS: 18 Muffins

STREUSEL	1/2 teaspoon salt
1/4 cup all-purpose flour	3/4 cup sour cream
1/4 cup packed brown sugar	1/2 cup butter or margarine, melted
2 tablespoons butter or margarine	1/4 cup milk
MUFFINS	1 tablespoon vanilla
2 cups all-purpose flour	1 egg
1/2 cup granulated sugar	1/2 cup chopped macadamia nuts
1 teaspoon baking powder	1/2 cup miniature semisweet chocolate chips
1/2 teaspoon baking soda	

1 Heat oven to 375°F. Grease 18 regular-size muffin cups or place paper baking cup in each muffin cup. In small bowl, mix all streusel ingredients with fork until mixture resembles coarse crumbs. Set aside.

2 In large bowl, mix 2 cups flour, the granulated sugar, baking powder, baking soda and salt. Add sour cream, 1/2 cup butter, the milk, vanilla and egg; stir just until dry particles are moistened. Fold in macadamia nuts and chocolate chips. Fill muffin cups 3/4 full; sprinkle each with 1-1/2 teaspoons streusel.

3 Bake 18 to 20 minutes or until toothpick inserted in center comes out clean. Remove from muffin cups immediately. Serve warm.

HIGH ALTITUDE (3500-6500 FT): Increase flour in muffins by 2 tablespoons.

NUTRITION INFORMATION PER SERVING: Calories 220 • Total Fat 12g • Saturated Fat 7g • Cholesterol 35mg • Sodium 190mg • Total Carbohydrate 25g • Dietary Fiber 1g • Sugars 12g • Protein 3g. DIETARY EXCHANGES: 1 Starch • 1/2 Other Carbohydrate • 2-1/2 Fat • 1-1/2 Carb Choices.

cook's notes

Give a batch of these treats as

a gift and make another batch

for your Christmas or New

Year's brunch.

peanut butter-brownie cookies

toasted almond tea cake

PREP TIME: 15 Minutes ✳ READY IN: 35 Minutes ✳ SERVINGS: 8

1 can (8 oz.) Pillsbury® refrigerated crescent dinner rolls	1/2 cup powdered sugar
2 tablespoons packed brown sugar	1/2 teaspoon almond extract
1/3 cup coarsely chopped almonds, toasted	3 to 4 teaspoons milk
1/4 cup golden raisins	Sliced almonds, toasted

1 Heat oven to 375°F. Lightly grease cookie sheet. Unroll dough into 2 long rectangles. Overlap long sides to form 1 large rectangle. Firmly press perforations and edges to seal. Sprinkle with brown sugar, 1/3 cup almonds and raisins, to within 1/2 inch of edges. Starting with longest side, roll up jelly-roll fashion. Place, seam side down, on cookie sheet.

2 Cut through roll at 1-inch intervals to within 1/8 inch of bottom, being careful not to cut all the way through. Fold down alternating slices from left to right, twisting slightly to show filling and forming a long loaf.

3 Bake 15 to 20 minutes or until deep golden brown. Immediately remove from cookie sheet to cooling rack.

4 In small bowl, mix powdered sugar, almond extract and enough milk for desired glaze consistency. Drizzle glaze over warm cake. Sprinkle with additional sliced almonds.

NUTRITION INFORMATION PER SERVING: Calories 200 • Total Fat 9g • Saturated Fat 2g • Cholesterol 0mg • Sodium 220mg • Total Carbohydrate 27g • Dietary Fiber 1g • Sugars 16g • Protein 3g. DIETARY EXCHANGES: 1 Starch • 1 Fruit • 2 Other Carbohydrate • 1-1/2 Fat.

tannenbaum coffee cakes

PREP TIME: 50 Minutes ✻ READY IN: 3 Hours 35 Minutes ✻ SERVINGS: 2 Cakes (24 slices each)

COFFEE CAKES

5 to 6	cups all-purpose flour
1/2	cup sugar
2	teaspoons salt
2	packages active dry yeast
1-1/2	cups milk
1/2	cup butter or margarine
2	eggs

FILLING

4	tablespoons butter or margarine, melted
1	cup sugar
1/2	cup chopped nuts
1	tablespoon cinnamon

TOPPING

1	cup powdered sugar
2 to 3	tablespoons milk
	Candied cherries, quartered or halved

1. In large bowl, combine 2 cups of the flour, 1/2 cup sugar, salt and yeast; blend well. In medium saucepan, heat 1-1/2 cups milk and 1/2 cup butter until very warm (120 to 130°F). Add warm liquid and eggs to flour mixture; blend with electric mixer at low speed until moistened. Beat 3 minutes at medium speed. By hand, stir in 2 to 2-1/2 cups flour to form a stiff dough.

2. On floured surface, knead in remaining 1 to 1-1/2 cups flour until dough is smooth and elastic, 5 to 8 minutes. Place dough in greased bowl; turn to grease all sides. Cover loosely with plastic wrap and cloth towel. Let rise in warm place (80 to 85°F) until light and doubled in size, 1 to 1-1/4 hours.

3. Generously grease two 15x10-inch baking pans with sides. Punch down dough several times to remove all air bubbles. Divide dough in half. On lightly floured surface, roll 1 half into a triangle with two 12-inch sides and a 16-inch base. Brush with 1 tablespoon of the melted butter.

4. In small bowl, combine 2 tablespoons melted butter and all remaining filling ingredients; mix well. Sprinkle half of filling evenly over dough.

5. To shape tree, starting at top point of dough triangle, fold 12-inch sides to meet in center, pressing all seams to seal. Invert, seam side down, into greased pan. With scissors or sharp knife, make 10 slits about 1 inch apart along each long outside edge of tree, cutting to within 1/2 inch of center of dough. (See diagrams below.)

6. Starting at bottom of tree, twist each strip so cut side is up to show filling. Cover; let rise in warm place until light and doubled in size, 30 to 40 minutes. Repeat with remaining dough, melted butter and filling for second tree.

7. Heat oven to 350°F. Uncover dough; bake 20 minutes or until golden brown. Cool in pans for 5 minutes. Remove coffee cakes from pans; place on wire racks. Cool 30 minutes or until completely cooled.

8. In small bowl, blend powdered sugar and enough milk for desired drizzling consistency. Drizzle over coffee cakes. Garnish with candied cherries.

NUTRITION INFORMATION PER SERVING: Calories 125 • Total Fat 4g • Saturated Fat 1g • Cholesterol 10mg • Sodium 135mg • Total Carbohydrate 20g • Dietary Fiber 0g • Sugars 10g • Protein 2g. DIETARY EXCHANGES: 1/2 Starch • 1/2 Other Carbohydrate • 1 Fat • 1 Carb Choice.

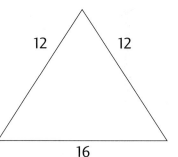

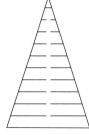

TANNENBAUM COFFEE CAKE DIAGRAMS

cook's notes

For easier shaping of each coffee cake, roll the dough on a lightly floured cookie sheet. When ready to place it in the baking pan, invert the pan over the tree on the cookie sheet. Then invert again and remove the cookie sheet.

cook's notes

Kick up the flavor of these nuts by adding 1/2 teaspoon red pepper sauce.

party almonds

PREP TIME: 10 Minutes ✳ READY IN: 30 Minutes ✳ SERVINGS: 8

1 tablespoon butter or margarine	1 tablespoon Worcestershire sauce
1 tablespoon olive oil	1/4 teaspoon red pepper sauce
1 teaspoon chili powder	2 cups whole almonds
1/2 teaspoon curry powder	1 to 2 teaspoons kosher (coarse) salt

1 Heat oven to 325°F. In 2-quart saucepan, melt butter over low heat; stir in oil, chili powder, curry powder, Worcestershire sauce and pepper sauce. Simmer gently 2 to 3 minutes to blend flavors.

2 Add almonds; toss to coat and spread in single layer in 15x10x1-inch pan. Bake 10 to 15 minutes, stirring once halfway through bake time.

3 Pour hot nuts into large bowl, toss with salt to coat. Spread in single layer in same pan; cool to room temperature. Store in airtight container.

NUTRITION INFORMATION PER SERVING: Calories 250 • Total Fat 21g • Saturated Fat 2.5g • Cholesterol 0mg • Sodium 330mg • Total Carbohydrate 8g • Dietary Fiber 4g • Sugars 2g • Protein 8g. DIETARY EXCHANGES: 1/2 Other Carbohydrate • 1 High-Fat Meat • 2-1/2 Fat • 1/2 Carb Choice.

kitchen tip

To test a candy thermometer for accuracy, insert it into a pan of water and bring the water to boiling. After it has boiled for 10 minutes, check the gauge. It should register 212°F at sea level (1 degree less for each 500 feet above sea level).

divinity

READY IN: 40 Minutes ✳ SERVINGS: 24 Candies

2 cups sugar	2 egg whites
1/4 teaspoon salt	1 teaspoon vanilla
1/2 cup water	1/2 to 1 cup chopped nuts
1/3 cup light corn syrup	

1 Line cookie sheet with waxed paper. In heavy medium saucepan, combine sugar, salt, water and corn syrup; cook and stir until sugar is dissolved. Bring to a full boil, stirring constantly. Cook uncovered without stirring until candy thermometer reaches hard-ball stage (250°F).

2 Meanwhile, in large bowl, beat egg whites until stiff peaks form. Pour syrup over egg whites in steady thin stream, beating continuously until mixture holds its shape and begins to lose its gloss. Stir in vanilla and nuts. Drop by teaspoonfuls onto waxed paper-lined cookie sheet. Store in tightly covered container.

HIGH ALTITUDE (3500-6500 FT): Cook until candy thermometer reaches 240°F.

NUTRITION INFORMATION PER SERVING: Calories 120 • Total Fat 3g • Saturated Fat 0g • Cholesterol 0mg • Sodium 35mg • Total Carbohydrate 21g • Dietary Fiber 0g • Sugars 19g • Protein 1g. DIETARY EXCHANGES: 1-1/2 Fruit • 1/2 Fat OR 1-1/2 Carbohydrate • 1/2 Fat.

silky chocolate-caramel sauce

READY IN: 10 Minutes ✳ SERVINGS: 16

3/4 cup packed brown sugar	10 tablespoons butter
2/3 cup whipping cream	4 oz. semisweet baking chocolate, chopped

1 In 2-quart saucepan, cook brown sugar, whipping cream and butter over medium heat 2 to 3 minutes, stirring constantly, until mixture comes to a full boil.

2 Add chocolate; cook about 2 minutes, stirring constantly, until chocolate is melted and sauce is smooth. Serve warm or cover and refrigerate until serving time.

NUTRITION INFORMATION PER SERVING: Calories 170 • Total Fat 12g • Saturated 8g • Cholesterol 30mg • Sodium 55mg • Total Carbohydrate 15g • Dietary Fiber 0g • Sugars 14g • Protein 1g.

party almonds

holiday bean
soup mix

holiday bean soup

cook's notes

Get a handle on the hustle and bustle of the Christmas season—invite friends over to create hostess gifts, such as this easy soup mix.

holiday bean soup mix

READY IN: 10 Minutes ✳ SERVINGS: 6 Jars of Mix

CONTAINERS
- 6 wide-mouth canning jars with lids (1 pint)
- 6 small resealable food storage plastic bags

SOUP MIX
- 1 package (16 oz.) dried black-eyed peas
- 1 package (16 oz.) dried yellow split peas
- 1 package (16 oz.) dried pinto beans
- 1 package (16 oz.) dried green split peas
- 1 package (16 oz.) dried navy beans
- 7 tablespoons chicken-flavor instant bouillon
- 3 tablespoons onion powder
- 1 tablespoon garlic powder
- 4 tablespoons dried thyme leaves
- 6 bay leaves

1 In each jar, layer 1/3 cup (about 4 heaping tablespoons) of each dried pea and dried bean in order given.

2 In medium bowl, combine bouillon, onion powder, garlic powder and thyme; mix well. Divide mixture evenly (about 2 tablespoons) into each plastic bag. Add 1 bay leaf to each; seal bags.

3 Seal jars with lids. Place seasoning bag on top of each jar. If desired, cover with decorative square of fabric and tie with ribbon. Include Holiday Bean Soup recipe (page 229).

NUTRITION INFORMATION PER SERVING: See Holiday Bean Soup recipe (page 229).

holiday bean soup

PREP TIME: 20 Minutes ✳ READY IN: 1 Hour 50 Minutes ✳ SERVINGS: 5

1   jar Holiday Bean Soup Mix (p. 228)
8   cups water

1 Pour dried pea/bean mixture into colander; rinse and sort. Place pea/bean mixture in large saucepan or Dutch oven.

2 Add water and contents of small plastic bag included with jar; stir to mix. Bring to a boil over medium-high heat. Reduce heat to medium-low; cover and cook 1-1/2 hours or until pinto beans are tender, stirring occasionally. If soup seems too thick, add 1/4 cup water. Split peas will be very soft and will thicken soup. Season to taste with salt and pepper. Discard bay leaf.

   HIGH ALTITUDE (3500-6500 FT): Cook, covered, for about 2 hours.

NUTRITION INFORMATION PER SERVING: Calories 195 • Total Fat 1g • Saturated Fat 0g • Cholesterol 0mg • Sodium 900mg • Total Carbohydrate 44g • Dietary Fiber 14g • Sugars 3g • Protein 16g. DIETARY EXCHANGES: 2 Starch • 1-1/2 Very Lean Meat • 2 Carb Choices.

cook's notes

Include a copy of this recipe when giving the Holiday Bean Soup Mix (p. 228) as a gift.

cherry almond bark

PREP TIME: 20 Minutes ✳ READY IN: 50 Minutes ✳ SERVINGS: 10 Dozen

1   jar (10 oz.) maraschino cherries, drained, chopped
1   package (24 oz.) vanilla-flavored candy coating (almond bark), coarsely chopped
1   cup chopped blanched almonds
1/2 teaspoon almond extract

1 Line 2 large cookie sheets with waxed paper. Spread chopped cherries on several layers of paper towels to drain completely.

2 Melt candy coating in heavy large saucepan over very low heat, stirring constantly. Stir in cherries, almonds and almond extract. Spread mixture thinly on waxed paper-lined cookie sheets. Let stand until set, about 30 minutes.

3 Break almond bark candy into pieces. Store in tightly covered container in refrigerator or cool, dry place.

NUTRITION INFORMATION PER SERVING: Calories 35 • Total Fat 2g • Saturated Fat 1g • Cholesterol 0mg • Sodium 5mg • Total Carbohydrate 4g • Dietary Fiber 0g • Sugars 4g • Protein 1g. DIETARY EXCHANGES: 1/2 Fruit • 1/2 Fat OR 1/2 Carbohydrate • 1/2 Fat.

cook's notes

Have fun experimenting with different fruits and nuts in this yummy recipe.

holiday snack mix

READY IN: 10 Minutes ✳ SERVINGS: 16

2   cups salted peanuts
1/2 cup candy-coated chocolate candies
1/2 cup whole almonds
1/2 cup raisins
1/2 cup chopped dates
2   tablespoons sunflower nuts

1 In large bowl or food-storage plastic bag, mix all ingredients. Store snack mix in airtight container.

NUTRITION INFORMATION PER SERVING: Calories 220 • Total Fat 14g • Saturated Fat 2.5g • Cholesterol 0mg • Sodium 60mg • Total Carbohydrate 16g • Dietary Fiber 3g • Sugars 11g • Protein 7g. DIETARY EXCHANGES: 1 Other Carbohydrate • 1 High-Fat Meat • 1 Fat • 1 Carb Choice.

Festive Cookies & Confections

For filling up holiday gift tins and treat trays during the holiday season, these Christmasy goodies just can't be beat. Don't forget to leave a plate for Santa, too!

p. 257

p. 233

p. 262

p. 261

p. 253

chocolate buttersweets p. 246

chocolate star gingersnaps

chocolate star gingersnaps

READY IN: 1 Hour 10 Minutes ❋ SERVINGS: 48 Cookies

1 cup packed brown sugar	1 teaspoon ground ginger
3/4 cup shortening	1 teaspoon ground cinnamon
1/4 cup molasses	1/4 teaspoon ground cloves
1 egg	1/4 cup granulated sugar
2-3/4 cups all-purpose flour	48 chocolate star candies
1 teaspoon baking soda	

1 Heat oven to 375°F. In large bowl, beat brown sugar, shortening and molasses with electric mixer on medium speed until smooth, scraping bowl occasionally. Beat in egg until well blended. On low speed, beat in flour, baking soda, ginger, cinnamon and cloves until well combined, scraping bowl occasionally.

2 Shape dough into 1-inch balls; roll in granulated sugar and place 2 inches apart on ungreased cookie sheets.

3 Bake 7 to 9 minutes or until tops are cracked and edges are set. Immediately press 1 candy in center of each cookie. Cool 1 minute; remove from cookie sheets.

HIGH ALTITUDE (3500-6500 FT): Decrease brown sugar to 3/4 cup.

NUTRITION INFORMATION PER SERVING: Calories 100 • Total Fat 4.5g • Saturated Fat 1.5g • Cholesterol 5mg • Sodium 35mg • Total Carbohydrate 15g • Dietary Fiber 0g • Sugars 9g • Protein 1g. DIETARY EXCHANGES: 1 Other Carbohydrate • 1 Fat • 1 Carb Choice.

kitchen tip

When using sticky liquids such as molasses, honey or corn syrup, spray the measuring cup with nonstick cooking spray before adding the liquid. This will make it easier to pour out the liquid and clean the cup.

pecan blondies with browned butter frosting

PREP TIME: 30 Minutes ❋ READY IN: 1 Hour 55 Minutes ❋ SERVINGS: 36 Bars

BARS

- 1 cup sugar
- 1/2 cup firmly packed brown sugar
- 1/2 cup butter, softened
- 1 teaspoon vanilla
- 2 eggs
- 1-1/2 cups all-purpose flour
- 1 teaspoon baking powder
- 1/2 teaspoon salt
- 1/2 cup chopped pecans

FROSTING

- 2 tablespoons butter (do not use margarine)
- 2 cups powdered sugar
- 1/4 teaspoon vanilla
- 2 to 4 tablespoons milk

GARNISH

- 36 pecan halves, if desired

1 Heat oven to 350°F. Grease 13x9-inch pan. In large bowl, combine sugar, brown sugar and 1/2 cup butter; beat until light and fluffy. Add 1 teaspoon vanilla and eggs; blend well. Add flour, baking powder and salt; mix well. Stir in 1/2 cup pecans. Spread in bottom of greased pan.

2 Bake at 350°F for 23 to 33 minutes or until toothpick inserted in center comes out clean. Cool 1 hour or until completely cooled.

3 Heat 2 tablespoons butter in medium saucepan over medium heat until light golden brown. Remove from heat. Stir in powdered sugar, 1/4 teaspoon vanilla and enough milk for desired spreading consistency; blend until smooth. Spread over cooled bars. Arrange pecan halves over frosting. Cut into bars.

HIGH ALTITUDE (3500-6500 FT): Increase flour to 1-3/4 cups; decrease granulated sugar to 1/2 cup. Bake as directed above.

NUTRITION INFORMATION PER SERVING: Calories 130 • Total Fat 5g • Saturated Fat 2g • Cholesterol 20mg • Sodium 80mg • Total Carbohydrate 20 g • Dietary Fiber 0g • Sugars 15g • Protein 1g. DIETARY EXCHANGES: 1-1/2 Fruit • 1 Fat OR 1-1/2 Carbohydrate • 1 Fat.

cook's notes

If you like, omit the frosting and pecan halves. When the bars are cool, sprinkle on some powdered sugar.

DICK BOULANGER
Williston, Vermont
Bake-Off® Contest 42, 2006
Prize Winner

sugar cookie-chocolate crunch fudge

PREP TIME: 15 Minutes ✳ READY IN: 2 Hours 15 Minutes ✳ SERVINGS: 48 Pieces

2 tablespoons light corn syrup	2 bags (12 oz. each) Hershey®'s semisweet chocolate chips
2 tablespoons butter or margarine	
1/4 teaspoon salt	5 teaspoons vanilla
1 can (14 oz.) sweetened condensed milk (not evaporated)	6 Nature Valley® pecan crunch crunchy granola bars (3 pouches from 8.9-oz. box), coarsely crushed (heaping 1 cup)
1 roll (16.5 oz.) Pillsbury® refrigerated sugar cookies, cut into small chunks	Fresh mint sprigs, if desired

1 In 3-quart heavy saucepan or deep 10-inch nonstick skillet, cook corn syrup, butter, salt and condensed milk over medium heat 2 to 3 minutes, stirring constantly with wooden spoon, until well blended. Reduce heat to medium-low; stir in cookie dough chunks. Cook 3 to 5 minutes, stirring constantly, until mixture is smooth and candy thermometer reads 160°F. Remove from heat.

2 Stir in chocolate chips and vanilla until chips are melted and mixture is smooth. Add crushed granola bars; stir until well blended. Cook over low heat 1 to 2 minutes, stirring constantly, until mixture is shiny. Spread in ungreased 12x8-inch or 13x9-inch pan. Refrigerate uncovered at least 2 hours or until firm.

3 Cut into 8 rows by 6 rows. Serve in decorative candy cups or mini paper baking cups on platter; garnish platter with mint sprigs.

NUTRITION INFORMATION PER SERVING: Calories 170 • Total Fat 8g • Saturated 4g • Cholesterol 5mg • Sodium 65mg • Total Carbohydrate 22g • Dietary Fiber 1g • Sugars 17g • Protein 2g.

cook's notes

These merry, gift-shaped treats

are perfect for a Christmas

cookie exchange.

holiday cookie packages

PREP TIME: 25 Minutes ✳ READY IN: 1 Hour 40 Minutes ✳ SERVINGS: 64 Cookies

COOKIES	FROSTING
1 cup butter, softened	2 cups powdered sugar
1/2 cup packed brown sugar	1/3 cup butter, softened
1/4 teaspoon ground cinnamon	1/2 teaspoon vanilla
1 teaspoon vanilla	1 to 2 tablespoons half-and-half or milk
2-1/4 cups all-purpose flour	Food color

1 Line 8-inch square pan with plastic wrap. In large bowl with electric mixer, beat all cookie ingredients except flour at medium speed, scraping bowl occasionally, until creamy. Reduce speed to low; beat in flour, scraping bowl occasionally, until mixture forms a dough. Press dough firmly and evenly in pan. Refrigerate 30 minutes.

2 Heat oven to 350°F. Using edges of plastic wrap, lift dough from pan. With sharp knife, cut into 8 rows in each direction to make 64 squares; carefully place squares 1 inch apart on ungreased cookie sheets.

3 Bake 13 to 17 minutes or until edges are lightly browned. Cool 5 minutes; remove from cookie sheets. Cool completely, about 10 minutes.

4 In medium bowl, mix all frosting ingredients except food color until smooth, adding enough half-and-half for desired spreading consistency. In small bowl, mix 1/3 cup of the frosting and enough food color until desired color and well blended; place in small resealable food storage plastic bag and partially seal.

5 Spread uncolored frosting over cooled cookies. Cut small hole in bottom corner of bag of colored frosting. Squeeze bag to pipe frosting onto each cookie to resemble bows.

NUTRITION INFORMATION PER SERVING: Calories 75 • Total Fat 4g • Saturated Fat 2g • Cholesterol 10mg • Sodium 25mg • Total Carbohydrate 9g • Dietary Fiber 0g • Sugars 5g • Protein 1g. DIETARY EXCHANGES: 1/2 Other Carbohydrate • 1 Fat • 1/2 Carb Choice.

sugar cookie-chocolate crunch fudge

chocolate-dipped
peanut butter fingers

chocolate-dipped peanut butter fingers

PREP TIME: 45 Minutes ✳ READY IN: 1 Hour ✳ SERVINGS: 32 Cookies

1 roll (16.5 oz.) Pillsbury® refrigerated peanut butter cookies

1/3 cup all-purpose flour

8 oz. sweet baking chocolate, broken into squares

1 tablespoon vegetable oil

Finely chopped peanuts and/or multicolored candy sprinkles

1 Heat oven to 375°F. In large bowl, break up cookie dough. Stir or knead in flour until well blended.

2 Divide dough into 32 equal pieces. Shape each into 2-1/2-inch-long log; place 2 inches apart on ungreased cookie sheets. With knife, make 3 shallow (about 1/4-inch-deep) cuts lengthwise in each log.

3 Bake 6 to 8 minutes or until golden brown. Immediately remove from cookie sheets; place on wire racks. Cool completely, about 15 minutes.

4 In microwavable measuring cup, microwave chocolate and oil on High 30 to 60 seconds, stirring every 15 seconds, until smooth. Dip 1/3 of each cookie into chocolate, allowing excess to drip off. Dip into peanuts or sprinkles; return to wire racks. Let stand until chocolate is set before storing.

NUTRITION INFORMATION PER SERVING: Calories 130 • Total Fat 7g • Saturated Fat 2.5g • Cholesterol 0mg • Sodium 80mg • Total Carbohydrate 15g • Dietary Fiber 0g • Sugars 9g • Protein 2g. DIETARY EXCHANGES: 1 Other Carbohydrate • 1-1/2 Fat.

cook's notes

Semisweet chocolate or milk chocolate would work equally well for dipping these cookies.

white chocolate-key lime calypso bars

PREP TIME: 20 Minutes ✳ READY IN: 3 Hours 5 Minutes ✳ SERVINGS: 36 Bars

1 roll (16.5 oz.) Pillsbury® refrigerated sugar cookies

1 cup chopped pistachio nuts

1 cup coconut

1-1/2 cups white vanilla baking chips (9 oz.)

1 can (14 oz.) sweetened condensed milk (not evaporated)

1/2 cup Key lime juice, fresh lime juice or frozen (thawed) limeade concentrate

3 egg yolks

1 teaspoon vegetable oil

DIDI FRAIOLI
Huntington, New York
Bake-Off® Contest 40, 2002

1 Heat oven to 350°F. Grease 13x9-inch pan with shortening or cooking spray. In large bowl, break up cookie dough. Stir or knead in nuts and coconut until well blended. Press dough mixture evenly in bottom of pan to form crust. Sprinkle 1 cup of the vanilla baking chips over dough; press lightly into dough.

2 Bake 14 to 16 minutes or until light golden brown. Meanwhile, in medium bowl, beat condensed milk, lime juice and egg yolks with spoon until well blended. Pour milk mixture evenly over crust. Bake 20 to 25 minutes longer or until filling is set.

3 In small microwavable bowl, microwave remaining 1/2 cup vanilla baking chips and the oil uncovered on High 45 seconds. Stir until smooth; if necessary, microwave 15 seconds longer. Drizzle over warm bars. Cool at room temperature 1 hour. Refrigerate until chilled, about 1 hour. For bars, cut into 6 rows by 6 rows. Cover and refrigerate any remaining bars.

HIGH ALTITUDE (3500-6500 FT): Bake crust 16 to 18 minutes.

NUTRITION INFORMATION PER SERVING: Calories 170 • Total Fat 8g • Saturated Fat 3.5g • Cholesterol 25mg • Sodium 70mg • Total Carbohydrate 20g • Dietary Fiber 0g. DIETARY EXCHANGES: 1/2 Starch • 1 Other Carbohydrate • 1-1/2 Fat • 1 Carb Choice.

cook's notes

Keep eggs in the refrigerator until you need them. Eggs will separate best when cold.

special touch

Any leftover vanilla coating

can be tinted pale pink using

a small amount of red food

color; drizzle the pink coating

over the covered cherries.

double chocolate-covered cherries

PREP TIME: 30 Minutes ✳ READY IN: 2 Hours 30 Minutes ✳ SERVINGS: 24 Cherries

CHERRIES
1 jar (10 oz.) maraschino cherries with stems (about 24)

CHOCOLATE FONDANT
3 tablespoons butter, softened

2 tablespoons light corn syrup

1 oz. unsweetened chocolate, melted

2 teaspoons half-and-half or milk

2 cups powdered sugar

COATING
1 bag (12 oz.) white vanilla baking chips

1 tablespoon shortening

1 Place cherries on several paper towels; gently press out excess moisture. Let stand at least 1 hour to drain.

2 Meanwhile, in medium bowl, beat butter, corn syrup, chocolate and half-and-half with electric mixer on medium speed until smooth. Stir in powdered sugar. Mixture will seem dry and crumbly. Turn fondant out onto work surface; knead until smooth. Divide fondant into 24 pieces. Shape each piece into ball. Flatten each ball slightly; mold around drained cherry, covering cherry completely. Refrigerate at least 1 hour or until very cold and firm.

3 Line large cookie sheet with waxed paper. In 1-quart saucepan over low heat, melt vanilla chips and shortening, stirring constantly until smooth. Place over pan of hot water to maintain dipping consistency. Holding stems, dip fondant-covered cherries into melted chips; draw bottoms of cherries lightly over edge of pan to remove excess coating. Place on paper-lined cookie sheet to set. Place cherries in small paper cups, if desired. Store in tightly covered container. Centers will soften slightly in 10 to 14 days.

NUTRITION INFORMATION PER SERVING: Calories 150 • Total Fat 7g • Saturated Fat 4g • Cholesterol 5mg • Sodium 30mg • Total Carbohydrate 21g • Dietary Fiber 0g • Sugars 20g • Protein 1g. DIETARY EXCHANGES: 1-1/2 Fruit • 1-1/2 Other Carbohydrate • 1-1/2 Fat.

cherry truffle bars

PREP TIME: 15 Minutes ✳ READY IN: 1 Hour 40 Minutes ✳ SERVINGS: 48 Bars

CRUST
1 package (16.5 oz.) Pillsbury® refrigerated sugar cookies

FILLING
1/3 cup semisweet chocolate chips

1/4 cup margarine or butter

1/4 cup unsweetened cocoa

3 tablespoons light corn syrup

1 tablespoon milk

2 cups powdered sugar

1 jar (10 oz.) maraschino cherries, drained, chopped (about 30 cherries)

TOPPING
1 cup white vanilla chips

2 tablespoons shortening

1 Heat oven to 350°F. Remove cookie dough from wrapper. With floured fingers, press dough evenly in bottom of ungreased 13x9-inch pan to form crust.

2 Bake at 350°F for 12 to 16 minutes or until light golden brown. Cool 45 minutes or until completely cooled.

3 In medium microwavable bowl, combine chocolate chips and margarine. Microwave on High for 1 to 2 minutes or until melted and smooth, stirring every 30 seconds. Add cocoa, corn syrup and milk; blend well. Add powdered sugar; mix until smooth. Press filling over cooled crust. Top with cherries; gently press into filling.

4 In small microwavable bowl, combine vanilla chips and shortening. Microwave on High for 1 to 2 minutes or until melted and smooth, stirring every 30 seconds. Spoon and spread over filling. Refrigerate 20 minutes or until set. Cut into bars.

NUTRITION INFORMATION PER SERVING: Calories 120 • Total Fat 5g • Saturated Fat 2g • Cholesterol 0mg • Sodium 55mg • Total Carbohydrate 18g • Dietary Fiber 0g • Sugars 15g • Protein 1g. DIETARY EXCHANGES: 1 Fruit • 1 Fat OR 1 Carbohydrate • 1 Fat • 1 Carb Choice.

cook's notes

These bars call for powdered

sugar, while some recipes list

"confectioners' sugar." There is

no difference between the two.

so-easy sugar cookies

PREP TIME: 15 Minutes ✳ READY IN: 35 Minutes ✳ SERVINGS: 48 Cookies

3/4 cup sugar

1/3 cup margarine or butter, softened, or shortening

1/3 cup oil

1 tablespoon milk

1 to 2 teaspoons almond extract

1 egg

1-1/2 cups all-purpose flour

1-1/2 teaspoons baking powder

1/4 teaspoon salt

1 tablespoon sugar or colored sugar

KATHRYN BLACKBURN
National Park, New Jersey
Bake-Off® Contest 30, 1982

1 Heat oven to 375°F. In large bowl, beat 3/4 cup sugar, margarine, oil, milk, almond extract and egg until light and fluffy. Stir in flour, baking powder and salt; blend well. Spread evenly in ungreased 15x10x1-inch baking pan; sprinkle with 1 tablespoon sugar. Bake at 375°F for 10 to 12 minutes or until light golden brown. Cool 5 minutes. Cut into bars.

HIGH ALTITUDE (3500-6500 FT): Decrease baking powder to 1 teaspoon.

NUTRITION INFORMATION PER SERVING: Calories 50 • Total Fat 3g • Sodium 40mg • Total Carbohydrate 6g • Protein 1g. DIETARY EXCHANGES: 1/2 Other Carbohydrate • 1/2 Fat • 1/2 Carb Choice.

peanut brittle bars

PREP TIME: 10 Minutes ✳ READY IN: 1 Hour 45 Minutes ✳ SERVINGS: 48 Bars

CRUST

2	cups all-purpose flour
1	cup packed brown sugar
1	teaspoon baking soda
1/4	teaspoon salt
1	cup butter or margarine

TOPPING

2	cups salted peanuts
1	cup milk chocolate chips
1	jar (12.5 oz.) caramel topping
3	tablespoons all-purpose flour

1 Heat oven to 350°F. Grease 15x10x1-inch pan with shortening. In large bowl, mix all crust ingredients except butter. With pastry blender or fork, cut in butter until crumbly. Press mixture evenly in bottom of pan. Bake 8 to 14 minutes or until golden brown.

2 Remove partially baked crust from oven. Sprinkle peanuts and chocolate chips over warm crust. In small bowl, mix caramel topping and 3 tablespoons flour until well blended. Drizzle evenly over chocolate chips and peanuts.

3 Return to oven; bake 12 to 18 minutes longer or until topping is set and golden brown. Cool completely, about 1 hour. Cut into bars.

NUTRITION INFORMATION PER SERVING: Calories 150 • Total Fat 8g • Saturated 3g • Cholesterol 10mg • Sodium 120mg • Total Carbohydrate 17g • Dietary Fiber 1g • Sugars 10g • Protein 3g.

hawaiian cookie tarts

PREP TIME: 35 Minutes ✳ READY IN: 1 Hour 45 Minutes ✳ SERVINGS: 36 Cookies

ELIZABETH ZEMELKO
Knox, Indiana
Bake-Off® Contest 34, 1990

COOKIES

1-3/4	cups all-purpose flour
1/2	cup powdered sugar
2	tablespoons cornstarch
1	cup butter or margarine, softened
1	teaspoon vanilla

FILLING

1	cup pineapple preserves
1/2	cup granulated sugar
1	egg
1-1/2	cups coconut
	Additional powdered sugar (about 2 tablespoons)

1. Heat oven to 350°F. In large bowl, stir together flour, 1/2 cup powdered sugar and the cornstarch. With spoon, beat in butter and vanilla until soft dough forms.

2. Shape dough into 1-inch balls. Place 1 ball in each of 36 ungreased mini muffin cups; press ball in bottom and up side of each muffin cup. Spoon 1 teaspoon pineapple preserves into each dough-lined cup.

3. In small bowl, beat granulated sugar and egg with fork until well blended. Stir in coconut until well coated with egg mixture. Spoon 1 teaspoon coconut mixture over preserves in each cup.

4. Bake 23 to 33 minutes or until cookie crusts are very light golden brown. Cool in pans on cooling racks 20 minutes.

5. To release cookies from cups, hold muffin pan upside down at an angle over cooling rack. With handle of table knife, firmly tap bottom of each cup until cookie releases. Cool completely, about 15 minutes. Just before serving, sprinkle with additional powdered sugar. Store in refrigerator.

NUTRITION INFORMATION PER SERVING: Calories 140 • Total Fat 7g • Saturated Fat 4.5g • Cholesterol 20mg • Sodium 50mg • Total Carbohydrate 18g • Dietary Fiber 0g. DIETARY EXCHANGES: 1 Other Carbohydrate • 1-1/2 Fat • 1 Carb Choice.

cook's notes

For Chocolate-Pistachio Bars,

press the dough mixture into an

ungreased 11 x 17-inch pan.

The bars are a little thicker, so

bake 14 to 16 minutes or until

golden brown.

JEAN OLSON
Wallingford, Iowa
Bake-Off® Contest 34, 1990
Prize Winner

kitchen tip

Candy coating—sometimes

called confectionery coating—

is available in many different

forms. At your store, you may

find large individual blocks,

packages of flat disks or chips

and boxes of individually

wrapped 1-ounce squares.

chocolate-pistachio wedges

PREP TIME: 20 Minutes ✳ READY IN: 1 Hour 5 Minutes ✳ SERVINGS: 32 Wedges

1 roll (16.5 oz.) Pillsbury® refrigerated chocolate chip cookies
1 box (3.4 oz.) pistachio instant pudding and pie filling mix

2 tablespoons milk
3/4 cup chopped shelled pistachios
1/2 cup white vanilla chips
2 teaspoons vegetable oil

1 Heat oven to 350°F. In large bowl, break up cookie dough. Stir in pudding mix and milk until well blended. Stir or knead in 1/2 cup of the pistachios. Divide dough into 4 pieces. On ungreased large cookie sheet, press each piece into 6-inch round.

2 Bake 11 to 16 minutes or until edges are golden brown. Immediately cut each round into 8 wedges. Remove from cookie sheet; place on wire racks. Cool completely, about 30 minutes.

3 In 1-quart saucepan, heat vanilla chips and oil over low heat about 2 minutes, stirring constantly, until chips are melted and smooth. Drizzle over cooled wedges. Immediately sprinkle with remaining 1/4 cup pistachios; press in lightly.

HIGH ALTITUDE (3500-6500 FT): Bake at 350°F 12 to 17 minutes. Continue as directed above.

NUTRITION INFORMATION PER SERVING: Calories 130 • Total Fat 6g • Saturated Fat 2g • Cholesterol 0mg • Sodium 120mg • Total Carbohydrate 17g • Dietary Fiber 0g • Sugars 10g • Protein 2g. DIETARY EXCHANGES: 1 Starch • 1 Fat • 1 Carb Choice.

caramel-filled chocolate cookies

PREP TIME: 1 Hour ✳ READY IN: 1 Hour 30 Minutes ✳ SERVINGS: 48 Cookies

2-1/2 cups all-purpose flour
3/4 cup unsweetened baking cocoa
1 teaspoon baking soda
1 cup granulated sugar
1 cup packed brown sugar
1 cup butter or margarine, softened
2 teaspoons vanilla

2 eggs
1 cup chopped pecans
1 tablespoon granulated sugar
48 round milk chocolate-covered caramels (from 12-oz. bag), unwrapped
4 oz. vanilla-flavored candy coating (almond bark), if desired

1 In small bowl, stir together flour, cocoa and baking soda; set aside. In large bowl, beat 1 cup granulated sugar, the brown sugar and butter with electric mixer on medium speed, scraping bowl occasionally, until light and fluffy. Beat in vanilla and eggs. On low speed, beat in flour mixture until well blended. Stir in 1/2 cup of the pecans. If necessary, cover with plastic wrap and refrigerate 30 minutes for easier handling.

2 Heat oven to 375°F. In small bowl, mix remaining 1/2 cup pecans and 1 tablespoon sugar. With floured hands, shape about 1 tablespoon dough around each caramel, covering completely. Press 1 side of each ball into pecan mixture. Place nut side up 2 inches apart on ungreased cookie sheets.

3 Bake 7 to 10 minutes or until set and slightly cracked. Cool 2 minutes; remove from cookie sheets to cooling rack. Cool completely, about 15 minutes.

4 In 1-quart saucepan, melt candy coating over low heat, stirring constantly until smooth. Drizzle over cookies.

HIGH ALTITUDE (3500-6500 FT): Increase all-purpose flour to 2-3/4 cups.

NUTRITION INFORMATION PER SERVING: Calories 150 • Total Fat 7g • Saturated Fat 3.5g • Cholesterol 20mg • Sodium 70mg • Total Carbohydrate 19g • Dietary Fiber 0g. DIETARY EXCHANGES: 1-1/2 Other Carbohydrate • 1-1/2 Fat • 1 Carb Choice.

chocolate-pistachio wedges

frosted reindeer cookies

frosted reindeer cookies

PREP TIME: 40 Minutes ✳ READY IN: 55 Minutes ✳ SERVINGS: 32 Cookies

1 roll (16.5 oz.) Pillsbury® refrigerated sugar cookies	64 small pretzel twists
1/4 cup all-purpose flour	64 semisweet chocolate chips (about 1/4 cup)
1 cup vanilla ready-to-spread frosting (from 1-lb. container)	16 gumdrops, cut in half

1 Heat oven to 350°F. In large bowl, break up cookie dough; work flour into dough until well blended. Shape roll of cookie dough into triangle-shaped log. (If dough is too soft to cut, place in freezer 30 minutes.)

2 With thin sharp knife, cut dough into 32 (1/4-inch-thick) triangular slices; place 2 inches apart on ungreased cookie sheet.

3 Bake 7 to 11 minutes or until set. Cool 1 minute; remove from cookie sheet to cooling rack. Cool completely, about 15 minutes.

4 Frost cookies with frosting. Place 2 pretzel twists on each triangle near corners for antlers. Lightly press 2 chocolate chips into each cookie for eyes and 1 halved gumdrop for nose. Store between sheets of waxed paper in tightly covered container.

NUTRITION INFORMATION PER SERVING: Calories 130 • Total Fat 5g • Saturated Fat 1.5g • Cholesterol 5mg • Sodium 95mg • Total Carbohydrate 19g • Dietary Fiber 0g • Sugars 11g • Protein 0g. DIETARY EXCHANGES: 1-1/2 Other Carbohydrate • 1 Fat • 1 Carb Choice.

cook's notes

For deer with a whole different taste, replace the sugar cookie dough with gingerbread dough.

lemon-glazed cashew shortbread

PREP TIME: 30 Minutes ✳ READY IN: 1 Hour 30 Minutes ✳ SERVINGS: 48 Cookies

COOKIES

- 3/4 cup powdered sugar
- 1-1/4 cups butter, softened
- 3 cups all-purpose flour
- 1/2 cup finely chopped cashews
- 1 teaspoon ginger
- 1/2 cup coarsely chopped cashews

GLAZE

- 1 cup powdered sugar
- 1 teaspoon grated lemon peel
- 4 to 6 teaspoons lemon juice

1 Heat oven to 325°F. In large bowl, combine 3/4 cup powdered sugar and butter; beat until light and fluffy. Add flour, 1/2 cup finely chopped cashews and ginger; mix well. Press dough evenly in ungreased 15x10x1-inch baking pan. Sprinkle with coarsely chopped cashews; press lightly into dough.

2 Bake at 325°F for 20 to 30 minutes or until edges are light golden brown. Place pan on wire rack. Immediately cut into 2-1/2-inch squares. Cut each square diagonally in half. Cool in pan 30 minutes or until completely cooled.

3 In small bowl, combine all glaze ingredients, adding enough lemon juice for desired drizzling consistency. Remove cooled cookies from pan; place on waxed paper. Drizzle with glaze.

HIGH ALTITUDE (3500-6500 FT): Decrease flour to 2-3/4 cups. Bake as directed above.

NUTRITION INFORMATION PER SERVING: Calories 100 • Total Fat 6g • Saturated Fat 3g • Cholesterol 15mg • Sodium 65mg • Total Carbohydrate 11g • Dietary Fiber 0g • Sugars 5g • Protein 1g. DIETARY EXCHANGES: 1/2 Fruit • 1-1/2 Fat OR 1/2 Carbohydrate • 1-1/2 Fat.

cook's notes

When the hustle and bustle of the holidays has cut down your kitchen time, try this recipe. It gives you 4 dozen cookies from just one pan.

VANCE FLETCHER
Indianapolis, Indiana
Bake-Off® Contest 16, 1964

chocolate buttersweets

PREP TIME: 1 Hour 35 Minutes ✳ READY IN: 2 Hours 15 Minutes ✳ SERVINGS: About 36 Cookies

COOKIES
1/2 cup butter or margarine, softened
1/2 cup powdered sugar
1/4 teaspoon salt
1 teaspoon vanilla
1 to 1-1/2 cups all-purpose flour

FILLING
1 package (3 oz.) cream cheese, softened
1 cup powdered sugar

2 tablespoons all-purpose flour
1 teaspoon vanilla
1/2 cup chopped walnuts
1/2 cup flaked coconut

FROSTING
1/2 cup semisweet chocolate chips
2 tablespoons butter or margarine
2 tablespoons water
1/2 cup powdered sugar

1 Heat oven to 350°F. In large bowl, beat 1/2 cup butter, 1/2 cup powdered sugar, the salt and 1 teaspoon vanilla with electric mixer on medium speed, scraping bowl occasionally, until blended. Gradually beat in 1 to 1-1/4 cups flour until soft dough forms.

2 Shape teaspoonfuls of dough into balls. On ungreased cookie sheets, place balls 2 inches apart. With thumb or handle of wooden spoon, make indentation in center of each cookie.

3 Bake 12 to 15 minutes or until edges are lightly browned. Meanwhile, in small bowl, beat cream cheese, 1 cup powdered sugar, 2 tablespoons flour and 1 teaspoon vanilla on medium speed until well blended. Stir in walnuts and coconut.

4 Immediately remove cookies from cookie sheets to cooling racks. Spoon about 1/2 teaspoon filling into each cookie. Cool completely, about 30 minutes.

5 In 1-quart saucepan, heat chocolate chips, 2 tablespoons butter and the water over low heat, stirring occasionally, until chips are melted. Remove from heat. With spoon, beat in 1/2 cup powdered sugar until smooth. Frost cooled cookies. Store covered in refrigerator.

HIGH ALTITUDE (3500-6500 FT): Bake 9 to 12 minutes.

NUTRITION INFORMATION PER SERVING: Calories 110 • Total Fat 6g • Saturated Fat 3.5g • Cholesterol 10mg • Sodium 50mg • Total Carbohydrate 12g • Dietary Fiber 0g • Sugars 8g • Protein 0g. DIETARY EXCHANGES: 1 Other Carbohydrate • 1 Fat • 1 Carb Choice.

candy and popcorn balls

PREP TIME: 50 Minutes ✳ SERVINGS: 10 Popcorn Balls

10 cups popped popcorn
1-1/2 cups small gumdrops
1/2 cup sugar
1/2 cup light corn syrup
2 tablespoons margarine or butter
1/4 teaspoon salt

1 Line cookie sheet with waxed paper. In large bowl, combine popcorn and gumdrops. In medium saucepan, combine sugar, corn syrup, margarine and salt; mix well. Bring to a boil. Cook over medium-high heat for 2 minutes, stirring constantly. Remove from heat. Add to popcorn mixture; mix well.

2 With hands dipped in cold water, shape popcorn mixture into 2-1/2-inch balls. Place on waxed paper-lined cookie sheets. Cool 15 minutes. Wrap individually in plastic wrap.

NUTRITION INFORMATION PER SERVING: Calories 180 • Total Fat 2g • Saturated Fat 1g • Cholesterol 2mg • Sodium 95mg • Total Carbohydrate 41g • Dietary Fiber 0g • Sugars 29g • Protein 0g. DIETARY EXCHANGES: 2-1/2 Fruit • 1/2 Fat OR 2-1/2 Carbohydrate • 1/2 Fat.

cook's notes

Use red and green gumdrops for a Christmasy look…and gumdrops of different colors to suit different holidays.

chocolate buttersweets

nutmeg cookie logs

nutmeg cookie logs

PREP TIME: 50 Minutes ✳ READY IN: 1 Hour 35 Minutes ✳ SERVINGS: 60 Cookies

Mrs. Robert J. Woods
South Charleston, West Virginia
Bake-Off® Contest 8, 1956

COOKIES

3/4	cup granulated sugar
1	cup butter or margarine, softened
2	teaspoons vanilla
2	teaspoons rum extract
1	egg
3	cups all-purpose flour
1	teaspoon ground nutmeg

FROSTING

2	cups powdered sugar
3	tablespoons butter or margarine, softened
3/4	teaspoon rum extract
1/4	teaspoon vanilla
2	to 3 tablespoons half-and-half or milk
	Additional ground nutmeg

1. In large bowl, beat granulated sugar, 1 cup butter, 2 teaspoons vanilla, 2 teaspoons rum extract and egg with electric mixer on medium speed until light and fluffy. With spoon, stir in flour and 1 teaspoon nutmeg. Cover with plastic wrap; refrigerate about 45 minutes for easier handling.

2. Heat oven to 350°F. Divide dough into 12 pieces. On floured surface, shape each piece of dough into long rope, 1/2 inch in diameter and about 15 inches long. Cut into 3-inch logs. On ungreased cookie sheets, place logs 1 inch apart.

3. Bake 12 to 15 minutes or until edges are light golden brown. Immediately remove from cookie sheets to cooling racks. Cool completely, about 20 minutes.

4. In small bowl, mix all frosting ingredients except nutmeg, adding enough half-and-half for desired spreading consistency. Spread on tops and sides of cookies. If desired, mark frosting with tines of fork to resemble bark. Sprinkle lightly with additional nutmeg. Let stand until frosting is set before storing.

NUTRITION INFORMATION PER SERVING: Calories 80 • Total Fat 4g • Saturated Fat 2.5g • Cholesterol 15mg • Sodium 25mg • Total Carbohydrate 11g • Dietary Fiber 0g • Sugars 6g • Protein 0g. DIETARY EXCHANGES: 1/2 Other Carbohydrate • 1 Fat • 1 Carb Choice.

microwave peanut brittle

PREP TIME: 25 Minutes ✳ READY IN: 55 Minutes ✳ SERVINGS: 16 Pieces

1	cup sugar
1/2	cup light corn syrup
1	cup roasted salted peanuts

1	teaspoon margarine or butter
1	teaspoon vanilla
1	teaspoon baking soda

1. Butter cookie sheet. In 1-1/2-quart microwavable casserole, combine sugar and corn syrup; mix well. Microwave on High for 4 minutes.

2. Stir in peanuts. Microwave on High for 3 to 5 minutes or until light brown. Stir in margarine and vanilla; blend well. Microwave on High for 1 to 2 minutes. (Peanuts should be lightly browned.)

3. Add baking soda; stir gently until light and foamy. Pour onto buttered cookie sheet. Cool 30 minutes. Break into pieces.

NUTRITION INFORMATION PER SERVING: Calories 140 • Total Fat 5g • Saturated Fat 1g • Cholesterol 0mg • Sodium 135mg • Total Carbohydrate 22g • Dietary Fiber 1g • Sugars 17g • Protein 2g. DIETARY EXCHANGES: 1/2 Starch • 1 Fruit • 1 Fat OR 1-1/2 Carbohydrate • 1 Fat.

cook's notes

Pack pieces of this yummy nut brittle in festive tins for quick and easy Christmas gifts.

ALICE REESE
Minneapolis, Minnesota
Bake-Off® Contest 13, 1961
Prize Winner

candy bar cookies

READY IN: 1 Hour 15 Minutes ✳ SERVINGS: 40 Cookies

BASE

3/4	cup powdered sugar
3/4	cup butter or margarine, softened
2	tablespoons whipping cream
1	teaspoon vanilla
2	cups all-purpose flour

FILLING

21	caramels, unwrapped
3	tablespoons whipping cream
3	tablespoons butter or margarine

3/4	cup powdered sugar
3/4	cup chopped pecans

GLAZE

1/3	cup semisweet chocolate chips
1	tablespoon whipping cream
2	teaspoons butter or margarine
3	tablespoons powdered sugar
1	teaspoon vanilla
40	pecan halves (1/2 cup), if desired

1 In large bowl, mix all base ingredients except flour with spoon until well blended. Stir in flour until dough forms. If necessary, cover dough with plastic wrap and refrigerate 1 hour for easier handling.

2 Heat oven to 325°F. On well-floured surface, roll out half of dough at a time into 10x8-inch rectangle. With pastry wheel or knife, cut into 2-inch squares. Place 1/2 inch apart on ungreased cookie sheets. Bake 10 to 13 minutes or until set. Immediately remove from cookie sheets to cooling racks. Cool completely, about 15 minutes.

3 In 2-quart saucepan, heat caramels, 3 tablespoons whipping cream and 3 tablespoons butter over low heat, stirring frequently, until caramels are melted and mixture is smooth. Remove from heat. Stir in 3/4 cup powdered sugar and the chopped pecans (add additional whipping cream a few drops at a time if needed for desired spreading consistency). Spread 1 teaspoon warm filling on each cookie square.

4 In 1-quart saucepan, heat chocolate chips, 1 tablespoon whipping cream and 2 teaspoons butter over low heat, stirring frequently, until chips are melted and mixture is smooth. Remove from heat. Stir in 3 tablespoons powdered sugar and 1 teaspoon vanilla. Spread glaze evenly over caramel filling on each cookie. Top each with pecan half.

NUTRITION INFORMATION PER SERVING: Calories 130 • Total Fat 8g • Saturated Fat 4g • Cholesterol 15mg • Sodium 45mg • Total Carbohydrate 15g • Dietary Fiber 0g. DIETARY EXCHANGES: 1 Other Carbohydrate • 1-1/2 Fat • 1 Carb Choice.

rocky road fudge

PREP TIME: 35 Minutes ✳ READY IN: 2 Hours 5 Minutes ✳ SERVINGS: 36 Pieces

2-1/2	cups sugar
1/2	cup butter or margarine
1	can (5 oz.) evaporated milk (2/3 cup)
1	jar (7 oz.) marshmallow creme (2 cups)

1	bag (12 oz.) semisweet chocolate chips (2 cups)
3/4	cup chopped walnuts
1	teaspoon vanilla
2	cups miniature marshmallows

1 Line 9-inch square or 13x9-inch pan with foil, extending foil over sides of pan; butter foil. In 3-quart saucepan, cook sugar, butter and milk over medium heat, stirring constantly, until mixture comes to a boil; boil 5 minutes, stirring constantly. Remove from heat.

2 Stir in marshmallow creme and chocolate chips until smooth. Stir in walnuts and vanilla. Stir in marshmallows (marshmallows should not melt completely). Quickly spread in pan. Cool completely, about 30 minutes. Refrigerate until firm, about 1 hour.

3 Using foil, lift fudge from pan; remove foil from fudge. With large knife, cut into squares. Store in refrigerator.

NUTRITION INFORMATION PER SERVING: Calories 175 • Total Fat 7g • Saturated Fat 4g • Cholesterol 10mg • Sodium 25mg • Total Carbohydrate 27g • Dietary Fiber 0g • Sugars 25g • Protein 1g. DIETARY EXCHANGES: 2 Other Carbohydrate • 1-1/2 Fat • 2 Carb Choices.

cook's notes

You can make this fudge about a week in advance and store it in the refrigerator.

turtles in a pretzel tree

PREP TIME: 25 Minutes ✳ READY IN: 35 Minutes ✳ SERVINGS: 24 Candies

- 24 small pretzel trees
- 24 vanilla caramels, unwrapped
- 3/4 cup milk chocolate chips, melted
- 24 pecan halves, toasted

1 Heat oven to 300°F. Line extra-large cookie sheet with foil; spray foil with cooking spray. Arrange pretzels 1 inch apart on cookie sheet. Top each pretzel with 1 caramel. Bake 5 to 8 minutes or just until caramels begin to melt.

2 Remove cookie sheet from oven. Spoon about 1 teaspoon melted chocolate onto each caramel; immediately press 1 pecan half onto each. Place cookie sheet in freezer until candy is set, about 10 minutes. Peel candies from foil.

NUTRITION INFORMATION PER SERVING: Calories 90 • Total Fat 4g • Saturated Fat 2g • Cholesterol 0mg • Sodium 55mg • Total Carbohydrate 12g • Dietary Fiber 0g • Sugars 8g • Protein 1g. DIETARY EXCHANGES: 1 Other Carbohydrate • 1/2 Fat • 1 Carb Choice.

cook's notes

If tree-shaped pretzels are not available, just use small pretzel twists instead.

cook's notes

To save a little time during the busy Christmas season, look for pistachio nuts that are already shelled.

cranberry-pistachio candy squares

PREP TIME: 20 Minutes ✳ READY IN: 4 Hours 10 Minutes ✳ SERVINGS: 96 Candies

- 1 bag (12 oz.) semisweet chocolate chips
- 1 cup butter or margarine
- 1 package (8 oz.) cream cheese, softened
- 1/2 cup evaporated milk
- 1 box (3.4 oz.) instant pistachio pudding and pie filling mix

- 4 cups powdered sugar
- 1/2 cup chopped shelled pistachios
- 1 package (20 oz.) vanilla-flavored candy coating or almond bark, chopped
- 3/4 cup sweetened dried cranberries

1 Line 13x9-inch pan with foil; spray foil with cooking spray. In 1-1/2-quart saucepan, melt chocolate chips and 1/2 cup of the butter over low heat, stirring frequently, until smooth. Remove from heat. With wire whisk, beat in 1/2 package (4 oz.) of the cream cheese until smooth. Spread in pan. Freeze until set, about 30 minutes.

2 In 2-quart saucepan, melt remaining 1/2 cup butter. Remove from heat. Stir in evaporated milk and pudding mix until blended. Stir in powdered sugar until smooth. Stir in pistachios. Carefully spread thick pudding mixture over frozen chocolate layer. Refrigerate 30 minutes.

3 Meanwhile, in another 2-quart saucepan, melt almond bark over low heat, stirring constantly, until smooth. Stir in remaining 1/2 package cream cheese and the cranberries. Pour over chilled pudding layer; spread to cover. Refrigerate until firm, at least 3 hours.

4 Remove candy from pan by lifting foil. Cut into 1-inch squares; remove from foil. Store in refrigerator.

NUTRITION INFORMATION PER SERVING: Calories 110 • Total Fat 6g • Saturated Fat 4g • Cholesterol 10mg • Sodium 45mg • Total Carbohydrate 13g • Dietary Fiber 0g • Sugars 12g • Protein 1g. DIETARY EXCHANGES: 1 Other Carbohydrate • 1 Fat • 1 Carb Choice.

white chocolate-ginger cookies

READY IN: 1 Hour 20 Minutes ✳ SERVINGS: 12 Large Cookies

COOKIES

1	roll (18 oz.) Pillsbury® refrigerated sugar cookies
1/4	cup packed dark brown sugar
1-1/4	teaspoons ground cinnamon
1/4	teaspoon ground ginger
1/4	teaspoon ground nutmeg
2	teaspoons grated orange peel

1	package (6 oz.) white chocolate baking bars, coarsely chopped
3/4	cup chopped pecans
1/3	cup finely chopped crystallized ginger

GLAZE

1/2	cup powdered sugar
1/8	teaspoon ground cinnamon
3	to 3-1/2 teaspoons orange juice

1 Heat oven to 350°F. In large bowl, break up cookie dough. Stir in brown sugar, 1-1/4 teaspoons cinnamon, the ginger, nutmeg and orange peel until well combined. Stir in white chocolate baking bars, pecans and crystallized ginger. Drop dough by 1/4 cupfuls 3 inches apart onto ungreased cookie sheets.

2 Bake at 350°F for 13 to 17 minutes or until edges are golden brown. Cool 2 minutes. Remove from cookie sheets; place on wire racks. Cool completely, about 15 minutes.

3 In small bowl, blend powdered sugar, 1/8 teaspoon cinnamon and enough orange juice for desired drizzling consistency. Drizzle glaze over cooled cookies; let stand until glaze is set before storing.

NUTRITION INFORMATION PER SERVING: Calories 350 • Total Fat 17g • Saturated 5g • Cholesterol 15mg • Sodium 120mg • Total Carbohydrate 44g • Dietary Fiber 0g. DIETARY EXCHANGES: 1/2 Starch • 2-1/2 Other Carbohydrate • 3-1/2 Fat • 3 Carb Choices.

ROBIN WILSON
Altamonte Springs, Florida
Bake-Off® Contest 41, 2004

kitchen tip

To easily chop crystallized ginger, use kitchen scissors to cut it into small pieces.

Mrs. Natalie Townes
Kriksville, Missouri
Bake-Off® Contest 2, 1950

missouri waltz brownies

PREP TIME: 45 Minutes ✳ READY IN: 2 Hours 50 Minutes ✳ SERVINGS: 20 Brownies

BROWNIES
3/4	cup all-purpose flour
1/2	teaspoon baking powder
1/2	teaspoon salt
1/2	cup shortening
1	cup granulated sugar
2	eggs
2-1/2	oz. unsweetened baking chocolate, melted, cooled
1	teaspoon vanilla
1/2	cup chopped nuts

MINT CREAM FROSTING
1-1/2	cups powdered sugar
1/2	cup half-and-half or evaporated milk
1	tablespoon butter or margarine
1/4	teaspoon peppermint extract
1	drop green food color
2	oz. unsweetened baking chocolate, melted, cooled

1 Heat oven to 350°F. Grease 9-inch square pan with shortening or cooking spray; lightly flour. In small bowl, stir together flour, baking powder and salt; set aside.

2 In medium bowl, beat shortening and granulated sugar with electric mixer on medium speed, scraping bowl occasionally, until well blended. Beat in eggs, 2-1/2 oz. melted chocolate and the vanilla. On low speed, beat in flour mixture and nuts until well blended. Pour into pan.

3 Bake 20 to 30 minutes or until toothpick inserted in center comes out clean. Cool completely, about 1 hour.

4 In 1-1/2-quart saucepan, mix powdered sugar and half-and-half. Cook over medium heat about 10 minutes until a small amount of mixture dropped into a cupful of very cold water forms a soft ball that flattens between fingers (232°F). Remove from heat. Stir in butter. Cool to lukewarm (120°F). Add peppermint extract and food color; beat on medium speed until thick and creamy. Spread over brownies.

5 Spread 2 oz. melted chocolate over frosting. Let stand about 45 minutes or until chocolate is set. For brownies, cut into 5 rows by 4 rows. Store in refrigerator.

HIGH ALTITUDE (3500-6500 FT): Bake 25 to 30 minutes.

NUTRITION INFORMATION PER SERVING: Calories 220 • Total Fat 12g • Saturated Fat 4.5g • Cholesterol 25mg • Sodium 85mg • Total Carbohydrate 25g • Dietary Fiber 1g • Sugars 19g • Protein 3g. DIETARY EXCHANGES: 1/2 Starch • 1 Other Carbohydrate • 2 Fat • 1-1/2 Carb Choices.

kahlúa cream truffles

PREP TIME: 30 Minutes ✳ READY IN: 1 Hour ✳ SERVINGS: 36 Truffles

6	oz. semisweet chocolate, cut into pieces
1/4	cup whipping cream
2	tablespoons coffee-flavored liqueur
3	tablespoons butter

2	tablespoons powdered sugar
2	tablespoons unsweetened cocoa or sifted powdered sugar

1 In small saucepan, combine all ingredients except unsweetened cocoa; mix well. Cook over low heat until chocolate is melted and mixture is smooth, stirring constantly. Place saucepan in bowl of ice water to speed chilling, stirring mixture occasionally. With small strainer, sift light layer of cocoa on cookie sheet.

2 When chocolate mixture is cooled and slightly thickened, spoon into decorating bag fitted with desired decorative tip. Squeeze small 1-inch truffles onto cocoa-dusted cookie sheet. Sift remaining cocoa over truffles. Store in tightly covered container in refrigerator. Let truffles stand at room temperature for 30 minutes before serving.

NUTRITION INFORMATION PER SERVING: Calories 45 • Total Fat 3g • Saturated Fat 2g • Cholesterol 5mg • Sodium 10mg • Total Carbohydrate 4g • Dietary Fiber 0g • Sugars 3g • Protein 0g. DIETARY EXCHANGES: 1/2 Fruit • 1/2 Fat OR 1/2 Carbohydrate • 1/2 Fat.

cook's notes

These special truffles can be dropped by teaspoonfuls onto cocoa-dusted cookie sheets and rolled with your hands to form balls.

missouri waltz brownies

russian tea cakes

russian tea cakes

PREP TIME: 35 Minutes ✷ READY IN: 55 Minutes ✷ SERVINGS: 54 Cookies

- 1 roll (16.5 oz.) Pillsbury® refrigerated sugar cookies
- 1/2 cup all-purpose flour
- 3/4 cup finely chopped pecans
- 1/2 teaspoon vanilla
- 1/2 cup plus 1 tablespoon powdered sugar

1 Heat oven to 350°F. In large bowl, break up cookie dough. Stir or knead in flour, pecans and vanilla until well blended. Shape dough into 54 (1-inch) balls. Place 1 inch apart on ungreased cookie sheets.

2 Bake 10 to 14 minutes or until set but not brown. Remove from cookie sheets. Cool slightly on cooling rack. Roll warm cookies in powdered sugar; cool on cooling rack. Roll in powdered sugar again.

NUTRITION INFORMATION PER SERVING: Calories 60 • Total Fat 3g • Saturated Fat 0.5g • Cholesterol 0mg • Sodium 25mg • Total Carbohydrate 8g • Dietary Fiber 0g • Sugars 4g • Protein 0g. DIETARY EXCHANGES: 1/2 Other Carbohydrate • 1/2 Fat • 1/2 Carb Choice.

cook's notes

These little "snowballs" make great treats at Christmastime, but keep them in mind for warm-weather tea parties and bridal showers, too.

MABEL PATENT
Kelseyville, California
Bake-Off® Contest 39, 2000

walnut fudge bars

PREP TIME: 15 Minutes ✷ READY IN: 4 Hours 20 Minutes ✷ SERVINGS: 36 Bars

- 1 box (19.5 oz.) Pillsbury® fudge brownie mix
- 1/2 cup butter or margarine, melted
- 1/4 cup water
- 2 eggs
- 2 cups quick-cooking oats

- 2 cups chopped walnuts
- 1 bag (12 oz.) semisweet chocolate chips (2 cups)
- 1 can (14 oz.) sweetened condensed milk (not evaporated)

1 Heat oven to 350°F. Grease 13x9-inch pan with shortening or cooking spray. In large bowl, mix brownie mix, butter, water and eggs; beat 50 strokes with spoon. Stir in oats and walnuts.

2 In medium microwavable bowl, mix chocolate chips and milk. Microwave uncovered on High 1 minute 30 seconds, stirring twice, until chips are melted and mixture is smooth.

3 Spread half of brownie batter in pan. Spread chocolate mixture over batter. Drop remaining brownie batter by teaspoonfuls over chocolate layer. (Brownie mixture will not completely cover chocolate layer.)

4 Bake 29 to 33 minutes or until brownie topping feels dry and edges begin to pull away from sides of pan. Do not overbake. Cool at room temperature 2 hours. Refrigerate 1 hour 30 minutes. For bars, cut into 6 rows by 6 rows. Serve cold or at room temperature. Store in refrigerator.

HIGH ALTITUDE (3500-6500 FT): Add 1/3 cup all-purpose flour to dry brownie mix.

NUTRITION INFORMATION PER SERVING: Calories 240 • Total Fat 13g • Saturated Fat 4.5g • Cholesterol 20mg • Sodium 80mg • Total Carbohydrate 29g • Dietary Fiber 2g • Sugars 20g • Protein 4g. DIETARY EXCHANGES: 1/2 Starch • 1-1/2 Other Carbohydrate • 2-1/2 Fat • 2 Carb Choices.

MARILYN BLANKSCHIEN
Clintonville, Wisconsin
Bake-Off® Contest 30, 1982

coconut-lemon-crescent bars

PREP TIME: 15 Minutes ✳ READY IN: 1 Hour 5 Minutes ✳ SERVINGS: 36 Bars

CRUST
- 1 can (8 oz.) Pillsbury® refrigerated crescent dinner rolls

FILLING
- 2 eggs, slightly beaten
- 1 cup sugar
- 1 cup flaked coconut
- 2 tablespoons all-purpose flour
- 1/2 teaspoon baking powder
- 1/2 teaspoon grated lemon peel
- 1/4 teaspoon salt
- 2 tablespoons lemon juice
- 2 tablespoons butter or margarine, melted

1 Heat oven to 375°F. Unroll dough into 2 long rectangles. Place in ungreased 13x9-inch pan; press in bottom and 1/2 inch up sides to form crust, firmly pressing perforations to seal. Bake 5 minutes.

2 Meanwhile, in medium bowl, mix all filling ingredients until well blended. Pour filling over partially baked crust; bake 12 to 17 minutes longer or until light golden brown. Cool completely in pan on cooling rack, about 30 minutes. For bars, cut into 6 rows by 6 rows.

HIGH ALTITUDE (3500-6500 FT): Bake 14 to 19 minutes.

NUTRITION INFORMATION PER SERVING: Calories 70 • Total Fat 3g • Saturated Fat 1.5g • Cholesterol 15mg • Sodium 85mg • Total Carbohydrate 9g • Dietary Fiber 0g • Sugars 7g • Protein 0g. DIETARY EXCHANGES: 1/2 Starch • 1/2 Fat • 1/2 Carb Choice.

ginger cookie cutouts

PREP TIME: 1 Hour 15 Minutes ✳ READY IN: 3 Hours 15 Minutes ✳ SERVINGS: 60 Cookies

- 3/4 cup sugar
- 1/2 cup shortening
- 1/2 cup molasses
- 1/4 cup warm coffee
- 1 teaspoon vanilla
- 1 egg
- 2-1/2 cups all-purpose flour
- 1 teaspoon baking soda
- 1/2 teaspoon ginger
- 1/2 teaspoon cinnamon
- 1/2 teaspoon allspice
- 1/4 teaspoon salt
- Sugar

1 In large bowl, combine 3/4 cup sugar and shortening; beat until light and fluffy. Add molasses, coffee, vanilla and egg; blend well. (Mixture may appear curdled.) Add flour, baking soda, ginger, cinnamon, allspice and salt; mix well. Cover with plastic wrap; refrigerate at least 2 hours for easier handling.

2 Heat oven to 350°F. On well-floured surface, roll out dough to 1/8- to 1/4-inch thickness. Cut with floured 2-inch cookie cutter. Place 1 inch apart on ungreased cookie sheets. Sprinkle lightly with sugar.

3 Bake at 350°F for 8 to 12 minutes or until cookies are set. Immediately remove from cookie sheets.

NUTRITION INFORMATION PER SERVING: Calories 60 • Total Fat 2g • Saturated Fat 0g • Cholesterol 4mg • Sodium 30mg • Total Carbohydrate 9g • Dietary Fiber 0g • Sugars 5g • Protein 1g. DIETARY EXCHANGES: 1/2 Starch • 1/2 Fat OR 1/2 Carbohydrate • 1/2 Fat.

cook's notes

Rolling the dough 1/8 inch thick will yield a thin, crisp cookie; rolling it to a 1/4-inch thickness will result in a more cakelike cookie.

coconut-lemon-crescent bars

fudgy-caramel cashew brownies

fudgy-caramel cashew brownies

PREP TIME: 25 Minutes ✳ READY IN: 2 Hours 25 Minutes ✳ SERVINGS: 36 Brownies

3 oz. bittersweet baking chocolate, chopped	1 teaspoon baking powder
1 cup butter	1/2 teaspoon salt
1 bag (12 oz.) semisweet chocolate chips	20 creme-filled chocolate sandwich cookies, crushed
4 eggs	40 round chewy caramels in milk chocolate (packaged in gold foil), unwrapped, each cut in half
1-1/2 cups sugar	
2 teaspoons vanilla	
1 cup all-purpose flour	3/4 cup coarsely chopped roasted cashews

1 Heat oven to 350°F (325°F for dark pan). Grease and flour 13x9-inch pan. In 1-quart microwavable bowl, place bittersweet chocolate, butter and 1 cup of the chocolate chips. Microwave on High 1-1/2 to 2 minutes, stirring twice, until melted and smooth. Cool slightly, about 5 minutes.

2 In large bowl with electric mixer, beat eggs, sugar and vanilla on medium speed until smooth. Add cooled chocolate mixture. Beat until well blended. Add flour, baking powder and salt. Beat on low speed until blended. By hand, stir in cookies and remaining chocolate chips. Pour into pan.

3 Bake 35 to 40 minutes or until edges begin to pull away from sides and center is set. Do not overbake. Immediately sprinkle candy on top of hot brownies. Let stand 10 minutes or until completely softened. Pull tip of toothpick through softened candy to spread and swirl. (It won't completely cover top.) Sprinkle with cashews. Cool until set, about 1 hour. Cut into 6 rows by 6 rows.

HIGH ALTITUDE (3500-6500 FT): Decrease butter to 3/4 cup, sugar to 1-1/4 cups and baking powder to 1/2 teaspoon. Bake 40 to 45 minutes.

NUTRITION INFORMATION PER SERVING: Calories 240 • Total Fat 14g • Saturated Fat 7g • Cholesterol 40mg • Sodium 140mg • Total Carbohydrate 27g • Dietary Fiber 1g • Sugars 20g • Protein 3g.

spicy spritz cookies

PREP TIME: 1 Hour ✳ READY IN: 1 Hour ✳ SERVINGS: About 96 Cookies

2 cups all-purpose flour	3/4 cup sugar
1 teaspoon ground ginger	3/4 cup shortening
1 teaspoon ground cloves	3 tablespoons molasses
1 teaspoon ground cinnamon	1 teaspoon lemon extract
1/2 teaspoon baking soda	1 egg
1/2 teaspoon salt	

1 Heat oven to 375°F. In medium bowl, stir together flour, ginger, cloves, cinnamon, baking soda and salt; set aside.

2 In large bowl, beat sugar and shortening with electric mixer on medium speed, scraping bowl occasionally, until light and fluffy. Beat in molasses, lemon extract and egg. On low speed, beat in flour mixture until well blended.

3 Attach template that has narrow slit with sawtooth edge to cookie press; place dough in cookie press. On ungreased large cookie sheets, press dough into 14-inch strips (on regular cookie sheets, press dough into 11-inch strips).

4 Bake 5 to 7 minutes or until edges are light golden. Cool 1 minute; cut into 2-1/2-inch strips. Remove from cookie sheets.

NUTRITION INFORMATION PER SERVING: Calories 35 • Total Fat 1.5g • Saturated Fat 0g • Cholesterol 0mg • Sodium 20mg • Total Carbohydrate 4g • Dietary Fiber 0g • Sugars 2g • Protein 0g. DIETARY EXCHANGE: 1/2 Other Carbohydrate.

cook's notes

To crush cookies, place them in a resealable food-storage plastic bag; seal the bag and finely crush with a rolling pin or meat mallet (or finely crush in a food processor). The cookies lend flavor and texture to the baked brownies but are not visible in them.

Pillsbury
Bake-Off

S.M. CAMPBELL
Northbrook, Illinois
Bake-Off® Contest 11, 1959

kitchen tip

Cookie-press dough must be firm enough so it doesn't stick to the inside of the press during shaping and stable enough to hold its shape when baked.

LAURA ROTT
Naperville, Illinois
Bake-Off® Contest 1, 1949
Prize Winner

starlight mint surprise cookies

PREP TIME: 1 Hour ✳ READY IN: 3 Hours ✳ SERVINGS: 60 Cookies

1 cup granulated sugar	3 cups all-purpose flour
1/2 cup packed brown sugar	1 teaspoon baking soda
3/4 cup butter or margarine, softened	1/2 teaspoon salt
2 tablespoons water	60 thin rectangular crème de menthe chocolate candies (from three 4.67-oz. pkgs.), unwrapped
1 teaspoon vanilla	
2 eggs	60 walnut halves or pieces

1 In large bowl, beat sugars, butter, water, vanilla and eggs with electric mixer on medium speed, scraping bowl occasionally, until blended. On low speed, beat in flour, baking soda and salt until well blended. Cover with plastic wrap; refrigerate at least 2 hours for easier handling.

2 Heat oven to 375°F. Using about 1 tablespoon dough, press dough around each chocolate candy to cover completely. Place 2 inches apart on ungreased cookie sheets. Top each with walnut half.

3 Bake 7 to 9 minutes or until light golden brown. Immediately remove from cookie sheets to cooling rack.

NUTRITION INFORMATION PER SERVING: Calories 110 • Total Fat 5g • Saturated Fat 2.5g • Cholesterol 15mg • Sodium 65mg • Total Carbohydrate 13g • Dietary Fiber 0g. DIETARY EXCHANGES: 1 Other Carbohydrate • 1 Fat • 1 Carb Choice.

maple nut goodie bars

PREP TIME: 50 Minutes ✳ READY IN: 4 Hours 20 Minutes ✳ SERVINGS: 64 Bars

1 package (12 oz.) semisweet chocolate chips (2 cups)	1/2 cup evaporated milk
1 package (11.5 oz.) milk chocolate chips (2 cups)	1 package (3 oz.) vanilla pudding and pie filling mix (not instant)
2 cups margarine or butter	1 package (2 lbs.) powdered sugar (7-1/2 cups)
1 cup peanut butter	2 teaspoons maple flavor
1 can (12 oz.) cocktail peanuts (2-1/2 cups)	

1 Line 15x10x1-inch baking pan with foil. Butter or spray foil with nonstick cooking spray. In large saucepan, melt chocolate chips and 1 cup of the margarine over low heat, stirring frequently. Remove saucepan from heat. Add peanut butter; mix well. Spread half of mixture in buttered foil-lined pan. Freeze 10 minutes or until set. Place pan in refrigerator.

2 Meanwhile, stir peanuts into remaining chocolate mixture. Set aside. Melt remaining 1 cup margarine in large saucepan over low heat. Gradually stir in evaporated milk. Stir in pudding mix. Cook until mixture is slightly thickened, stirring constantly. Do not boil. Remove saucepan from heat. Add powdered sugar and maple flavor; mix well. Cool about 10 minutes or until slightly cooled.

3 Carefully spread pudding mixture over chilled chocolate layer. Refrigerate 30 minutes. Stir reserved chocolate-peanut mixture. Drop by spoonfuls onto chilled pudding layer; spread to cover. Refrigerate at least 3 hours or until firm. Cut into bars. Store in refrigerator.

NUTRITION INFORMATION PER SERVING: Calories 230 • Total Fat 14g • Saturated Fat 4g • Cholesterol 0mg • Sodium 125mg • Total Carbohydrate 24g • Dietary Fiber 1g • Sugars 21g • Protein 3g. DIETARY EXCHANGES: 1-1/2 Fruit • 1/2 High-Fat Meat • 2 Fat OR 1-1/2 Carbohydrate • 1/2 High-Fat Meat • 2 Fat.

Kitchen tip

If you'd like to save leftover evaporated milk, transfer the milk from its can to another container for storage. If stored in a covered container in the refrigerator, the milk can be used safely within 3 days.

starlight mint surprise cookies

chocolate-drizzled walnut cookies

READY IN: 1 Hour 15 Minutes ✳ SERVINGS: 36 Cookies

1 cup butter, softened	1/4 teaspoon salt
1/2 cup powdered sugar	3/4 cup finely chopped walnuts
1 teaspoon vanilla	2 oz. semisweet baking chocolate, chopped
2-1/4 cups all-purpose flour	

1 Heat oven to 375°F. In medium bowl, beat butter and powdered sugar with electric mixer on medium speed until creamy. Beat in vanilla. On low speed, beat in flour and salt until mixture is crumbly. Stir in 1/2 cup of the walnuts.

2 Shape dough into walnut-sized balls; roll each into 3x3/4-inch log. Place on ungreased cookie sheets.

3 Bake 9 to 12 minutes or until set and bottoms are golden brown. Immediately remove from cookie sheets; place on wire racks. Cool completely, about 10 minutes.

4 Meanwhile, in small microwavable bowl, microwave chocolate on High 30 seconds; stir until smooth.

5 Place cooled cookies on sheet of waxed paper. Drizzle chocolate over cookies; sprinkle with remaining 1/4 cup walnuts.

NUTRITION INFORMATION PER SERVING: Calories 100 • Total Fat 7g • Saturated Fat 4g • Cholesterol 15mg • Sodium 70mg • Total Carbohydrate 9g • Dietary Fiber 0g • Sugars 3g • Protein 1g. DIETARY EXCHANGES: 1/2 Starch • 1-1/2 Fat OR 1/2 Carbohydrate • 1/2 Carb Choice.

PENELOPE WEISS
Pleasant Grove, Utah
Bake-Off® Contest 35, 1992

black and white brownies

PREP TIME: 15 Minutes ✳ READY IN: 2 Hours 30 Minutes ✳ SERVINGS: 36 Brownies

BROWNIES

- 1 box (19.5 oz.) Pillsbury® traditional fudge brownie mix
- 1/4 cup water
- 1/2 cup vegetable oil
- 2 eggs
- 1-1/2 cups chopped pecans
- 1 cup semisweet chocolate chips (6 oz.)
- 1 bag (12 oz.) white vanilla baking chips (2 cups)

FROSTING

- 2 cups powdered sugar
- 1/4 cup unsweetened baking cocoa
- 3 to 4 tablespoons hot water
- 1/4 cup butter or margarine, melted
- 1 teaspoon vanilla
- 1/2 to 1 cup pecan halves

1 Heat oven to 350°F. Grease bottom only of 13x9-inch pan with shortening or cooking spray. In large bowl, beat brownie mix, 1/4 cup water, the oil and eggs 50 strokes with spoon. Stir in chopped pecans, chocolate chips and 1 cup of the vanilla baking chips. Spread in pan.

2 Bake 28 to 34 minutes or until center is set. Remove from oven; immediately sprinkle with remaining 1 cup vanilla baking chips. Let stand 1 minute to soften chips; spread evenly over brownies.

3 In small bowl, beat all frosting ingredients except pecan halves with electric mixer on medium speed until smooth (mixture will be thin). Spoon over melted vanilla baking chips; spread to cover. Arrange pecan halves on frosting. Cool completely, about 1 hour 30 minutes. For brownies, cut into 6 rows by 6 rows.

HIGH ALTITUDE (3500-6500 FT): Add 1/2 cup all-purpose flour to dry brownie mix. Increase water in brownies to 1/3 cup.

NUTRITION INFORMATION PER SERVING: Calories 260 • Total Fat 14g • Saturated Fat 5g • Cholesterol 15mg • Sodium 75mg • Total Carbohydrate 29g • Dietary Fiber 1g • Sugars 24g • Protein 2g. DIETARY EXCHANGES: 2 Other Carbohydrate • 3 Fat • 2 Carb Choices.

vanilla fudge

PREP TIME: 40 Minutes ✳ READY IN: 2 Hours 10 Minutes ✳ SERVINGS: 36 Squares

- 2-1/2 cups sugar
- 1/2 cup butter
- 1 can (5 oz.) evaporated milk (2/3 cup)
- 1 jar (7 oz.) marshmallow creme (2 cups)

- 8 oz. vanilla-flavored candy coating (almond bark), cut into pieces
- 1 teaspoon vanilla
- 3/4 cup chopped walnuts

1 Line 9-inch square or 13x9-inch pan with foil so foil extends over sides of pan; butter foil. In large saucepan, combine sugar, butter and evaporated milk; cook and stir over medium heat until sugar is dissolved. Bring to a full boil, stirring constantly. Boil over medium heat for 5 minutes, stirring constantly.

2 Remove saucepan from heat. Add marshmallow creme and candy coating; stir until candy coating is melted and mixture is smooth. Stir in vanilla and walnuts. Pour into buttered foil-lined pan, spreading evenly. Cool 1 hour or until completely cooled.

3 Score fudge into 36 squares. Refrigerate until firm, about 30 minutes. Remove fudge from pan by lifting foil; remove foil from sides of fudge. With long knife, cut through scored lines. Store in refrigerator.

NUTRITION INFORMATION PER SERVING: Calories 150 • Total Fat 6g • Saturated Fat 3g • Cholesterol 10mg • Sodium 40mg • Total Carbohydrate 23g • Dietary Fiber 0g • Sugars 21g • Protein 1g. DIETARY EXCHANGES: 1-1/2 Fruit • 1-1/2 Fat OR 1-1/2 Carbohydrate • 1-1/2 Fat.

cook's notes

Dampen the bottom of the inside of the pan to help hold the foil in place.

cook's notes

These bars are a yummy way to use a can of cranberry sauce left over from Thanksgiving.

BEATRICE HARLIB
Lincolnwood, Illinois
Bake-Off® Contest 4, 1952

kitchen tip

With three cookie sheets, you can bake one pan while you prepare another and cool a third.

quick cranberry-orange bars

PREP TIME: 20 Minutes ✷ READY IN: 1 Hour 55 Minutes ✷ SERVINGS: 16 Bars

BASE
- 1 package (15.6 oz.) cranberry quick bread mix
- 1/3 cup margarine or butter, softened
- 1 egg

FILLING
- 1 can (16 oz.) whole berry cranberry sauce
- 1 tablespoon grated orange peel
- 1 tablespoon cornstarch

1. Heat oven to 350°F. Grease 9-inch square pan. In large bowl, combine all base ingredients; mix well with pastry blender or fork until crumbly. Reserve 1 cup mixture for topping. Press remaining mixture evenly in bottom of greased pan.

2. In medium bowl, combine all filling ingredients; blend well. Spread filling evenly over base. Sprinkle evenly with reserved crumb mixture; press lightly.

3. Bake at 350°F for 30 to 35 minutes or until top is golden brown. Cool 1 hour or until completely cooled. Cut into bars.

NUTRITION INFORMATION PER SERVING: Calories 200 • Total Fat 6g • Saturated Fat 1g • Cholesterol 15mg • Sodium 170mg • Total Carbohydrate 34g • Dietary Fiber 1g • Sugars 22g • Protein 2g. DIETARY EXCHANGES: 1/2 Starch • 2 Fruit • 1 Fat OR 2-1/2 Carbohydrate • 1 Fat.

snappy turtle cookies

PREP TIME: 1 Hour 30 Minutes ✷ READY IN: 2 Hours 45 Minutes ✷ SERVINGS: 42 Cookies

COOKIES
- 1/2 cup packed brown sugar
- 1/2 cup butter or margarine, softened
- 1/4 teaspoon vanilla
- 1/8 teaspoon maple flavor, if desired
- 1 egg
- 1 egg, separated
- 1-1/2 cups all-purpose flour
- 1/4 teaspoon baking soda
- 1/4 teaspoon salt
- 1 cup pecan halves, each broken lengthwise into 2 pieces

FROSTING
- 1/3 cup semisweet chocolate chips
- 3 tablespoons milk
- 1 tablespoon butter or margarine
- 1 cup powdered sugar

1. In large bowl, beat brown sugar and 1/2 cup butter with electric mixer on medium speed, scraping bowl occasionally, until light and fluffy. Beat in vanilla, maple flavor, 1 whole egg and 1 egg yolk until well blended. On low speed, beat in flour, baking soda and salt. Cover with plastic wrap; refrigerate at least 1 hour for easier handling.

2. Heat oven to 350°F. Grease cookie sheets with shortening or cooking spray. Arrange pecan pieces in groups of 5 on cookie sheets to resemble head and legs of turtle. In small bowl, beat egg white with fork or wire whisk. Shape dough into 1-inch balls. Dip bottoms in beaten egg white; press lightly onto pecans (tips of pecans should show).

3. Bake 10 to 12 minutes or until edges are light golden brown. Immediately remove from cookie sheets to cooling racks. Cool completely, about 15 minutes.

4. Meanwhile, in 1-quart saucepan, heat chocolate chips, milk and 1 tablespoon butter over low heat, stirring constantly, until chips are melted and mixture is smooth. Remove from heat. Stir in powdered sugar. If necessary, add additional powdered sugar until frosting is spreadable. Frost cooled cookies. Let frosting set before storing in tightly covered container.

NUTRITION INFORMATION PER SERVING: Calories 90 • Total Fat 5g • Saturated Fat 2g • Cholesterol 15mg • Sodium 45mg • Total Carbohydrate 10g • Dietary Fiber 0g • Sugars 6g • Protein 1g. DIETARY EXCHANGES: 1 Other Carbohydrate • 1 Fat • 1/2 Carb Choice.

quick cranberry-orange bars

easy oatmeal caramel bars

NIELA FRANTELLIZZI
Boca Raton, Florida
Bake-Off® Contest 37, 1996

easy oatmeal caramel bars

PREP TIME: 35 Minutes ✳ READY IN: 2 Hours 45 Minutes ✳ SERVINGS: 16 Bars

1 roll (16.5 oz.) Pillsbury® refrigerated chocolate chip cookies

1 cup quick-cooking oats

Dash salt, if desired

2/3 cup caramel topping

5 tablespoons all-purpose flour

1 teaspoon vanilla

3/4 cup chopped walnuts

1 bag (6 oz.) semisweet chocolate chips (1 cup)

1 Heat oven to 350°F. Into large bowl, break up cookie dough. Add oats and salt; mix well. Reserve 1/2 cup dough mixture for topping. Press remaining dough mixture evenly in bottom of ungreased 9-inch square pan to form crust.

2 Bake 10 to 12 minutes or until dough puffs and appears dry. Meanwhile, in small bowl, mix caramel topping, flour and vanilla; blend well.

3 Sprinkle walnuts and chocolate chips evenly over crust. Drizzle evenly with caramel mixture. Crumble reserved 1/2 cup dough mixture over caramel.

4 Bake 20 to 25 minutes longer or until golden brown. Cool 10 minutes. Run knife around sides of pan to loosen. Cool completely, about 1-1/2 hours. For bars, cut into 4 rows by 4 rows.

HIGH ALTITUDE (3500-6500 FT): Bake crust 12 to 14 minutes. After topping crust, bake 22 to 27 minutes.

NUTRITION INFORMATION PER SERVING: Calories 290 • Total Fat 13g • Saturated Fat 4g • Cholesterol 10mg • Sodium 140mg • Total Carbohydrate 40g • Dietary Fiber 1g • Sugars 23g • Protein 3g. DIETARY EXCHANGES: 1 Starch • 1-1/2 Other Carbohydrate • 2-1/2 Fat • 2-1/2 Carb Choices.

special touch

For an especially indulgent dessert, use the cookie squares as the base for a rich sundae. Top each square with a scoop of ice cream, a generous drizzle of hot fudge or caramel topping and whipped cream.

old-fashioned caramels

PREP TIME: 1 Hour ✳ READY IN: 1 Hour 30 Minutes ✳ SERVINGS: 48 Squares

1 cup butter

2-1/4 cups firmly packed brown sugar

1 cup light corn syrup

1 can (14 oz.) sweetened condensed milk (not evaporated)

1-1/2 teaspoons vanilla

1 Line 9-inch square pan with foil so foil extends over sides of pan; lightly butter foil. In heavy 3-quart saucepan, melt butter. Add brown sugar; mix well. Stir in corn syrup. Cook over medium-low heat until sugar dissolves and mixture is well blended.

2 Remove saucepan from heat; stir in sweetened condensed milk. Cook over medium heat for 20 to 30 minutes, stirring constantly, until candy thermometer reaches firm-ball stage (244°F).

3 Remove saucepan from heat; stir in vanilla. Pour into buttered foil-lined pan. Cool about 30 minutes.

4 When candy has completely set, carefully remove from pan by lifting foil; remove foil sides of candy. With thin-bladed knife, cut candy into pieces, using a light sawing motion. Wrap individual pieces in waxed paper. Store in refrigerator.

HIGH ALTITUDE (3500-6500 FT): Cook until candy thermometer reaches 234°F.

NUTRITION INFORMATION PER SERVING: Calories 130 • Total Fat 5g • Saturated Fat 3g • Cholesterol 15mg • Sodium 60mg • Total Carbohydrate 20g • Dietary Fiber 0g • Sugars 17g • Protein 1g. DIETARY EXCHANGES: 1-1/2 Fruit • 1 Fat OR 1-1/2 Carbohydrate • 1 Fat.

cook's notes

Want chocolaty caramels? After stirring in the sweetened condensed milk, cook over medium heat for about 20 minutes, stirring constantly, until a candy thermometer reaches 230°F. Then stir in 2 oz. unsweetened chocolate, coarsely chopped; continue cooking and stirring for about 15 minutes or until the mixture reaches 240°F. Continue as directed in the recipe.

cook's notes

There's no need for a cookie cutter because you form these cute houses with your hands. Follow the shaping directions in Step 2.

santa's sweet houses

PREP TIME: 1 Hour ✳ READY IN: 1 Hour 30 Minutes ✳ SERVINGS: 8 Cookies

1 roll (16.5 oz.) Pillsbury® refrigerated gingerbread cookies

Decorating icing (from 6.4-oz. aerosol can)

Multi-Bran Chex® cereal

Assorted small candies

1 Heat oven to 350°F. Cut cookie dough into 8 equal pieces. Work with 1 piece of dough at a time; refrigerate remaining dough pieces until needed.

2 For each cookie, cut 1 piece of dough into 3 equal slices. Place 2 slices side by side on ungreased cookie sheet; press into 3x3-1/2-inch rectangle. Place third slice on center of long side of rectangle; press slice into triangle for roof (house should be about 5 inches tall). Repeat with remaining dough, making a total of 8 house shapes 1-1/2 inches apart on cookie sheets.

3 Bake 8 to 11 minutes or until light golden brown. Cool 2 minutes; remove from cookie sheets. Cool completely, about 15 minutes.

4 Decorate with decorating icing; use cereal for shingles and candy for house features. Let stand until frosting is set, about 30 minutes. Store between sheets of waxed paper in tightly covered container.

NUTRITION INFORMATION PER SERVING: Calories 260 • Total Fat 13g • Saturated Fat 4g • Cholesterol 20mg • Sodium 200mg • Total Carbohydrate 34g • Dietary Fiber 0g • Sugars 17g • Protein 2g. DIETARY EXCHANGES: 1 Starch • 1 Other Carbohydrate • 2-1/2 Fat • 2 Carb Choices.

Pillsbury Bake-Off®

DOROTHY SHAFFER
Prosser, Washington
Bake-Off® Contest 31, 1984

sugar-crusted meltaways

READY IN: 1 Hour 35 Minutes ✳ SERVINGS: 42 Cookies

1 tablespoon grated orange peel

1/4 cup orange juice

1/4 cup sugar

1/8 teaspoon salt

3/4 cup butter or margarine, softened

1 tablespoon water

1 teaspoon vanilla

1-3/4 cups all-purpose flour

1 cup semisweet chocolate chips (6 oz.)

1 cup finely chopped nuts

Additional sugar (about 1/2 cup)

1 Heat oven to 325°F. In small bowl, mix orange peel and orange juice; set aside. In large bowl, beat 1/4 cup sugar, the salt, butter, water and vanilla with electric mixer on medium speed, scraping bowl occasionally, until well blended. On low speed, beat in flour. Stir in chocolate chips and nuts.

2 Shape dough into 1-inch balls. Place 2 inches apart on ungreased cookie sheets. Bake 15 to 20 minutes or until firm to the touch. Remove from cookie sheets to cooling racks. Cool completely, about 15 minutes.

3 Place fine strainer over another small bowl. Pour orange juice mixture through strainer to remove peel. Dip cooled cookies into orange juice; roll in additional sugar. Let stand until dry and sugar shell forms on each cookie.

NUTRITION INFORMATION PER SERVING: Calories 100 • Total Fat 6g • Saturated Fat 3g • Cholesterol 10mg • Sodium 30mg • Total Carbohydrate 11g • Dietary Fiber 0g • Sugars 6g • Protein 1g. DIETARY EXCHANGES: 1 Other Carbohydrate • 1 Fat • 1 Carb Choice.

santa's sweet houses

Heavenly Desserts

At Christmastime, everyone saves room in anticipation of an extra-special, seasonal treat. Make eyes light up with the holiday cakes, pies and other delights here.

p. 307

p. 279

p. 280

p. 308

p. 282

chocolate streusel
banana-carrot cake p. 292

almond crumble cherry pie

PREP TIME: 15 Minutes ✳ READY IN: 55 Minutes ✳ SERVINGS: 8

Cook's Notes

Marzipan is a mixture of egg whites, sugar and almond paste. It adds almond flavor and a crumbly texture to the cherry pie topping. Look for marzipan in your grocery store's baking section.

CRUST

  1 Pillsbury® refrigerated pie crust (from 15-oz. box), softened as directed on box

TOPPING

  1/3 cup marzipan (about 4 oz.)

  3 tablespoons butter or margarine, softened

  1/2 cup old-fashioned oats

  2 tablespoons all-purpose flour

FILLING

  2 cans (21 oz. each) cherry pie filling

  1/4 teaspoon almond extract

1 Heat oven to 375°F. Make pie crust as directed on box for one-crust baked shell using 9-inch glass pie pan. Bake 8 to 10 minutes or just until set but not brown.

2 Meanwhile, in small bowl, place marzipan and butter; with pastry blender or fork, mix until well blended. Stir in oats and flour until crumbly. In large bowl, mix filling ingredients.

3 Remove partially baked shell from oven. Pour pie filling into shell. Crumble marzipan topping over filling.

4 Return to oven; bake 30 to 40 minutes longer or until topping is golden brown and filling is bubbly around edges. If necessary, after 15 minutes of baking, cover edge of crust with strips of foil to prevent excessive browning.

HIGH ALTITUDE (3500-6500 FT): Use 9-inch deep-dish pie pan. In Step 1, bake crust at 375°F 10 to 12 minutes. In Step 4, bake 35 to 45 minutes and continue as directed.

NUTRITION INFORMATION PER SERVING: Calories 430 • Total Fat 16g • Saturated 6g • Cholesterol 20mg • Sodium 160mg • Total Carbohydrate 68g • Dietary Fiber 2g • Sugars 43g • Protein 4g.

mint cheesecake squares

PREP TIME: 30 Minutes ✳ READY IN: 4 Hours ✳ SERVINGS: 20

CRUST
- 1 package (9 oz.) thin chocolate wafer cookies, crushed (1-3/4 cups)
- 1/2 cup margarine or butter, melted

FILLING
- 2 packages (8 oz. each) cream cheese, softened
- 1/2 cup dairy sour cream

- 4 eggs
- 2/3 cup sugar
- 1/2 cup creme de menthe syrup
- 1/4 teaspoon mint extract

TOPPING
- 4 oz. semisweet baking chocolate, chopped
- 1/2 cup dairy sour cream

cook's notes

These bars can be made up to

two days before serving; store

in refrigerator.

1. Heat oven to 350°F. In medium bowl, mix crust ingredients. Press in bottom of ungreased 13x9-inch pan. Freeze crust while preparing filling.

2. In large bowl with electric mixer, beat all filling ingredients on low speed until smooth. Pour into crust-lined pan. Bake 30 to 35 minutes or until knife inserted in center comes out clean. Cool on wire rack.

3. Meanwhile, in 1-quart saucepan, melt chocolate over low heat, stirring constantly. Cool 5 minutes; beat in sour cream with spoon. Spread over warm cheesecake. Refrigerate 3 hours or until firm. Cut into squares. Store in refrigerator.

HIGH ALTITUDE (3500-6500 FT): Bake at 350°F 35-40 minutes.

NUTRITION INFORMATION PER SERVING: Calories 300 • Total Fat 21g • Saturated Fat 10g • Cholesterol 75mg • Sodium 220mg • Total Carbohydrate 25g • Dietary Fiber 1g • Sugars 14g • Protein 5g. DIETARY EXCHANGES: 1/2 Starch • 1 Other Carbohydrate • 1/2 Medium-Fat Meat • 3-1/2 Fat • 1-1/2 Carb Choices.

pumpkin bread pudding with ginger cream

PREP TIME: 15 Minutes ✳ READY IN: 1 Hour 45 Minutes ✳ SERVINGS: 9

PUDDING
- 3 eggs
- 1-1/4 cups sugar
- 1-1/2 teaspoons ground cinnamon
- 1/2 to 1-1/2 teaspoons ground nutmeg
- 1/4 cup butter or margarine, melted
- 1-1/2 teaspoons vanilla
- 1 container (8 oz.) plain dry bread crumbs (1-3/4 cups)

- 2 cups milk
- 1 cup canned pumpkin (not pumpkin pie mix)
- 1/2 cup raisins

GINGER CREAM
- 1 cup whipping cream
- 3 tablespoons sugar
- 1/2 teaspoon ground ginger

CANDICE MERRILL
Pasadena, California
Bake-Off® Contest 38, 1998

1. Heat oven to 350°F. Spray 8- or 9-inch square pan with cooking spray. In large bowl, beat eggs until well blended.

2. Add 1-1/4 cups sugar, the cinnamon, nutmeg, butter and vanilla; beat with electric mixer on medium speed until smooth. Add crumbs, milk and pumpkin; mix well. Let stand 10 minutes.

3. Add raisins to batter; mix well. Spread evenly in pan. Bake 37 to 47 minutes or until knife inserted 1-1/2 inches from edge comes out clean. Cool 30 minutes.

4. In small bowl, beat whipping cream, gradually adding 3 tablespoons sugar and ginger until soft peaks form. To serve, cut pudding into squares. Serve warm or cool topped with ginger cream. Store covered in refrigerator.

HIGH ALTITUDE (3500-6500 FT): Heat oven to 375°F. Bake 35 to 45 minutes.

NUTRITION INFORMATION PER SERVING: Calories 430 • Total Fat 17g • Saturated Fat 10g • Cholesterol 120mg • Sodium 240mg • Total Carbohydrate 60g • Dietary Fiber 2g. DIETARY EXCHANGES: 1 Starch • 3 Other Carbohydrate • 1/2 Medium-Fat Meat • 3 Fat • 4 Carb Choices.

maple-apple cake

PREP TIME: 30 Minutes ✳ READY IN: 2 Hours 50 Minutes ✳ SERVINGS: 16

CAKE

1	cup granulated sugar
1/2	cup packed brown sugar
3/4	cup butter or margarine, softened
3/4	cup maple-flavored syrup
4	eggs
3	cups all-purpose flour
2	teaspoons baking powder
1	teaspoon ground cinnamon
1/2	teaspoon salt
1/2	teaspoon ground nutmeg
1/4	teaspoon ground allspice
3	cups chopped peeled apples (3 medium)
1/2	cup chopped walnuts

GLAZE

1/2	cup powdered sugar
3	tablespoons maple-flavored syrup
1	tablespoon butter or margarine, softened

GARNISH

1	tablespoon chopped walnuts

1 Heat oven to 350°F. Grease and flour 12-cup fluted tube pan. In large bowl, beat granulated sugar, brown sugar and 3/4 cup butter until smooth. Beat in 3/4 cup syrup and eggs until blended.

2 Beat in flour, baking powder, cinnamon, salt, nutmeg and allspice until combined. Stir in apples and 1/2 cup walnuts. Spread batter evenly in pan.

3 Bake 55 to 65 minutes or until toothpick inserted in center comes out clean. Cool 15 minutes. Remove from pan. Cool completely, about 1 hour.

4 In small bowl, mix glaze ingredients until smooth. Spoon over top of cake. Sprinkle with 1 tablespoon walnuts.

HIGH ALTITUDE (3500-6500 FT): Decrease granulated sugar to 3/4 cup; increase flour to 3-1/2 cups. Bake at 375°F 50 to 60 minutes.

NUTRITION INFORMATION PER SERVING: Calories 380 • Total Fat 14g • Saturated Fat 7g • Cholesterol 80mg • Sodium 230mg • Total Carbohydrate 58g • Dietary Fiber 1g • Sugars 33g • Protein 5g.

strawberry-rhubarb crescent shortcakes

READY IN: 50 Minutes ✳ SERVINGS: 6

TOPPING

2	cups chopped fresh or frozen rhubarb, thawed
1	cup sugar
1/4	cup orange juice
2	cups sliced fresh or frozen strawberries, thawed

SHORTCAKES

4	teaspoons sugar
1	teaspoon grated orange peel
1	can (8 oz.) Pillsbury® refrigerated crescent dinner rolls

1 In medium saucepan, combine rhubarb, 1 cup sugar and orange juice; mix well. Cook over medium heat for 15 to 17 minutes or until rhubarb is very tender and mixture is thick and syrupy, stirring occasionally. Cool 25 minutes or until room temperature. Fold in strawberries.

2 Meanwhile, heat oven to 375°F. Grease cookie sheet. In small bowl, combine 3 teaspoons of the sugar and orange peel; mix well.

3 Unroll dough into 1 large rectangle. Press perforations to seal. Sprinkle dough with sugar-orange peel mixture. Starting at short side of rectangle, roll up dough; seal edges. Cut roll crosswise into 6 slices; place cut side down on greased cookie sheet. Sprinkle evenly with remaining teaspoon sugar.

4 Bake at 375°F for 13 to 17 minutes or until golden brown. Cool 10 minutes. To serve, place shortcakes in individual dessert bowls. Spoon topping over shortcakes. Store in refrigerator.

NUTRITION INFORMATION PER SERVING: Calories 305 • Total Fat 6g • Saturated Fat 1g • Cholesterol 0mg • Sodium 460mg • Total Carbohydrate 60g • Dietary Fiber 2g • Sugars 46g • Protein 3g. DIETARY EXCHANGES: 1 Starch • 3 Fruit • 1 Fat OR 4 Carbohydrate • 1 Fat • 4 Carb Choices.

maple-apple cake

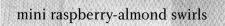

mini raspberry-almond swirls

mini raspberry-almond swirls

PREP TIME: 20 Minutes ✳ READY IN: 40 Minutes ✳ SERVINGS: 24 Rolls

1/4 cup sugar	1 can (8 oz.) refrigerated crescent dinner rolls
1/2 cup slivered almonds	1/4 cup seedless red raspberry jam
1 package (3 oz.) cream cheese, softened, cut into pieces	24 fresh raspberries, if desired
1/4 teaspoon vanilla	3 tablespoons semisweet chocolate chips
1/8 teaspoon almond extract	1 teaspoon shortening
1 egg yolk	

1 Heat oven to 375°F. Spray 24 mini muffin cups with cooking spray. In food processor, place sugar and almonds. Cover; process about 30 seconds or until almonds are finely ground. Add cream cheese, vanilla, almond extract and egg yolk. Cover; process about 10 seconds or until well blended.

2 On lightly floured surface, unroll dough into 1 large rectangle. With floured rolling pin or fingers, roll or press dough into 12x9-inch rectangle, firmly pressing perforations to seal.

3 Spread cream cheese mixture evenly over dough rectangle. With pizza cutter or knife, cut rectangle lengthwise into 2 narrow rectangles. Starting with cut edge, roll up each narrow dough rectangle (filling will be soft). Repeat with remaining half. With serrated knife, cut each roll into 12 slices; place cut side up in muffin cups.

4 Bake 11 to 13 minutes or until light golden brown. Remove rolls from oven. With handle of wooden spoon, make indentation in center of each roll; spoon 1 teaspoon jam into each.

5 Bake 2 to 4 minutes longer or until golden brown. Run knife around edge of each muffin cup to loosen. Remove rolls from cups; place on cooling racks.

6 Place 1 raspberry over jam on each roll. In 1-cup microwavable measuring cup, microwave chocolate chips and shortening uncovered on High 30 to 45 seconds, stirring once, until melted. Drizzle chocolate over warm rolls. Serve warm or cool. Store rolls in refrigerator.

HIGH ALTITUDE (3500-6500 FT): Increase first bake time to 13 to 15 minutes.

NUTRITION INFORMATION PER SERVING: Calories 90 • Total Fat 5g • Saturated Fat 2g • Cholesterol 10mg • Sodium 85mg • Total Carbohydrate 9g • Dietary Fiber 0g • Sugars 5g • Protein 2g. DIETARY EXCHANGES: 1/2 Starch • 1 Fat • 1/2 Carb Choice.

lemon pudding cake

PREP TIME: 15 Minutes ✳ READY IN: 50 Minutes ✳ SERVINGS: 6

3 eggs, separated	1/2 cup sugar
1/2 cup milk	1/3 cup all-purpose flour
1/4 cup lemon juice	1/8 teaspoon salt
1 teaspoon grated lemon peel	

1 Heat oven to 350°F. Grease 1-quart casserole. In small bowl, beat egg yolks; stir in milk, lemon juice and lemon peel. Add sugar, flour and salt; beat until smooth.

2 In another small bowl, beat egg whites until stiff peaks form. Gently fold yolk mixture into beaten egg whites. Do not over-mix. Pour into greased casserole. Place casserole in 13x9-inch pan; place in oven. Pour hot water into pan around casserole to a depth of 1 inch. Bake at 350°F for 25 to 35 minutes or until light golden brown. Serve warm or cool.

NUTRITION INFORMATION PER SERVING: Calories 140 • Total Fat 3g • Saturated Fat 1g • Cholesterol 110mg • Sodium 90mg • Total Carbohydrate 24g • Dietary Fiber 0g • Sugars 18g • Protein 5g. DIETARY EXCHANGES: 1/2 Starch • 1 Fruit • 1/2 Medium-Fat Meat OR 1-1/2 Carbohydrate • 1/2 Medium-Fat Meat.

BRENDA ELSEA
Tuscon, Arizona
Bake-Off® Contest 38, 1998
Prize Winner

cook's notes

To substitute for the light rum,

mix 1/2 teaspoon rum extract

with 4 teaspoons water.

bananas foster tart

PREP TIME: 30 Minutes ✳ READY IN: 1 Hour ✳ SERVINGS: 10

CRUST

1　Pillsbury® refrigerated pie crust (from 15-oz. box), softened as directed on box

FILLING

2　medium bananas, cut into 1/4-inch slices

4-1/2　teaspoons light rum

2　teaspoons grated orange peel

2/3　cup chopped pecans

2/3　cup packed brown sugar

1/4　cup whipping cream

1/4　cup butter or margarine

1/2　teaspoon vanilla

Vanilla ice cream

1　Heat oven to 450°F. Bake pie crust as directed on box for One-Crust Baked Shell, using 9-inch tart pan with removable bottom or 9-inch glass pie plate. Cool 5 minutes.

2　In small bowl, gently mix bananas and rum to coat. Sprinkle orange peel evenly in bottom of shell. Arrange bananas in single layer over peel. Sprinkle with pecans.

3　In 2-quart heavy saucepan, mix brown sugar, whipping cream and butter. Cook and stir over medium-high heat 2 to 3 minutes or until mixture boils. Cook 2 to 4 minutes longer, stirring constantly, until mixture has thickened and is deep golden brown. Remove from heat; stir in vanilla. Spoon warm filling over bananas and pecans. Cool 30 minutes. Serve warm or cool with ice cream. Cover and refrigerate any remaining tart.

NUTRITION INFORMATION PER SERVING: Calories 290 • Total Fat 17g • Saturated Fat 7g • Cholesterol 20mg • Sodium 130mg • Total Carbohydrate 31 g • Dietary Fiber 1 g • Sugars 18g • Protein 1g. DIETARY EXCHANGES: 1/2 Starch • 1-1/2 Other Carbohydrate • 3-1/2 Fat • 2 Carb Choices.

chocolate cream angel slices with cherry-berry sauce

READY IN: 20 Minutes ✳ SERVINGS: 8

SAUCE

1　can (21 oz.) cherry pie filling

1　cup frozen whole raspberries (from 12- to 14-oz. bag)

2　tablespoons amaretto, if desired

ANGEL SLICES

2　oz. semisweet chocolate

1　cup whipping cream

1　tablespoon amaretto, if desired

1　loaf (10.5 oz.) angel food cake (about 7x3x3-inch)

TOPPING

8　teaspoons chocolate-flavored syrup

1　In small bowl, mix all sauce ingredients. Cover; refrigerate until serving time. In 1-quart saucepan, heat chocolate over low heat, stirring occasionally, just until melted. Remove from heat. Stir in 1/4 cup of the whipping cream.

2　In medium bowl, beat remaining 3/4 cup whipping cream with electric mixer on high speed until stiff peaks form. Beat in chocolate mixture and amaretto. Serve immediately or cover and refrigerate up to 2 hours.

3　To serve, cut cake into 8 slices; place on individual dessert plates. Spoon about 1/3 cup sauce over each slice. Top each with about 1/4 cup chocolate cream mixture; drizzle with 1 teaspoon chocolate syrup.

NUTRITION INFORMATION PER SERVING: Calories 340 • Total Fat 12g • Saturated Fat 7g • Cholesterol 35mg • Sodium 290mg • Total Carbohydrate 56g • Dietary Fiber 5g • Sugars 47g • Protein 5g.

bananas foster tart

BESSIE E. MILLER
Tampa, Florida
Bake-Off® Contest 32, 1986

apple berry pie

PREP TIME: 30 Minutes ✳ READY IN: 1 Hour 20 Minutes ✳ SERVINGS: 6 to 8

CRUST
- 1 box (15 oz.) Pillsbury® refrigerated pie crusts, softened as directed on box

FILLING
- 3 cups chopped, peeled apples
- 1/2 cup sugar
- 1/4 cup chopped pecans or walnuts
- 1/4 cup raisins
- 3 tablespoons all-purpose flour
- 1/2 teaspoon ground cinnamon
- 1/4 teaspoon ground nutmeg
- 2 tablespoons butter or margarine, melted
- 1 can (16 oz.) whole berry cranberry sauce

1 Heat oven to 425°F. Make pie crusts as directed on box for Two-Crust Pie, using 9-inch glass pie plate. Cut second crust into 6 or 8 wedges; set aside.

2 In large bowl, mix filling ingredients. Spoon into crust-lined pie plate. Arrange pie crust wedges over berry mixture, points of wedges meeting in center. (Do not overlap.) Fold outer edge of each wedge under bottom crust; flute.

3 Bake 40 to 50 minutes or until crust is golden brown and apples are tender. Cover edge of pie crust with strip of foil during last 10 to 15 minutes of bake time if necessary to prevent excessive browning.

NUTRITION INFORMATION PER SERVING: Calories 630 • Total Fat 26g • Saturated Fat 9g • Cholesterol 20mg • Sodium 340mg • Total Carbohydrate 97g • Dietary Fiber 2g. DIETARY EXCHANGES: 1/2 Starch • 1/2 Fruit • 5-1/2 Other Carbohydrate • 5 Fat • 6-1/2 Carb Choices.

spiced cider cheesecake

PREP TIME: 1 Hour ✳ READY IN: 6 Hours ✳ SERVINGS: 16

CRUST

- 1 cup finely crushed gingerbread cookies or gingersnaps
- 1 cup graham cracker crumbs
- 1/4 cup sugar
- 1/4 cup butter, melted

FILLING

- 1 can (12 oz.) frozen apple juice concentrate, thawed
- 2 tablespoons mulling spices

- 3/4 cup chopped dried apples
- 3 packages (8 oz. each) cream cheese, softened
- 3/4 cup sugar
- 2 tablespoons cornstarch
- 4 eggs

TOPPING

- 1-1/2 cups sour cream
- 2 tablespoons sugar

cook's notes

Mulling spices contain nutmeg, cloves, cinnamon and allspice. Keep the spice blend on hand during the holiday season to add flavor to hot cider or wine.

1 Heat oven to 350°F. In medium bowl, combine gingerbread cookie crumbs, graham cracker crumbs and 1/4 cup sugar; mix well. Stir in butter. Reserve 2 tablespoons crumb mixture for cheesecake garnish. Press remaining crumb mixture in bottom and 2 inches up sides of ungreased 9-inch springform pan.

2 Bake at 350°F for 10 minutes. Cool 10 minutes. Wrap outside of pan, bottom and sides, with heavy-duty foil.

3 Meanwhile, in small saucepan, bring apple juice concentrate and mulling spices to a boil over medium-high heat. Boil 10 minutes. Place dried apples in medium bowl. Strain apple juice mixture over apples; discard spices. Cool 15 minutes or until lukewarm, stirring occasionally.

4 Beat cream cheese in large bowl at medium speed until creamy. Beat in 3/4 cup sugar and cornstarch until smooth. Reduce speed to low; beat in eggs one at a time, beating just until combined and scraping down sides of bowl after each addition. Beat in lukewarm apple mixture. Pour into crust-lined pan.

5 Bake at 350°F for 50 to 55 minutes or until sides of cheesecake are set and puffed, top is golden brown and center still moves slightly when pan is tapped. Meanwhile, in small bowl, combine topping ingredients; blend well.

6 Remove cheesecake from oven. Gently spread sour cream topping over cheesecake. Return to oven; bake an additional 5 minutes. Center will still move slightly when pan is tapped. Turn off oven; let cheesecake stand in oven with door slightly ajar for 10 minutes. Remove cheesecake from oven. Cool in pan on wire rack for 1 hour.

7 Sprinkle reserved 2 tablespoons of crumb mixture over top of cheesecake. Cover; refrigerate at least 3 hours or overnight before serving. To serve, remove sides of pan. Cut cheesecake into wedges.

HIGH ALTITUDE (3500-6500 FT): Bake cheesecake at 350°F for 60 to 65 minutes.

NUTRITION INFORMATION PER SERVING: Calories 395 • Total Fat 25g • Saturated Fat 15g • Cholesterol 120mg • Sodium 250mg • Total Carbohydrate 38g • Dietary Fiber 1g • Sugars 30g • Protein 6g. DIETARY EXCHANGES: 2 Starch • 1/2 Fruit • 2-1/2 Other Carbohydrate • 4-1/2 Fat.

amaretto peach tart

PREP TIME: 35 Minutes ✳ READY IN: 2 Hours 40 Minutes ✳ SERVINGS: 10

CRUST
- 1 Pillsbury® refrigerated pie crust (from 15-oz. box), softened as directed on box

FILLING
- 1 package (8 oz.) cream cheese, softened
- 1/3 cup sugar
- 2 tablespoons amaretto or 1/4 teaspoon almond extract
- 2 eggs

TOPPING
- 2 tablespoons peach preserves
- 1 tablespoon amaretto or 1/8 teaspoon almond extract
- 2 cups thinly sliced, peeled peaches (2 to 3 medium)

1 Heat oven to 450°F. Bake pie crust as directed on box for One-Crust Baked Shell, using 10-inch tart pan with removable bottom. Cool on cooling rack 15 minutes.

2 Reduce oven temperature to 375°F. In medium bowl, beat cream cheese and sugar with electric mixer on medium speed until light and fluffy. Beat in 2 tablespoons amaretto and the eggs until well blended. Pour into baked shell.

3 Bake 18 to 22 minutes or until filling is set. Cool 10 minutes. Refrigerate at least 1 hour until completely cooled and set.

4 Just before serving, in medium microwavable bowl, microwave preserves on High 20 seconds. Stir in 1 tablespoon amaretto. Stir in peaches to coat. Arrange peach slices over top of tart. Cover and refrigerate any remaining tart.

NUTRITION INFORMATION PER SERVING: Calories 250 • Total Fat 15g • Saturated Fat 7g • Cholesterol 70mg • Sodium 170mg • Total Carbohydrate 25g • Dietary Fiber 0g • Sugars 13g • Protein 3g. DIETARY EXCHANGES: 1 Starch • 1/2 Other Carbohydrate • 3 Fat • 1-1/2 Carb Choices.

pineapple upside-down cake

PREP TIME: 20 Minutes ✳ READY IN: 1 Hour ✳ SERVINGS: 6

- 1/2 cup firmly packed brown sugar
- 1/4 cup margarine or butter, melted
- 6 canned pineapple slices, drained
- 6 maraschino cherries
- 2 eggs, separated
- 1/2 cup sugar
- 3/4 cup all-purpose flour
- 1/2 teaspoon baking powder
- 1/4 teaspoon salt
- 1/4 cup pineapple juice
- Whipped cream

1 Heat oven to 350°F. In small bowl, combine brown sugar and margarine; blend well. Spread in bottom of ungreased 9-inch round cake pan. Arrange pineapple slices and maraschino cherries over brown sugar mixture. Set aside.

2 In small bowl, beat egg yolks until thick and lemon-colored. Gradually add sugar; beat well. Add flour, baking powder, salt and pineapple juice; mix well.

3 In another small bowl, beat egg whites until stiff peaks form. Fold into batter. Pour batter evenly over pineapple slices and cherries.

4 Bake at 350°F for 30 to 35 minutes or until toothpick inserted in center comes out clean. Cool upright in pan 2 minutes. Invert cake onto serving plate. Serve warm with whipped cream.

HIGH ALTITUDE (3500-6500 FT): Increase flour to 3/4 cup plus 3 tablespoons. Bake at 375°F for 30 to 35 minutes.

NUTRITION INFORMATION PER SERVING: Calories 370 • Total Fat 15g • Saturated Fat 5g • Cholesterol 90mg • Sodium 250mg • Total Carbohydrate 55g • Dietary Fiber 1g • Sugars 43g • Protein 4g. DIETARY EXCHANGES: 1 Starch • 2-1/2 Fruit • 3 Fat OR 3-1/2 Carbohydrate • 3 Fat.

amaretto peach tart

pear and ginger cream tart

PREP TIME: 45 Minutes ✳ READY IN: 1 Hour 45 Minutes ✳ SERVINGS: 8

PASTRY CREAM
1-1/2 cups milk
   1 tablespoon grated gingerroot
   4 egg yolks
 3/4 cup sugar
 1/2 cup all-purpose flour
   2 tablespoons butter
1-1/2 teaspoons vanilla

CRUST
   1 Pillsbury® refrigerated pie crust (from 15-oz. box), softened as directed on box

TOPPING
   2 cans (15 oz. each) pear halves in juice, drained
   1 oz. white chocolate baking bar (from 6-oz. box)
   1 teaspoon shortening

1 In 3-quart saucepan, heat milk and grated gingerroot over low heat about 5 minutes, stirring frequently, until very hot but not boiling.

2 In medium bowl with electric mixer, beat egg yolks and sugar on medium speed 4 to 6 minutes or until pale yellow. Beat in flour. Gradually beat in warm milk mixture until well blended.

3 Return mixture to saucepan; cook over medium-low heat about 5 minutes, stirring constantly, until mixture is very thick and begins to boil. Boil 1 minute, stirring constantly. Remove from heat; stir in butter and vanilla. Pour into medium bowl; place plastic wrap on surface of pastry cream. Refrigerate until completely cooled, about 1 hour.

4 Meanwhile, heat oven to 450°F. Prepare pie crust as directed on package for one-crust baked shell using 9-inch tart pan with removable bottom or 9-inch pie pan. Trim edges if necessary. Bake 9 to 11 minutes or until lightly browned. Cool completely, about 15 minutes.

5 Fill baked shell with prepared pastry cream. Cut pear halves into thin slices; arrange pear slices on top of tart.

6 In small microwavable bowl, microwave baking bar and shortening on High 45 to 60 seconds, stirring once halfway through microwaving, until melted. If necessary, continue to microwave on High in 15-second increments, stirring until smooth. Drizzle over tart. Store in refrigerator.

NUTRITION INFORMATION PER SERVING: Calories 380 • Total Fat 15g • Saturated Fat 7g • Cholesterol 125mg • Sodium 160mg • Total Carbohydrate 56g • Dietary Fiber 1g • Sugars 35g • Protein 5g. DIETARY EXCHANGES: 1 Starch • 3 Other Carbohydrate • 3 Fat • 4 Carb Choices.

pumpkin pie squares

PREP TIME: 15 Minutes ✳ READY IN: 2 Hours ✳ SERVINGS: 12

CRUST

- 3/4 cup all-purpose flour
- 3/4 cup quick-cooking or old-fashioned oats
- 1/2 to 1 cup chopped nuts
- 1/2 cup butter or margarine, softened
- 1 box (3.5 oz.) butterscotch pudding and pie filling mix (not instant)

FILLING

- 2 eggs
- 1 cup flaked or shredded coconut, if desired
- 1-1/2 teaspoons pumpkin pie spice
- 1 can (15 oz.) pumpkin (2 cups)
- 1 can (14 oz.) sweetened condensed milk (not evaporated)

1 Heat oven to 350°F. In large bowl, mix all crust ingredients until well combined. Press mixture in bottom of ungreased 13x9-inch pan. In same bowl, beat eggs. Stir in all remaining filling ingredients until blended. Pour over crust.

2 Bake 35 to 45 minutes or until knife inserted in center comes out clean. Cool completely, about 1 hour. Cut into squares. If desired, serve topped with whipped cream or ice cream and sprinkle with pumpkin pie spice. Store in refrigerator.

HIGH ALTITUDE (3500-6500 FT): Bake crust at 375°F about 8 minutes. Add filling; bake 38 to 48 minutes.

NUTRITION INFORMATION PER SERVING: Calories 315 • Total Fat 15g • Saturated Fat 7g • Cholesterol 65mg • Sodium 150mg • Total Carbohydrate 38g • Dietary Fiber 2g • Sugars 25g • Protein 7g.

cook's notes

Pecans are a good choice for the chopped nuts in this recipe, but you can also use walnuts or almonds.

chocolate bread pudding
with cherry-raspberry sauce

PREP TIME: 30 Minutes ✳ READY IN: 1 Hour 10 Minutes ✳ SERVINGS: 20

BREAD PUDDING

- 1 bag (6 oz.) semisweet chocolate chips (1 cup)
- 1 cup whipping cream
- 2/3 cup packed brown sugar
- 5 eggs, separated
- 1/2 cup butter or margarine, cut into pieces
- 1 teaspoon vanilla
- 4 cups soft bread cubes

CHERRY-RASPBERRY SAUCE

- 2 tablespoons granulated sugar
- 4 teaspoons cornstarch
- 1 can (16 oz.) pitted dark sweet cherries in syrup, drained, liquid reserved
- 1 box (10 oz.) frozen raspberries in syrup, thawed, drained, liquid reserved

1 Heat oven to 350°F. Grease 12x8-inch (2-quart) glass baking dish with shortening. In large saucepan, heat chocolate chips and whipping cream over medium-low heat, stirring occasionally, until chips are melted. Stir in 1/3 cup of the brown sugar. Beat in 1 egg yolk at a time until well blended. Continue cooking until slightly thickened. Add butter and vanilla; stir until smooth. Remove from heat; stir in bread cubes.

2 In large bowl, beat egg whites with electric mixer on medium speed until soft peaks form. Gradually add remaining 1/3 cup brown sugar, beating on highest speed until stiff peaks form. Fold egg whites into chocolate mixture. Pour into baking dish; place baking dish on 15x10x1-inch pan. Place pan in oven; pour boiling water into 15x10x1-inch pan until water is 1/2 to 3/4 inch deep. Bake 35 to 40 minutes or until center is set.

3 In medium saucepan, mix granulated sugar and cornstarch. Gradually stir in reserved liquids from fruits. Cook over medium-high heat, stirring constantly, until mixture boils and thickens. Cool slightly; stir in fruit. Serve over warm bread pudding. Store any remaining bread pudding and sauce in refrigerator.

NUTRITION INFORMATION PER SERVING: Calories 230 • Total Fat 12g • Saturated Fat 7g • Cholesterol 80mg • Sodium 105mg • Total Carbohydrate 27g • Dietary Fiber 2g • Sugars 21g • Protein 3g. DIETARY EXCHANGES: 1 Starch • 1 Other Carbohydrate • 2 Fat • 2 Carb Choices.

special touch

To really impress guests with a "to-die-for" dessert, spoon generous dollops of whipped cream on each serving and then drizzle on warm chocolate sauce or hot fudge sauce. Go all out by topping it off with a chocolate-covered cherry!

blueberry-lemon tart

PREP TIME: 20 Minutes ✳ READY IN: 1 Hour 15 Minutes ✳ SERVINGS: 16

1 box (15 oz.) Pillsbury® refrigerated pie crusts, softened as directed on box

2 containers (6 oz. each) Yoplait® Original 99% Fat Free lemon burst yogurt

1 package (8 oz.) cream cheese, softened

1 can (21 oz.) blueberry pie filling with more fruit

1 cup fresh blueberries

1 Heat oven to 375°F. Unroll 1 pie crust on center of ungreased large cookie sheet. Unroll second pie crust and place over first crust, matching edges and pressing to seal. With rolling pin, roll out into 14-inch round.

2 Fold 1/2 inch of crust edge under, forming border; press to seal seam (if desired, flute edge). Prick crust generously with fork. Bake 20 to 25 minutes or until golden brown. Cool completely, about 30 minutes.

3 In medium bowl, beat yogurt and cream cheese with electric mixer on medium speed until blended. Spread evenly over crust. Spread pie filling evenly over yogurt mixture. Top with blueberries. Cut into wedges to serve. Cover and refrigerate any remaining tart.

HIGH ALTITUDE (3500-6500 FT): Bake 17 to 22 minutes.

NUTRITION INFORMATION PER SERVING: Calories 230 • Total Fat 12g • Saturated Fat 6g • Cholesterol 20mg • Sodium 160mg • Total Carbohydrate 29g • Dietary Fiber 0g • Sugars 13g • Protein 2g. DIETARY EXCHANGES: 1/2 Starch • 1-1/2 Other Carbohydrate • 2-1/2 Fat • 2 Carb Choices.

elegant cherry cups

PREP TIME: 30 Minutes ✳ READY IN: 50 Minutes ✳ SERVINGS: 16

CUPS

1 box (15 oz.) Pillsbury® refrigerated pie crusts, softened as directed on box

1 teaspoon sugar

1/3 cup chopped white chocolate baking bar

FILLING

1 carton (7 oz.) crème fraîche (about 1 cup)

1 cup cherry pie filling

1 tablespoon kirsch or maraschino cherry juice

3 tablespoons chopped white chocolate baking bar

1 Heat oven to 450°F. Unroll pie crusts on work surface. Sprinkle crusts with sugar; press in lightly. Cut 16 rounds from crusts with 3-3/8- to 3-1/2-inch round cookie cutter. Press sugared side up in bottoms and up sides of 16 regular-size muffin cups, without going to top edge of cups. Prick each crust generously with fork.

2 Bake 6 to 8 minutes or until lightly browned. Sprinkle 1 teaspoon chopped white chocolate in each cup; cool 10 minutes. Remove tart shells from muffin cups. Place shells on serving platter.

3 To serve, drop about 1 tablespoon crème fraîche into each shell. In small bowl, mix cherry pie filling with kirsch; top each with cherry mixture. Sprinkle about 1/2 teaspoon chopped white chocolate on filling.

NUTRITION INFORMATION PER SERVING: Calories 190 • Total Fat 12g • Saturated Fat 6g • Cholesterol 20mg • Sodium 90mg • Total Carbohydrate 19g • Dietary Fiber 0g • Sugars 10g • Protein 0g. DIETARY EXCHANGES: 1-1/2 Other Carbohydrate • 2-1/2 Fat • 1 Carb Choice.

blueberry-lemon tart

raspberry-lemon meringue tart

raspberry-lemon meringue tart

PREP TIME: 1 Hour ❋ READY IN: 4 Hours ❋ SERVINGS: 8

RASPBERRY FILLING
- 1 bag (12 oz.) frozen whole raspberries
- 1/4 cup sugar
- 2 tablespoons cornstarch

CRUST
- 1 Pillsbury® refrigerated pie crust (from 15-oz. box), softened as directed on box

LEMON FILLING
- 1 cup sugar
- 2 tablespoons cornstarch
- 2 tablespoons all-purpose flour
- 1/4 teaspoon salt
- 1-1/2 cups water
- 3 egg yolks, beaten
- 1 tablespoon grated lemon peel
- 1/3 cup lemon juice
- 1 tablespoon butter or margarine

MERINGUE
- 1/3 cup sugar
- 1 tablespoon cornstarch
- 1/3 cup water
- 3 egg whites
- 1/8 teaspoon salt

1 Place raspberries on large platter to thaw, about 1 hour. When thawed, place in strainer over bowl to collect juices.

2 Heat oven to 450°F. Bake pie crust as directed on box for One-Crust Baked Shell, using 9-inch tart pan with removable bottom or 9-inch glass pie plate. Cool on cooling rack 15 minutes.

3 In 2-quart saucepan, mix 1/4 cup sugar and 2 tablespoons cornstarch. If necessary, add water to reserved raspberry liquid to measure 1/2 cup; gradually add raspberry liquid to sugar mixture. Cook over medium heat, stirring constantly, until thickened. Gently fold in raspberries. Cool 10 minutes. Spread in crust.

4 In 2-quart saucepan, mix 1 cup sugar, 2 tablespoons cornstarch, the flour and 1/4 teaspoon salt. Gradually stir in 1-1/2 cups water, stirring until smooth. Heat to boiling over medium heat; cook and stir 1 minute longer. Remove from heat. Quickly stir about 1/2 cup hot mixture into beaten egg yolks; mix well. Gradually stir egg mixture back into hot mixture. Stir in lemon peel and juice. Cook over medium heat about 5 minutes, stirring constantly. Remove from heat. Add butter; stir until melted. Let stand 10 minutes.

5 Meanwhile, heat oven to 350°F. In 1-quart saucepan, mix 1/3 cup sugar and 1 tablespoon cornstarch. Stir in 1/3 cup water; cook and stir over medium heat until thickened. Cool completely by placing in freezer about 15 minutes. In small bowl, beat egg whites and 1/8 teaspoon salt with electric mixer on high speed until soft peaks form. Add cooled cornstarch mixture, beating on medium speed until stiff peaks form. Carefully pour hot lemon filling over raspberry mixture in crust. Gently spread meringue over filling. Bake 20 to 25 minutes or until meringue reaches 160°F. Cool 2 hours; refrigerate until serving time. Remove side of pan. Cover and refrigerate any remaining tart.

HIGH ALTITUDE (3500-6500 FT): Not recommended.

NUTRITION INFORMATION PER SERVING: Calories 370 • Total Fat 10g • Saturated Fat 4g • Cholesterol 85mg • Sodium 260mg • Total Carbohydrate 65g • Dietary Fiber 3g • Sugars 42g • Protein 3g. DIETARY EXCHANGES: 1 Starch • 3-1/2 Other Carbohydrate • 2 Fat • 4 Carb Choices.

kitchen tip

Egg whites will really fluff up during beating if you let them stand at room temperature for about 30 minutes first.

chocolate streusel banana-carrot cake

PREP TIME: 20 Minutes ❋ READY IN: 2 Hours ❋ SERVINGS: 12

STREUSEL
- 1/2 cup chopped walnuts
- 1/4 cup firmly packed brown sugar
- 2 tablespoons Gold Medal® all-purpose flour
- 2 tablespoons butter or margarine, melted
- 1/2 cup semisweet chocolate chips

CAKE
- 1-1/2 cups sliced very ripe bananas (about 3 medium)
- 1/2 cup sour cream
- 4 eggs
- 1 package (18 oz.) carrot cake mix with pudding
- 1/2 cup semisweet chocolate chips

1 Heat oven to 350°F. Grease and flour 13x9-inch pan. In medium bowl, combine all streusel ingredients except 1/2 cup chocolate chips; mix well. Stir in chocolate chips. Set aside.

2 In large bowl, combine bananas, sour cream and eggs; beat with electric mixer at medium speed until well blended. Add cake mix; beat at low speed until combined. Beat 2 minutes at medium speed. Stir in 1/2 cup chocolate chips. Spoon into greased and floured pan. Sprinkle with streusel.

3 Bake at 350°F for 30 to 40 minutes or until toothpick inserted in center comes out clean. Cool 1 hour or until completely cooled.

HIGH ALTITUDE (3500-6500 FT): Add 1/3 cup flour to dry cake mix. Bake at 375°F for 30 to 40 minutes.

NUTRITION INFORMATION PER SERVING: Calories 395 • Total Fat 17g • Saturated Fat 7g • Cholesterol 80mg • Sodium 330mg • Total Carbohydrate 54g • Dietary Fiber 1g • Sugars 41g • Protein 6g. DIETARY EXCHANGES: 2 Starch • 1-1/2 Other Carbohydrate • 3-1/2 Fat • 3-1/2 Carb Choices.

glazed almond amaretto cheesecake

PREP TIME: 20 Minutes ❋ READY IN: 8 Hours ❋ SERVINGS: 16

TOPPING
- 1/2 cup sugar
- 1/4 cup water
- 1 cup sliced almonds
- 1 teaspoon amaretto

CRUST
- 2 cups graham cracker crumbs (about 32 squares)
- 1/4 cup finely chopped almonds
- 1/3 cup butter or margarine, melted

FILLING
- 2 packages (8 oz. each) cream cheese, softened
- 1 cup sugar
- 3 eggs
- 1 cup sour cream
- 1/2 cup whipping cream
- 1/4 cup amaretto
- 1/2 teaspoon almond extract

1 In small saucepan, heat 1/2 cup sugar and the water to boiling; boil 2 minutes. Remove from heat. Stir in sliced almonds and 1 teaspoon amaretto. With slotted spoon, remove almonds and place on waxed paper; separate with fork. Cool.

2 Heat oven to 350°F. In medium bowl, mix all crust ingredients. Press mixture in bottom and 1-1/2 inches up side of ungreased 10-inch springform pan.

3 In large bowl, beat cream cheese and 1 cup sugar with electric mixer on medium speed until smooth and creamy. At low speed, beat in 1 egg at a time until well blended. Add all remaining filling ingredients; blend well. Pour into crust-lined pan.

4 Bake 45 to 60 minutes; arrange sliced almonds in 2-inch-wide circle around outer edge of cheesecake. Bake 15 minutes longer or until center is set. Cool 15 minutes. Run knife around edge of pan; carefully remove side of pan. Cool completely. Refrigerate several hours or overnight before serving. Store in refrigerator.

NUTRITION INFORMATION PER SERVING: Calories 370 • Total Fat 25g • Saturated Fat 13g • Cholesterol 100mg • Sodium 190mg • Total Carbohydrate 30g • Dietary Fiber 1g • Sugars 25g • Protein 6g. DIETARY EXCHANGES: 1 Starch • 1 Other Carbohydrate • 1/2 High-Fat Meat • 4 Fat • 2 Carb Choices.

chocolate streusel
banana-carrot cake

cook's notes

If the cakes cool after being removed from the custard cups, reheat each in the microwave for 15 to 20 seconds or until they're warm.

saucy center chocolate cakes

PREP TIME: 20 Minutes ✳ READY IN: 40 Minutes ✳ SERVINGS: 7

1/2 cup butter	1/2 cup granulated sugar
8 oz. semisweet baking chocolate, chopped	2 tablespoons all-purpose flour
4 eggs	Powdered sugar
2 tablespoons hazelnut coffee drink syrup	

1 Heat oven to 400°F. Generously grease 7 (6-oz.) custard cups with shortening; lightly flour. In 2-quart saucepan, melt butter and chocolate over low heat, stirring frequently, until smooth; set aside.

2 In medium bowl, beat eggs and syrup with electric mixer on high speed until foamy. Gradually beat in granulated sugar. Beat on high speed 2 minutes or until light and thickened, scraping bowl occasionally. On low speed, beat in flour and chocolate mixture just until blended, scraping bowl occasionally. Divide batter evenly among cups, filling each about 3/4 full. Place on cookie sheet.

3 Bake 11 to 15 minutes or until cakes have formed top crust but are still soft in center. Cool 5 minutes. Place individual dessert plate over each custard cup; turn plate and cup over. Remove cup. Sift powdered sugar over cakes; serve warm.

HIGH ALTITUDE (3500-6500 FT): Bake 13 to 15 minutes.

NUTRITION INFORMATION PER SERVING: Calories 420 • Total Fat 26g • Saturated Fat 13g • Cholesterol 155mg • Sodium 125mg • Total Carbohydrate 41g • Dietary Fiber 2g • Sugars 37g • Protein 5g. DIETARY EXCHANGES: 1 Starch • 2 Other Carbohydrate • 5 Fat.

mocha-hazelnut cream-filled cake

PREP TIME: 35 Minutes ✳ READY IN: 3 Hours ✳ SERVINGS: 16

1 box (1 lb. 2.25 oz.) butter recipe chocolate cake mix	2 bags (12 oz. each) semisweet chocolate chips (4 cups)
1-1/3 cups water	1 bottle (16 oz.) refrigerated hazelnut-flavor coffee creamer
1/2 cup butter, softened	1 package (8 oz.) cream cheese, softened
3 eggs	2 tablespoons chopped hazelnuts (filberts)
2 teaspoons instant coffee granules or crystals	

1 Heat oven to 350°F (325°F for dark or nonstick pans). Grease bottoms only of two 9-inch round pans with shortening. In large bowl, beat cake mix, water, butter, eggs and coffee granules with electric mixer on low speed about 30 seconds or until blended. Beat on medium speed 2 minutes, scraping bowl occasionally. Pour batter into pan.

2 Bake 28 to 33 minutes or until toothpick inserted in center comes out clean. Cool 10 minutes; turn upside down onto cooling rack.

3 In 3-quart saucepan, cook chocolate chips and coffee creamer over medium-low heat about 8 minutes, stirring constantly, until melted. Remove from heat; beat in cream cheese with wire whisk until smooth. Cover; refrigerate about 30 minutes.

4 In small microwavable bowl, reserve 1/2 cup of the chocolate mixture. Beat remaining mixture with electric mixer on medium-high speed about 8 minutes or until light and fluffy.

5 Place 1 cake layer on serving plate, rounded side down. Spread 1-inch-thick layer of frosting over cake. Top with second cake layer, rounded side up. Spread frosting on side and top of cake.

6 Microwave reserved 1/2 cup chocolate mixture on High about 30 seconds or until soft; spread over top of cake. Sprinkle hazelnuts around top edge. Cover loosely; refrigerate at least 1 hour before serving. Store in refrigerator.

HIGH ALTITUDE (3500-6500 FT): When making the cake, follow High Altitude directions on box. Continue as directed above.

NUTRITION INFORMATION PER SERVING: Calories 550 • Total Fat 32g • Saturated 16g • Cholesterol 70mg • Sodium 400mg • Total Carbohydrate 63g • Dietary Fiber 4g • Sugars 45g • Protein 6g.

kitchen tip

To keep frosting from sticking to plastic wrap, simply poke toothpicks around the outside edge of the frosted cake before covering it with wrap. Remove the toothpicks before serving.

make-ahead brownie delight

PREP TIME: 20 Minutes ✳ READY IN: 4 Hours ✳ SERVINGS: 16

BROWNIE BASE

- 1 box (1 lb. 2.3 oz.) fudge brownie mix
- 1/2 cup vegetable oil
- 1/4 cup water
- 2 eggs
- 3/4 cup large chocolate chips or chunks

FILLING

- 2 cups whipping cream
- 4 oz. cream cheese, softened
- 1/4 cup powdered sugar
- 1/2 cup white vanilla baking chips, melted

SAUCE

- 1 package (10 oz.) frozen raspberries in syrup, thawed
- 3 tablespoons sugar
- 1 teaspoon cornstarch
- 1 cup fresh raspberries

1 Heat oven to 350°F. Grease bottom and sides of 9-inch springform pan. In large bowl, beat brownie mix, oil, water and eggs 50 strokes with spoon. Stir in chocolate chips. Spread batter in pan. Bake 40 to 45 minutes or until center is almost set. Cool 1 hour or until completely cooled.

2 In large bowl, beat cream until stiff peaks form. In another large bowl, beat cream cheese and powdered sugar until smooth. Stir in melted vanilla baking chips. Fold in 1/3 of whipped cream; fold in remaining whipped cream. Reserve 1 cup mixture for piped edge; spread remaining mixture over brownie. Using decorating bag fitted with star tip (1/4- to 3/8-inch opening), pipe decorative border around edge of brownie, making sure border doesn't touch side of pan. Cover; refrigerate at least 2 hours.

3 Meanwhile, in food processor bowl with metal blade or blender container, process raspberries with syrup until smooth. Strain to remove seeds. In small saucepan, mix 3 tablespoons sugar, the cornstarch and raspberry purée. Cook and stir over medium heat until mixture boils and thickens. Cool to room temperature.

4 About 1 hour before serving, arrange fresh raspberries over filling. Refrigerate until serving time. With sharp knife, loosen dessert from side of pan; remove side of pan. Cut into wedges. Serve with raspberry sauce. Store in refrigerator.

NUTRITION INFORMATION PER SERVING: Calories 450 • Total Fat 26g • Saturated Fat 12g • Cholesterol 65mg • Sodium 180mg • Total Carbohydrate 51g • Dietary Fiber 2g • Sugars 39g • Protein 4g. DIETARY EXCHANGES: 1 Starch • 2-1/2 Other Carbohydrate • 5 Fat • 3-1/2 Carb Choices.

cook's notes

To make this dessert several weeks ahead of time, prepare the brownie base and filling as directed in the recipe. Top the brownie base with filling as directed and store it, tightly covered, in the freezer. Allow the dessert to thaw completely in the refrigerator. Add the raspberries and sauce shortly before serving.

crescent macadamia truffle cups

crescent macadamia truffle cups

PREP TIME: 40 Minutes ❋ READY IN: 3 Hours ❋ SERVINGS: 24

4 oz. sweet baking chocolate, cut into pieces	24 whole macadamia nuts
1/4 cup unsalted butter, regular butter or margarine	3 oz. white chocolate baking bar, cut into pieces
1/4 cup packed brown sugar	1/3 cup cream cheese spread (from 8-oz. container)
2 tablespoons all-purpose flour	1/2 cup whipping cream
2 tablespoons coffee-flavored liqueur or cold brewed coffee	2 tablespoons powdered sugar
1 egg	1 teaspoon vanilla
1 can (8 oz.) Pillsbury® refrigerated crescent dinner rolls	

special touch

Lightly dust the tops of the truffle cups with unsweetened baking cocoa.

1 Heat oven to 350°F. In 1-quart saucepan, melt sweet chocolate and 1/4 cup butter over low heat, stirring constantly, until smooth. Remove from heat. Stir in brown sugar, flour, liqueur and egg; set aside.

2 Unroll dough into 2 long rectangles; firmly press perforations to seal. Cut each rectangle in half lengthwise. Cut each half crosswise into 6 (2-inch) squares. Press or roll out each square to 2-3/4-inch square. Place 1 square in each of 24 ungreased mini muffin cups; firmly press in bottom and up side, leaving corners of dough extended over edge of each cup.

3 Place 1 macadamia nut in each dough-lined cup. Spoon about 2 teaspoons filling mixture over nut in each cup.

4 Bake 12 to 15 minutes or until filling is set and corners of dough are golden brown. Cool 5 minutes. Remove from pan; place on cooling racks. Cool completely, about 30 minutes. Refrigerate until thoroughly chilled, about 1 hour.

5 Meanwhile, in 1-quart saucepan, melt baking bar and cream cheese spread over low heat, stirring constantly, until smooth. Cover with plastic wrap; refrigerate until thoroughly chilled, about 1 hour, stirring occasionally.

6 In small bowl, beat whipping cream, powdered sugar and vanilla with electric mixer on high speed just until soft peaks form. Add chilled baking bar mixture; beat on low speed just until well blended. Pipe or spoon topping over tops of chilled cups. Refrigerate until topping is set, about 30 minutes. Store truffle cups in refrigerator.

NUTRITION INFORMATION PER SERVING: Calories 170 • Total Fat 12g • Saturated Fat 6g • Cholesterol 25mg • Sodium 105mg • Total Carbohydrate 11g • Dietary Fiber 1g • Sugars 6g • Protein 2g. DIETARY EXCHANGES: 1 Other Carbohydrate • 2-1/2 Fat • 1 Carb Choice.

cook's notes

For a taste variation, substitute raspberry-flavored liqueur for the coffee liqueur.

triple-chocolate torte

PREP TIME: 30 Minutes ✻ READY IN: 2 Hours 45 Minutes ✻ SERVINGS: 16

CAKE

3/4	cup butter or margarine
12	oz. bittersweet baking chocolate, coarsely chopped
3	tablespoons coffee-flavored liqueur or strong brewed coffee
4	eggs
2/3	cup sugar
1/4	teaspoon salt
1/3	cup all-purpose flour

GANACHE AND TOPPING

3	tablespoons whipping cream
4	oz. white chocolate baking bars, chopped
1/4	cup milk chocolate chips or 1 oz. milk chocolate, chopped

1 Heat oven to 350°F. Spray bottom only of 9-inch round cake pan with baking spray and flour, then line bottom of pan with cooking parchment paper or waxed paper and spray again.

2 In 2-quart saucepan, heat butter and bittersweet chocolate over low heat, stirring occasionally, until melted. Remove from heat; stir in liqueur. Cool slightly, stirring occasionally.

3 Meanwhile, in large bowl, beat eggs, sugar and salt with electric mixer on medium-high speed about 4 minutes or until pale and thickened. Gradually beat in chocolate mixture until blended. Beat in flour, scraping bowl occasionally, just until blended. Pour into pan.

4 Bake about 30 minutes or until center is set. (Toothpick inserted in center may not come out clean.) Place pan on cooling rack. With sharp knife, loosen cake from side of pan. Cool 30 minutes. Carefully remove cake from pan to cooling rack. Cool completely, about 1 hour.

5 In 1-quart saucepan, heat whipping cream just to boiling. Remove from heat; stir in white chocolate until melted and mixture is smooth. (If necessary, stir mixture over low heat for a few seconds until chocolate is completely melted and mixture is smooth.) Pour into small bowl; refrigerate 15 minutes or until mixture is thickened and spreadable.

6 Place cake on serving plate. Spread white chocolate mixture just over top of cake. In small freezer plastic bag, place milk chocolate chips; seal bag slightly. Microwave on High 45 to 60 seconds; squeeze bag until chocolate is smooth. Cut off small corner of bag; squeeze bag to drizzle chocolate over cake.

7 To serve, cut cake into slices with sharp knife, wiping off knife after each cut. Store covered in refrigerator. If refrigerated, let stand at room temperature 20 minutes before serving.

NUTRITION INFORMATION PER SERVING: Calories 340 • Total Fat 25g • Saturated Fat 15g • Cholesterol 80mg • Sodium 130mg • Total Carbohydrate 23g • Dietary Fiber 3g • Sugars 15g • Protein 5g. DIETARY EXCHANGES: 1/2 Starch • 1 Other Carbohydrate • 1/2 High-Fat Meat • 4 Fat • 1-1/2 Carb Choices.

triple-chocolate torte

brownie trifle

brownie trifle

PREP TIME: 10 Minutes ✳ READY IN: 1 Hour 40 Minutes ✳ SERVINGS: 6

1 pouch (10.25 oz.) fudge brownie mix	1 egg
1/4 cup vegetable oil	2 cups frozen (thawed) whipped topping
2 tablespoons water	1-1/2 cups fresh raspberries (6 oz.)
1/2 teaspoon almond extract	1/4 cup sliced almonds

1 Heat oven to 325°F. Spray bottom only of 8-inch square pan with cooking spray or grease with shortening. In large bowl, stir brownie mix, oil, water, almond extract and egg with spoon about 50 times (batter may be lumpy). Spread in pan.

2 Bake 26 to 28 minutes or until toothpick inserted in center comes out almost clean. Cool completely, about 1 hour.

3 Break cooled brownies into bite-size pieces, placing half of pieces in 2-quart straight-sided serving bowl. Top with half of the whipped topping and half of the raspberries; repeat layers. Sprinkle almonds over top.

HIGH ALTITUDE (3500-6500 FT): Follow High Altitude directions on brownie mix pouch.

NUTRITION INFORMATION PER SERVING: Calories 390 • Total Fat 19g • Saturated Fat 6g • Cholesterol 35mg • Sodium 180mg • Total Carbohydrate 51g • Dietary Fiber 4g • Sugars 34g • Protein 4g.

cook's notes

Experiment with a different brownie flavor for this trifle. You could also substitute sliced fresh strawberries for the fresh raspberries.

dixie spice cake with caramel frosting

PREP TIME: 30 Minutes ✳ READY IN: 2 Hours 15 Minutes ✳ SERVINGS: 12

CAKE

2-1/4 cups all-purpose flour	1 teaspoon vanilla
1-1/4 cups firmly packed brown sugar	3 eggs
1/2 cup sugar	1 cup chopped walnuts or pecans
1 teaspoon baking soda	**FROSTING**
1/2 teaspoon salt	1/2 cup margarine or butter
1/2 teaspoon nutmeg	1 cup firmly packed brown sugar
1/2 teaspoon allspice	1/4 cup milk
1 cup buttermilk	3 cups powdered sugar
2/3 cup shortening	1/2 teaspoon vanilla

1 Heat oven to 350°F. Generously grease and flour bottom only of 13x9-inch pan. In large bowl, combine all cake ingredients except walnuts; beat at low speed until moistened. Beat 3 minutes at medium speed. Stir in walnuts. Pour batter into greased and floured pan.

2 Bake at 350°F for 40 to 45 minutes or until top springs back when touched lightly in center. Cool 1 hour or until completely cooled.

3 In medium saucepan, melt margarine. Add brown sugar; cook over low heat for 2 minutes, stirring constantly. Add milk; continue cooking until mixture comes to a rolling boil. Remove from heat. Gradually add powdered sugar and vanilla; mix well. If needed, add a few drops of milk for desired spreading consistency. Spread over cooled cake.

HIGH ALTITUDE (3500-6500 FT): Increase flour to 2-1/4 cups plus 3 tablespoons; decrease brown sugar in cake to 1 cup. Bake at 375°F for 35 to 40 minutes.

NUTRITION INFORMATION PER SERVING: Calories 670 • Total Fat 27g • Saturated Fat 5g • Cholesterol 55mg • Sodium 340mg • Total Carbohydrate 100g • Dietary Fiber 1g • Sugars 79g • Protein 6g. DIETARY EXCHANGES: 2 Starch • 4-1/2 Fruit • 5-1/2 Fat OR 6-1/2 Carbohydrate • 5-1/2 Fat.

cook's notes

For Dixie Spice Cupcakes, fill 24 to 30 paper-lined muffin cups 2/3 full with batter. Bake at 350°F for 20 to 25 minutes. Frost with caramel frosting.

turtle pumpkin cheesecake

PREP TIME: 20 Minutes ✻ READY IN: 9 Hours 5 Minutes ✻ SERVINGS: 16

CRUST

1-1/2	cups thin chocolate wafer cookie crumbs (about 30 cookies)
1/4	cup butter or margarine, melted

FILLING

1/4	cup all-purpose flour
2	teaspoons pumpkin pie spice
1	can (15 oz.) pumpkin (not pumpkin pie mix)
4	packages (8 oz. each) cream cheese, softened
1	cup packed brown sugar
2/3	cup granulated sugar
5	eggs

TOPPING

1/2	cup chopped pecans, toasted
2	oz. bittersweet baking chocolate, coarsely chopped
1	tablespoon vegetable oil
1	cup caramel topping

1 Heat oven to 300°F. Wrap foil around outside of bottom and side of 9-inch springform pan to prevent drips. Spray bottom and 1 inch up side of pan with cooking spray. In small bowl, mix cookie crumbs and melted butter. Press crumb mixture on bottom and 1 inch up side of pan. Bake crust 8 to 10 minutes or until set. Cool at room temperature 5 minutes. Refrigerate about 5 minutes or until completely cooled.

2 Meanwhile, in another small bowl, mix flour, pumpkin pie spice and pumpkin; set aside. In large bowl, beat cream cheese with electric mixer on medium speed until smooth and creamy. Gradually beat in brown sugar and granulated sugar until smooth. On low speed, beat in eggs, one at a time, just until blended. Gradually beat in pumpkin mixture until smooth. Pour filling over crust.

3 Bake 1 hour 15 minutes to 1 hour 25 minutes or until edge of cheesecake is set but center still jiggles slightly when moved. Run knife around edge of pan to loosen cheesecake. Turn oven off; open oven door at least 4 inches. Let cheesecake remain in oven 30 minutes.

4 Cool cheesecake in pan on cooling rack 30 minutes. Refrigerate at least 6 hours or overnight before serving.

5 Just before serving, sprinkle pecans over top of cheesecake. In small microwavable bowl, microwave chocolate and oil uncovered on High 1 minute to 1 minute 30 seconds, stirring every 15 seconds, until melted. Drizzle chocolate over pecans.

6 To serve, run knife around edge of pan to loosen cheesecake; carefully remove side of pan. Drizzle caramel topping over each serving. Store covered in refrigerator.

HIGH ALTITUDE (3500-6500 FT): Before preheating oven, place pan of water on oven rack below rack cheesecake will be baked on. In Step 3, bake 1 hour 20 minutes to 1 hour 30 minutes. Do not run knife around edge of pan until after cheesecake has cooled 30 minutes.

NUTRITION INFORMATION PER SERVING: Calories 510 • Total Fat 31g • Saturated Fat 17g • Cholesterol 140mg • Sodium 360mg • Total Carbohydrate 50g • Dietary Fiber 2g • Sugars 38g • Protein 8g. DIETARY EXCHANGES: 3-1/2 Other Carbohydrate • 1 High-Fat Meat • 4-1/2 Fat • 3 Carb Choices.

cook's notes

To toast pecans, sprinkle them in an ungreased heavy skillet. Cook over medium heat 5 to 7 minutes, stirring frequently until pecans begin to brown, then stirring constantly until light brown.

festive pound cake with fruit compote

PREP TIME: 45 Minutes ✳ READY IN: 3 Hours 20 Minutes ✳ SERVINGS: 16

CAKE

2-1/2 cups sugar

1-1/2 cups butter, softened

1 teaspoon vanilla

6 eggs

3 cups all-purpose flour

1/2 teaspoon baking powder

1/2 teaspoon salt

2 tablespoons grated orange peel

1/2 cup milk

COMPOTE

3/4 cup cut-up dried apricots

1 package (3.5 oz.) sweetened dried cherries (2/3 cup)

1/2 cup sugar

3/4 cup orange juice

1 tablespoon brandy

1 medium orange, peeled, chopped (about 1 cup)

Ice cream, if desired

1 Heat oven to 350°F. Generously grease 10-inch angel food (tube cake) pan with shortening; lightly flour. In large bowl, beat 2-1/2 cups sugar and the butter until light and fluffy. Add vanilla; mix well. Beat in 1 egg at a time until well blended.

2 In small bowl, mix flour, baking powder and salt. Add flour mixture alternately with orange peel and milk, beating well after each addition. Pour batter into pan.

3 Bake 55 to 65 minutes or until toothpick inserted in center comes out clean. Cool 15 minutes. Invert cake onto serving plate. Cool completely, about 1-1/2 hours.

4 In medium saucepan, mix apricots, cherries, 1/2 cup sugar and the orange juice. Heat to boiling; simmer 10 to 15 minutes or until most of liquid is absorbed. Stir in brandy and chopped orange. Serve warm compote with cake and ice cream.

HIGH ALTITUDE (3500-6500 FT): Decrease sugar in cake to 2-1/4 cups.

NUTRITION INFORMATION PER SERVING: Calories 470 • Total Fat 20g • Saturated Fat 12g • Cholesterol 125mg • Sodium 240mg • Total Carbohydrate 68g • Dietary Fiber 2g • Sugars 47g • Protein 6g. DIETARY EXCHANGES: 1-1/2 Starch • 3 Other Carbohydrate • 4 Fat • 4-1/2 Carb Choices.

cook's notes

Dried cherries are delicious but can sometimes be a bit difficult to find. If you can't find them, just substitute cherry-flavored dried cranberries.

butterscotch cream cheese-apple pie

PREP TIME: 20 Minutes ✳ READY IN: 1 Hour 35 Minutes ✳ SERVINGS: 8

CRUST

1 Pillsbury® refrigerated pie crust (from 15-oz. box), softened as directed on box

FILLING

1 package (8 oz.) cream cheese, softened

1-1/2 cups milk

1 box (4-serving size) butterscotch instant pudding and pie filling mix

TOPPING

1 can (21 oz.) apple pie filling with more fruit

1 cup frozen (thawed) whipped topping

Fresh apple pieces, if desired

1 Heat oven to 450°F. Bake pie crust as directed on box for One-Crust Baked Shell, using 9-inch glass pie plate. Cool on cooling rack 15 minutes.

2 Meanwhile, in small bowl, beat cream cheese with electric mixer on medium speed until fluffy. In medium bowl, beat milk and pudding mix with electric mixer on medium speed until well blended. Add cream cheese; beat until smooth.

3 Spread cream cheese-pudding mixture in shell. Refrigerate 1 hour. Top individual servings with apple pie filling; garnish with whipped topping and apple pieces. Cover and refrigerate any remaining pie.

cook's notes

To make this pie a day ahead, prepare the recipe through Step 3. Cover and refrigerate overnight; top as directed.

ice cream-filled puffs

ice cream-filled puffs

PREP TIME: 30 Minutes ✳ READY IN: 1 Hour 35 Minutes ✳ SERVINGS: 8

CREAM PUFFS
- 1/2 cup water
- 1/4 cup butter
- 1/4 cup milk
- 1 teaspoon sugar
- 1/4 teaspoon salt
- 3/4 cup all-purpose or unbleached flour
- 3 eggs

FILLING
- 1-1/2 pints (3 cups) mint chip ice cream

TOPPING
- 6 oz. semisweet chocolate, chopped
- 2/3 cup whipping cream
- Crushed peppermint candies

1 Heat oven to 425°F. Grease cookie sheet. In 2-quart saucepan, mix water, butter, milk, sugar and salt. Heat to a full rolling boil, allowing butter to melt completely.

2 Immediately add flour, stirring vigorously until mixture leaves sides of saucepan in smooth ball. Remove from heat; cool 5 minutes.

3 Add eggs, 1 at a time, beating well after each addition. Mixture will be soft and shiny. Drop dough into 8 mounds onto cookie sheet.

4 Bake 10 minutes. Reduce oven temperature to 375°F; bake 15 minutes. Slit cream puffs with tip of knife. Bake about 5 minutes or until set and golden brown. Place on cooling rack; cool completely, about 15 minutes. Split cream puffs; remove any soft portions.

5 Meanwhile, line large cookie sheet with waxed paper. Scoop ice cream into 32 small balls, about 1-1/2 inches in diameter. Place on paper-lined cookie sheets. Freeze until serving time.

6 In 1-quart saucepan, mix chocolate and cream; cook over low heat until chocolate is melted. Stir until smooth. Cool until lukewarm, about 15 minutes.

7 When ready to serve, place bottom halves of cream puffs on dessert plates. Place 3 balls of ice cream in each bottom half. Top with additional ball of ice cream to form pyramid. Cover with top halves of cream puffs, placing slightly off center. Drizzle with chocolate sauce; sprinkle with candies.

NUTRITION INFORMATION PER SERVING: Calories 420 • Total Fat 26g • Saturated Fat 15g • Cholesterol 140mg • Sodium 190mg • Total Carbohydrate 41g • Dietary Fiber 2g • Sugars 27g • Protein 7g. DIETARY EXCHANGES: 1 Starch • 1-1/2 Other Carbohydrate • 1/2 Milk • 4 Fat • 3 Carb Choices.

kitchen tip

For perfect cream puffs, make sure to heat the oven 10 to 15 minutes before baking. Bake the puffs until they're golden brown and their shape is set. Slitting the puffs with the tip of a knife will allow steam to escape and prevent a soggy interior.

maple baked apples

PREP TIME: 20 Minutes ✳ READY IN: 1 Hour 10 Minutes ✳ SERVINGS: 6

- 6 large baking apples
- 2 tablespoons lemon juice
- 1/2 cup raisins
- 1/2 teaspoon cinnamon
- 1 cup real maple or maple-flavored syrup
- 1/4 cup water

1 Heat oven to 350°F. Core apples and remove a 1-inch strip of peel around top to prevent splitting. Brush tops and insides with lemon juice. Place apples in ungreased 8-inch square (2-quart) baking dish.

2 In small bowl, combine raisins and cinnamon; fill center of each apple with mixture. Pour maple syrup over apples. Add 1/4 cup water to baking dish.

3 Bake at 350°F for 45 to 50 minutes or until apples are tender, occasionally spooning syrup mixture over apples.

NUTRITION INFORMATION PER SERVING: Calories 320 • Total Fat 1g • Saturated Fat 0g • Cholesterol 0mg • Sodium 5mg • Total Carbohydrate 78g • Dietary Fiber 6g • Sugars 70g • Protein 1g. DIETARY EXCHANGES: 5-1/2 Fruit OR 5-1/2 Carbohydrate.

sour cream cherry bars

PREP TIME: 15 Minutes ✳ READY IN: 2 Hours 30 Minutes ✳ SERVINGS: 60 Bars

BASE AND TOPPING

1	cup packed brown sugar
1	cup butter, softened
2	cups quick-cooking oats
1-1/2	cups all-purpose flour
1	teaspoon baking soda

FILLING

3/4	cup granulated sugar
1/4	cup all-purpose flour
1	tablespoon grated orange peel
1	cup sour cream
1	teaspoon almond extract
1	egg
4-1/2	cups frozen pitted tart cherries, thawed (24 oz.)

1 Heat oven to 350°F. In large bowl, blend brown sugar and butter. Add oats, 1-1/2 cups flour and the baking soda; mix until crumbs form. Press half of crumb mixture in bottom of ungreased 15x10x1-inch pan; reserve remaining mixture for topping. Bake 10 minutes.

2 Meanwhile, in large bowl, mix all filling ingredients except cherries. Stir in cherries. Pour filling over partially baked crust. Crumble and sprinkle remaining half of crumb mixture over filling.

3 Bake 25 to 35 minutes longer or until center is set. Cool completely, about 1-1/2 hours. For bars, cut into 10 rows by 6 rows. Store in refrigerator.

NUTRITION INFORMATION PER SERVING: Calories 90 • Total Fat 4g • Saturated Fat 2.5g • Cholesterol 15mg • Sodium 45mg • Total Carbohydrate 13g • Dietary Fiber 0g • Sugars 8g • Protein 1g. DIETARY EXCHANGES: 1/2 Starch • 1/2 Other Carbohydrate • 1/2 Fat • 1 Carb Choice.

pecan pie ginger cheesecake

PREP TIME: 20 Minutes ✳ READY IN: 4 Hours 10 Minutes ✳ SERVINGS: 12

CRUST

1	Pillsbury® refrigerated pie crust (from 15-oz. pkg.), softened as directed on package

FILLING

1	package (8 oz.) cream cheese, softened
6	tablespoons sugar
1/2	teaspoon vanilla
1	egg
1/4	cup finely chopped crystallized ginger

TOPPING

2	tablespoons all-purpose flour
1/4	cup margarine or butter, melted
3/4	cup firmly packed brown sugar
1	teaspoon vanilla
2	eggs
2	cups pecan halves or pieces

1 Heat oven to 350°F. Place pie crust in 9-inch glass pie pan or 9-inch deep-dish glass pie pan as directed on package for one-crust filled pie. In medium bowl, combine cream cheese, sugar, 1/2 teaspoon vanilla and 1 egg; beat at medium speed until smooth. Stir in ginger. Spoon and spread filling in crust-lined pan.

2 In large bowl, combine flour and margarine; mix well. Add brown sugar, 1 teaspoon vanilla and 2 eggs; mix well. Stir in pecans. Carefully spoon mixture evenly over filling.

3 Bake at 350°F for 40 to 50 minutes or until center is set and crust is golden brown. Cool 1 hour. Refrigerate 2 hours or until thoroughly chilled. Store in refrigerator.

NUTRITION INFORMATION PER SERVING: Calories 415 • Total Fat 29g • Saturated Fat 8g • Cholesterol 75mg • Sodium 190mg • Total Carbohydrate 33g • Dietary Fiber 2g • Sugars 22g • Protein 6g. DIETARY EXCHANGES: 2 Starch • 6 Fat OR 2 Carbohydrate • 6 Fat • 2 Carb Choices.

gingered apple-berry crisp

PREP TIME: 15 Minutes ✳ READY IN: 55 Minutes ✳ SERVINGS: 6

TOPPING
- 3/4 cup quick-cooking oats
- 3/4 cup crushed gingersnap cookies
- 1/2 cup all-purpose flour
- 1/4 cup packed brown sugar
- 1/2 cup butter or margarine, cut into small pieces

FRUIT MIXTURE
- 1 cup frozen unsweetened blueberries
- 1 cup frozen unsweetened raspberries
- 1/2 teaspoon ground ginger
- 1 can (21 oz.) apple pie filling

1 Heat oven to 350°F. Spray 12x8-inch (2-quart) glass baking dish with cooking spray. In large bowl, combine all topping ingredients except butter. With pastry blender or fork, cut in butter until crumbly.

2 In large bowl, mix all fruit mixture ingredients; pour into baking dish. Sprinkle topping evenly over fruit.

3 Bake 35 to 40 minutes or until fruit mixture is bubbly and topping is golden brown. If necessary, cover with foil during last 15 to 20 minutes of baking to prevent excessive browning.

HIGH ALTITUDE (3500-6500 FT): Heat oven to 375°F. Continue as directed above.

NUTRITION INFORMATION PER SERVING: Calories 480 • Total Fat 18g • Saturated Fat 10g • Cholesterol 40mg • Sodium • 200mg • Total Carbohydrate 74g • Dietary Fiber 6g • Sugars 46g • Protein 5g.

kitchen tip

To crush cookies, place them in a resealable food-storage plastic bag; seal the bag and finely crush with a rolling pin or meat mallet (or finely crush in a food processor).

JOAN WITTAN
North Potomac, Maryland
Bake-Off® Contest 35, 1992

cook's notes

To extract the most juice from

a lime, roll it on the countertop

using your hand, applying

medium pressure. Then slice

the lime and extract the juice.

key lime cream torte

PREP TIME: 35 Minutes ✳ READY IN: 4 Hours 35 Minutes ✳ SERVINGS: 12

CAKE
1   box (18.25 oz.) Pillsbury® Moist Supreme® golden butter recipe cake mix

2   tablespoons lime juice plus water to equal 1 cup

1/2 cup butter or margarine, softened

3   eggs

FILLING
1   can (14 oz.) sweetened condensed milk (not evaporated)

1/2 cup lime juice

2   cups whipping cream

GARNISH, IF DESIRED
Lime slices

1   Heat oven to 350°F. Grease two 9- or 8-inch round cake pans with shortening; lightly flour. In large bowl, beat cake ingredients with electric mixer on low speed about 30 seconds or until moistened. Beat on medium speed 2 minutes, scraping bowl occasionally. Pour batter evenly into pans.

2   Bake the 9-inch pans 27 to 32 minutes and the 8-inch pans 32 to 37 minutes or until toothpick inserted in center comes out clean. Cool 15 minutes. Remove from pans to cooling racks. Cool completely, about 1 hour.

3   In small bowl, mix condensed milk and 1/2 cup lime juice until well blended. In large bowl, beat whipping cream with electric mixer on high speed until stiff peaks form. Reserve 1 cup of the whipped cream. Fold condensed milk mixture into remaining whipped cream just until blended.

4   To assemble torte, cut each layer in half horizontally to make 4 layers. Place 1 cake layer, cut side up, on serving plate. Spread with 1/3 of the whipped cream filling. Repeat with second and third cake layers. Top with remaining cake layer. Pipe in decorative pattern or spread reserved whipped cream over top of torte. Refrigerate at least 2 hours before serving. Garnish with lime slices. Cover and refrigerate any remaining torte.

HIGH ALTITUDE (3500-6500 FT): Add water to lime juice to equal 1-1/4 cups.

NUTRITION INFORMATION PER SERVING: Calories 490 • Total Fat 27g • Saturated Fat 16g • Cholesterol 130mg • Sodium 410mg • Total Carbohydrate 55g • Dietary Fiber 0g • Sugars 39g • Protein 6g. DIETARY EXCHANGES: 1 Starch • 2-1/2 Other Carbohydrate • 1/2 High-Fat Meat • 4-1/2 Fat • 3-1/2 Carb Choices.

strawberry-mango margarita dessert

PREP TIME: 25 Minutes ✳ READY IN: 3 Hours 25 Minutes ✳ SERVINGS: 10

CRUST
1-1/4 cups crushed pretzels

1/4 cup sugar

1/2 cup butter or margarine, melted

FILLING
1   pint mango sorbet, softened slightly

2   boxes (10 oz. each) frozen strawberries in syrup, thawed

1/2 cup frozen (thawed) margarita mix concentrate

1   cup whipping cream, whipped

10 fresh strawberries, halved

1   small ripe mango, cut into cubes

Coarse sugar, if desired

Fresh strawberry slices, if desired

cook's notes

Add a little "Olé!" to a casual

Christmas gathering by making

it a "Feliz Navidad" party—

and feature this fun dessert.

To make cutting the pie easier,

wait to place the fruit skewers

on top until after slicing it.

1   In small bowl, mix crust ingredients. Press firmly in bottom of ungreased 9- or 8-in. springform pan; refrigerate 10 minutes. Spoon sorbet over crust; spread evenly with metal spatula. Freeze 30 minutes.

2   In large bowl, mix thawed strawberries, using wire whisk, until broken into small pieces. Beat in margarita mix until well blended. Fold in whipped cream. Carefully pour into pan over sorbet. Freeze at least 3 hours until firm.

3   Using 4-inch wooden skewers, place strawberry half and mango cube on each of 10 skewers. Sprinkle with coarse sugar. Place skewers into top of dessert for garnish. Top with fresh stawberry slices. To serve, cut into wedges.

NUTRITION INFORMATION PER SERVING: Calories 360 • Total Fat 17g • Sodium 180mg • Dietary Fiber 2g. DIETARY EXCHANGES: 1/2 Starch • 3 Other Carbohydrate • 3 Fat • 3 Carb Choices.

key lime cream torte

christmas angel cake

christmas angel cake

PREP TIME: 1 Hour ✳ READY IN: 2 Hours 15 Minutes ✳ SERVINGS: 10

CAKE

1 package (18.25 oz.) white cake mix with pudding

1-1/4 cups water

1/3 cup oil

3 egg whites

FROSTING AND DECORATIONS

1 foil baking cup

1 can (16 oz.) vanilla frosting

2 cups frozen whipped topping, thawed

1/4 cup flaked coconut

Edible glitter

Small candies

Yellow food color

1 wafer cookie

cook's notes

To keep the serving platter clean, use waxed or parchment paper. Before frosting the cake, tuck strips of the paper under the cake all around the base. Pull away the strips before the frosting sets.

1 Heat oven to 350°F. Spray bottom only of 13x9-inch pan with nonstick cooking spray. Line bottom with waxed paper; spray and lightly flour paper. Generously spray and flour 10-oz. custard cup.

2 In large bowl, combine cake mix, water, oil and egg whites; beat at low speed until moistened. Beat 2 minutes at medium speed. Pour 1/2 cup batter into sprayed and floured custard cup. Pour remaining batter evenly into sprayed and floured paper-lined pan.

3 Bake at 350°F until cake springs back when touched lightly in center. Bake custard cup for 20 to 30 minutes; bake 13x9-inch pan for 28 to 33 minutes. Cool cakes in pan and cup for 15 minutes. Invert cakes onto wire rack; remove pan, cup and paper. Cool 30 minutes or until completely cooled.

4 Invert large cake into flat serving tray or foil-covered 20x15-inch cardboard. To form angel shape, starting at center of one short side, make 2 diagonal cuts to corners of opposite short side, forming a triangular piece in center. Separate pieces 1 and 2 from piece 3 at bottom of cake to form wings. (See diagrams below.)

5 For angel's halo and head, flatten foil baking cup; place at point of center triangle between wings. Invert small round cake onto halo.

6 In medium bowl, combine frosting and whipped topping; blend well. Reserve 1/4 cup frosting mixture for hair. Frost sides and tops of cake pieces. Sprinkle coconut over wings. Sprinkle wings with edible glitter.

7 Place candies on cake for eyes, mouth and buttons. Add yellow food color to reserved frosting; blend well. Spread or pipe frosting on head for hair. Cut wafer cookie and add to cake for songbook. Attach small candies with frosting for hands. Store in refrigerator.

HIGH ALTITUDE (3500-6500 FT): See package for directions for preparing batter and baking 13x9-inch cake. Bake custard cup for 22 to 32 minutes.

NUTRITION INFORMATION PER SERVING: Calories 550 • Total Fat 24g • Saturated Fat 9g • Cholesterol 0mg • Sodium 390mg • Total Carbohydrate 80g • Dietary Fiber 1g • Sugars 58g • Protein 3g. DIETARY EXCHANGES: 1 Starch • 4-1/2 Fruit • 4-1/2 Fat OR 5-1/2 Carbohydrate • 4-1/2 Fat.

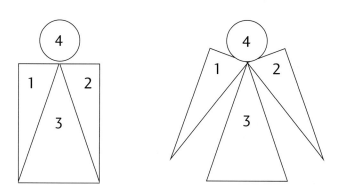

CHRISTMAS ANGEL CAKE DIAGRAMS

general recipe index

alphabetical recipe index